The Pulse in Cinema

The Pulse in Cinema

The Aesthetics of Horror

Sharon Jane Mee

EDINBURGH
University Press

Edinburgh University Press is one of the leading university presses in the UK. We publish academic books and journals in our selected subject areas across the humanities and social sciences, combining cutting-edge scholarship with high editorial and production values to produce academic works of lasting importance. For more information visit our website: edinburghuniversitypress.com

© Sharon Jane Mee, 2020, 2022

Edinburgh University Press Ltd
The Tun – Holyrood Road
12 (2f) Jackson's Entry
Edinburgh EH8 8PJ

First published in hardback by Edinburgh University Press 2020

Typeset in 11/13 Monotype Ehrhardt by
IDSUK (DataConnection) Ltd

A CIP record for this book is available from the British Library

ISBN 978 1 4744 7584 6 (hardback)
ISBN 978 1 4744 7585 3 (paperback)
ISBN 978 1 4744 7586 0 (webready PDF)
ISBN 978 1 4744 7587 7 (epub)

The right of Sharon Jane Mee to be identified as the author of this work has been asserted in accordance with the Copyright, Designs and Patents Act 1988, and the Copyright and Related Rights Regulations 2003 (SI No. 2498).

Contents

List of Figures vii
Acknowledgements ix

Introduction 1
   Rosalind E. Krauss's Theory of the Pulse 2
   Rhythm and Pulse 4
   The Pulse: A Philosophical Enquiry 7
   Body Horror 12

1. The Rhythm of Life: The Pulse in the Image 25
   Rhythm and Pulse 26
   Rhythm in Experimental Cinema 30
   Protocinema: Étienne-Jules Marey 40
   The Pulse in Psychoanalysis: Sigmund Freud 49

2. The Rhythm of Life: The Pulse in the Spectator 63
   Surfaces of Inscription and Passages of Intensity 65
   Movement, and an Opening 74
   The Logic of Sensation as a Diastolic–Systolic Opening 78
   The Aesthetics of the Open: Georges Franju's
      Le Sang des bêtes/ Blood of the Beasts (1949) 82
   A Libidinal Economy, and an Opening 85
   Candour as the Body's Openness to an Outside 90

3. *Aisthesis* and *Dispositif*: The Pulse and Its Analogues 97
   Extracting the Fear that Tingles the Spine: The Hype,
      the Buzz of the Gimmick, and the Bottom Line 98
   The Execution: *The Tingler* (1959) 100
   Aisthesis and Prescribed Lines 103
   Prescription and the Aesthetics of Blood Spilled 107
   The Pulse 'Exposed' 110
   Dispositif: Lines of Fright 111
   Figural Analogues or 'a Metonymy Without End':
      The Heart that Throbs, the Spine that Tingles,
      the Mouth that Screams. Do you have the Guts? 121

CONTENTS

4. Automutilation and Metonymy: The Economy of the Pulse 130
   General Economy as Energetic Expenditure 132
   Two General Economies of Communication and Communion 135
   Automutilation and George A. Romero's *Dawn of the Dead* (1978) 143
   An Operation in the Morgue: Lucio Fulci's *L'aldilà/
      The Beyond* (1981) 147
   The Sovereign Operation as Affective Experience 152
   The Pulse as a Sovereign Operation in Horror Cinema 156

5. Blood and Convulsive Affect: Vectors of the Pulse as
   Sovereign Operations 166
   Andrzej Żuławski's *Possession* (1981) 169
   Possession and Dispossession 170
   Body Horror and Convulsive Affect 176
   The Copula and the Copulation of Bodies: The Convulsions of
      Language and Self, Even (Fucking Language) 178
   The Movement-Image and Vectors of Sensation 181
   The Machinic and the Non-Machinic 185
   The Vector and Communication 188
   The Magnitude and Direction of Vectors that Result in
      Possession and Dispossession 191
   Material Vectors and their (Non)sense 193

Bibliography 202
Filmography 213
Index 215

Figures

1.1	Mapping the pulse (Dr Susann Beier, 2020)	28
1.2	Spiralling discs in *Anémic Cinéma* (Marcel Duchamp, 1926)	39
1.3	Spiralling discs in *Anémic Cinéma* (Marcel Duchamp, 1926)	40
1.4	A man running (chronophotography) (Étienne-Jules Marey, 1894)	43
1.5	A man running (geometrical chronophotography) (Étienne-Jules Marey, 1894)	43
1.6	A man running (graphic inscription) (Étienne-Jules Marey, 1874)	45
1.7	Recording the trace of the pulse (Étienne-Jules Marey, 1878)	46
2.1	*Le Sang des bêtes/Blood of the Beasts* (Georges Franju, 1949)	63
2.2	*Le Sang des bêtes/Blood of the Beasts* (Georges Franju, 1949)	63
2.3	*Le Sang des bêtes/Blood of the Beasts* (Georges Franju, 1949)	64
2.4	*Le Sang des bêtes/Blood of the Beasts* (Georges Franju, 1949)	64
2.5	The 'felt' vibrations of the image. *Figure with Meat* (Francis Bacon, 1954)	80
2.6	Sheep lined up on a rack their legs kicking like a crazy centipede. *Le Sang des bêtes/Blood of the Beasts* (Georges Franju, 1949)	83
2.7	The heads of calves: a rhythmic tableau. *Le Sang des bêtes/Blood of the Beasts* (Georges Franju, 1949)	84
3.1	'Do you have the guts to sit in this chair?' A theatrical film poster from *The Tingler* (William Castle, 1959)	113
3.2	Audience participation: the collapse of the theatrical space into the cinema space in *The Tingler* (William Castle, 1959)	122
4.1	The surplus of the sun. *The Sower* (Vincent van Gogh, November 1888)	137
4.2	Blood splatter on a shop front window. *Dawn of the Dead* (George A. Romero, 1978)	144
4.3	A biker disembowelled. *Dawn of the Dead* (George A. Romero, 1978)	145
4.4	The biker screams. *Dawn of the Dead* (George A. Romero, 1978)	145

4.5 The 'chowdown'. *Dawn of the Dead* (George A. Romero, 1978) 146
4.6 Acid pouring from a beaker. *L'aldilà / The Beyond* (Lucio Fulci, 1981) 149
4.7 Mary-Ann's disintegrating face. *L'aldilà / The Beyond* (Lucio Fulci, 1981) 150
4.8 The advancing tide of blood. *L'aldilà / The Beyond* (Lucio Fulci, 1981) 150
4.9 Jill screams. *L'aldilà / The Beyond* (Lucio Fulci, 1981) 150
5.1 Mark thrashes back and forth on the bed. *Possession* (Andrzej Żuławski, 1981) 173
5.2 Anna grinding meat turns the electric knife on her own throat. *Possession* (Andrzej Żuławski, 1981) 173
5.3 Anna throwing herself, milk and eggs, against the walls of the subway tunnel. *Possession* (Andrzej Żuławski, 1981) 174
5.4 Anna seized by convulsions. *Possession* (Andrzej Żuławski, 1981) 175
5.5 Anna's miscarriage in the subway tunnel. *Possession* (Andrzej Żuławski, 1981) 175
5.6 Mark and Anna in Café Einstein. *Possession* (Andrzej Żuławski, 1981) 183
5.7 The tide of blood approaches Jill's feet. *L'aldilà / The Beyond* (Lucio Fulci, 1981) 195

Acknowledgements

This book has been written with support from the University of New South Wales. Chapter 2 or parts thereof first appeared as 'The Rhythm of Life as an Opening to Sensation in Georges Franju's *Le Sang des bêtes/ Blood of the Beasts* (1949)' in *SubStance* 49, no. 3, 2020 pp. 54–70, and Chapter 3 as 'The Originary Sensations of *Aisthesis* "Exposed" in William Castle's *The Tingler* (1959)' in *Screening the Past* 45, 2020. Various thoughts and ideas were published in 'The Scream Itself: Masochistic *Jouissance* and a Cinema of Speechlessness in *La Grande Bouffe*', *Film-Philosophy* 24, no. 3, 2020, pp. 321–40, and early work completed for Chapter 4 was published in 'A Terrifying Spectatorship: Jean-François Lyotard's *Dispositif* and the Expenditure of Intensities in Steven Kastrissios's *The Horseman*', *Philament* 21, February 2016, pp. 19–44. I would like to thank the publishers for permission to reprint material from these articles.

I am deeply grateful to Lisa Trahair for enabling this project as my PhD supervisor and for her advice and support. I thank Sigi Jöttkandt and Erin Brannigan for their helpful comments on earlier drafts of this book. Sigi was also instrumental in supporting this book's publication. Special thanks are due to peers, colleagues, and friends for their intellectual input. I especially give thanks to Luke Robinson, Adam Daniel, Melanie Robson, Gabrielle Lowe and Fiona Ransom. I am grateful to Steven Shaviro (Wayne State University) and Tom Cohen (University at Albany, SUNY) for their kind comments and for supporting the publication of this book. I would also like to thank Rob Garbutt (Southern Cross University) for his mentorship in the past year.

Bill Hunt, artist of the cover image of this book, I consider a true friend. I thank Gillian Leslie, Richard Strachan and Fiona Conn at Edinburgh University Press for their support and their work on this book. Images from Marcel Duchamp's *Anémic Cinéma* (1926), Étienne-Jules Marey's chronophotographic work, and the film poster from William Castle's

The Tingler (1959) would not have made their way into this book without the help of the George Eastman Museum, Huntington Library and *Fangoria*, respectively.

This book would not have been possible without the support of James Dahlstrom and my family, Lorna, Graeme, Michelle and Brendan.

Introduction

This book theorises cinema in relation to the pulse. It has been an imperative for the theorists of film spectatorship to prioritise the body. Such theorists describe the embodied and corporealised nature of film spectatorship. To consider a pulse in cinema is to put film spectatorship in the body. Where the pulse in cinema may be found in the heartbeat of the spectator as they respond to affective or moving scenes in the film, how can we begin to think beyond this simply physiological response? This book expands on theoretical considerations in film spectatorship to locate a pulse comprised of affects and sensations that are unseen in the image and the spectator, but that has the force of intensities within the energetic arrangement.

The importance of the pulse for film spectatorship theory means that this book explores the pulse as the registration of affection in the spectator, and a means of approaching sensation. The pulse is affective because, as Gilles Deleuze writes about affection: 'It is a coincidence of subject and object, or the way in which the subject perceives itself, or rather experiences itself or feels itself "from the inside".'[1] Like affection, the pulse seizes the body from within. The pulse is, moreover, a response in the body to cinema that does not simply filter the world through the sense organs and turn the experience of sensation into something that is cognitive but is an organic response to cinema's sensations through the beat of the heart. That is, sensation and affection are not first and foremost a cognitive process but a bodily process. The pulse is the index of sensation and affection. My theory of the pulse in this book reveals that just as the pulse is the minimal condition of sensation in the body, it is also the condition for sensation in cinema.

The pulse can be described as the cumulative effect of 'sensings' and the speed of its rhythm a response of the body to the world. This responsiveness does not treat cinema as mediating the body in the world but as part of the world, as an Open receptiveness of the body to the world that overlaps with the Open receptiveness of the world to the body. Because the pulse is as much found in an experience of the world as it is found in the cinema experience, the pulse in cinema is no different from the quotidian pulse. The image and the world are in this sense synonymous because both the image and the world affect the pulse. *The Pulse in Cinema* explores a pulse that is extensive as well as intensive. The pulse seizes the body whose movement extends into the image/world and the pulse seizes the image/world whose movement extends into the body. This is how I describe the pulse in cinema, both in the image/world and in the viewer.

Thus, expanding upon a film spectatorship theory of corporealisation, the pulse puts film spectatorship in the body, but the pulse of the body is also an Open receptiveness to the image/world. That is, the pulse is in the image/world inasmuch as the pulse extends to and seizes, by investing with affection, the image/world. Deleuze describes the action of a vital and diastolic–systolic rhythm and its relation to sensation as the opening of the self to the world that opens the world to the self.[2] The action of the diastole–systole rhythm in contact with sensation, Deleuze writes, exceeds the levels or domains of the senses – rhythm invests our auditory senses to produce music and invests our visual senses to produce painting, but rhythm itself is in excess of any one sense.[3] Rhythm also allows sensation to exceed a particular work of art. Deleuze describes the diastole–systole of rhythm in contact with sensation as the 'vital power that exceeds every domain and traverses them all'.[4] Like the action of the diastole–systole rhythm that opens the self to the world and opens the world to the self, equally, the diastole–systole rhythm of the pulse is found in the opening of the body that opens the image/world. When we attribute the pulse simply to the physiological body we must see that the conditions of the pulse are dependent on the conditions of the world. We must also see that the forces of matter and their vibrations are continuous in the world. With respect to the pulse as it appears in the body and in the image/world, Chapter 1 will focus on the pulse as it is found in the image and Chapter 2 will focus on the pulse as it is found in the spectator.

Rosalind E. Krauss's Theory of the Pulse

Rosalind E. Krauss has described the pulse as a 'force [that] wells up within the density and thickness of the carnal being'.[5] She makes it the cornerstone of her theory of corporeal spectatorship. For her, the pulse presumes a kind of 'carnal being': a body not limited to the relationship between the sense organs and the brain, but sensible and sensual in its relation to the world. Carnality is libidinous: it refers to needs or appetites, and a 'carnal being' entails a being impelled towards sensuality in the world.

The pulse resides in the dense material of the body's tissue, itself the site from which vision extends. Referring to the dense material, 'opacity or carnal density' of the body, Jonathan Crary writes about a 'new type of observer' that had come out of the 'reconfiguration of vision' by the 1840s through the work of Hermholtz: 'The body which had been a neutral or invisible term in vision now was the thickness from which knowledge of vision was derived.'[6] However, just as the body 'loomed . . . into view', the 'stability of visual space' was brought into question.[7] Krauss writes in her essay 'The Im/Pulse to See': 'this beat [of the pulse] has the power to decompose and dissolve the very coherence of form on which visuality may be thought to depend'.[8] For Krauss, to 'corporealize the visual' is also to acknowledge that the eye is available to the 'force of eroticization'.[9] By this eroticisation, desire is invested in vision and the pulse becomes an alternative to the 'claims of modernist opticality to have both abstracted vision and rationalized form'.[10]

Given Krauss's reading of Jean-François Lyotard's 'Fiscourse Digure: The Utopia behind the Scenes of the Phantasy' later in her essay, the 'density' or 'thickness' of 'carnal being' that Krauss describes can also be linked to a 'blocking' of desire that occurs as a fact of the pleasure principle.[11] In the scene of the phantasy such as the one analysed by Sigmund Freud in 'A Child is Being Beaten', this 'blocking' of desire makes different desires and different positions for desire interchangeable and concurrently present, whereby 'spanking' is simultaneously a 'caress' and the 'child' is simultaneously a spectator of the scene.[12] By this 'blocking' of desire we can conceptualise the 'simultaneous' and often 'contradictory' directions of the energetic flow in the phantasy, which Krauss understands as taking the form of 'rhythmic oppositions' but that will help us to understand the force, magnitude, and direction of the pulse in the investment of desire.[13]

Krauss trials several theories across several essays and texts to describe her theory of the pulse. These include the essay 'The Im/Pulse to See', the book *The Optical Unconscious*, and Krauss's section titled 'Pulse' in Yve-Alain Bois and Krauss's book *Formless: A User's Guide*. Themes recur across these three texts, most notably the pulse's relation to modern technology in an investigation of artistic practice and product. Krauss finds the pulse in a number of artistic productions and works by Surrealist and Dada artists Max Ernst and Marcel Duchamp, Alberto Giacometti, and Cubist artist Pablo Picasso. However, it is most notable that works by such artists are indebted to the pulses, Krauss writes, of city landscapes: in the flicker of 'its neon signs, its hysterical sirens, its crawling metallic scrap heap, its entire mechanical ballet'.[14] The pulse in the age of mechanical reproduction is in the 'television, discos, transistor radios'.[15] And while

Krauss engages with Walter Benjamin's essay 'The Work of Art in the Age of Mechanical Reproduction', Krauss also reads Freud, Lyotard and Georges Bataille to describe the pulse.

Krauss's theory of the pulse is far from exhaustive and only hints at a starting point for a theory of the pulse as it relates to cinema. She nevertheless presents us with a series of compelling statements that will provide a way to conceptualise the pulse as an energetics in cinema by which the image and spectator are invested with desire. She relates the pulse both to a corporeal spectatorship as a spectatorship of desire, and to modern technology that tends towards a particular 'beat' in relation to which one can talk about mass art. She also elaborates on the transgressive aspect of the beat.

However, there are limitations in Krauss's work. In assimilating the beat as the throb of on/off, on/off, on/off to the spanking of the child in Freud's 'A Child is Being Beaten' essay, Krauss confuses rhythm (the beat against a surface/flesh) and the pulse (the force of intensity).[16] Furthermore, her conception of the *dispositif* as a relation between the work and the artist that includes the viewer is too mechanistic in its failure to heed the energetic stakes of the arrangement. Finally, she makes little headway in integrating Bataille's conception of the formless (*informe*) to the pulse. For Krauss, the pulse as a characteristic of the *informe* is the way it 'desublimate[s] . . . vision through the shock effect of the beat'.[17] Bataille's conception of the *informe* refers to operations or 'tasks' rather than determinate meanings for things.[18] As a bodily and energetic process rather than a cognitive process, the pulse can be understood as one such operation or 'task'. In my analysis, the pulse works at the level of the *informe* because pulsatile cinema does not bring about a spectator subject that recognises objects and subjects in the world and gives them meaning, but there is an Open relation that apprehends the spectator as just another process among the multifarious energetic and material interactions of the world. This concern – of the *informe* with operations or 'tasks' – means that what one refers to is economy, and specifically, general economy.

Rhythm and Pulse

In this book, I distinguish between rhythm and the pulse. Whereas the cinematic apparatus that mediates the film viewing experience is rhythmic, a cinema in which the spectator and the image are Open is pulsatile. For rhythm there is a surface on which the 'beat' hits: in cinema, the cinema screen or the spectator subject. Rhythm is a way of thinking about the mediation or reconciling of differences between contact and release, charge and discharge, excitation and enervation. The pulse, because of its simultaneous libidinal investments means that it entails processes of desire in the flow of energy that make up the *dispositif*. The film and the spectator are components in the flow of energy and are simultaneously invested in what is an Open relationship.

And yet, notwithstanding this distinction between rhythm and the pulse, the two also exist in an imbricated relation to each other: there is the rhythm of the pulse. Imbrication is the embeddedness in each other of subjects and objects, and means that subjects and objects are not discrete entities; that is, subjects are not unified subjects defined by their stasis, fixity or enclosure. Subjects are even 'partial and momentary' components in the flow of cathetic energy in the *dispositif*.[19] Imbrication is what underlies the relationship between *Eros* and *Thanatos*, cognition and sensation, restricted economy and general economy, rhythm and the pulse. Rhythm is the only means of describing the pulse's interaction with the exterior world. The exterior world interacts with the body via rhythm – the twenty-four frames per second of the filmstrip rely on the fusion and phi-phenomenon of the eye. The pulse is felt as rhythm on the skin – we measure the pulse in rhythm when we 'take the pulse' such that the pulse of the body is 'understood' by its rhythm. The cardiograph mechanically inscribes the pulse as rhythm. Conversely, the life of the pulse is what is mapped in rhythm so that rhythm can also be said to involve the intensities of the pulse. In this examination of cinema, rhythm will be the indication of a pulse 'exposed' because rhythm is what inscribes the movement of the pulse.

The action of rhythmic excitations upon perception means that the 'feeling' body can be conceived as the site of external beats of reality – like the skin of a drum, for touch, from the outside, and not just by other bodies, but by the atmosphere, and even the image – but it is also responsive to the internal workings of the body. The action of rhythmic excitations upon perception promotes thinking about the interval while the pulse promotes thinking about the flow of excitations as duration. Because excitations occur from without as well as within the body the skin acts as a system of communication between the organic body and the exterior world. The pulse is thus not only found in the flux of excitations and enervations of the internal workings of the body, but is also the communication between the body and the image/world. In short, the image/world is composed of others – other pulses – in filmmakers and spectators such that the pulse is not simply attributed to the body but is found in communication, and even communion, with other pulses in the image/world.

The pulse is an autonomic response in the body. The movement of the pulse is also, as the *Oxford Dictionary* defines it, 'a throb or thrill of life, emotion'.[20] It is in this sense that I define the movement of the pulse as 'felt'. The pulse's rhythms mean that the feeling body is alternately excited and pacified. In the flux of the movement of energy there is excitation and enervation that occurs at the site of the body. Such enervation is a management mechanism of the body so that the body does not overload with sensation. In *Beyond the Pleasure Principle* Freud calls this management mechanism 'inertia' and later Jacques Lacan calls it 'homeostasis',[21] and it is the way that the flow of energy is regulated, even if the beyond of the pleasure principle works outside this model. This excitation and pacification or enervation, tension and release, dilation and contraction, is also the flux of the pulse and the method by which energetic movement proceeds.

Rhythm is in the image in sequential space, the inscription upon material frames or forms, an abstract and metric measure of time, and series or sets of images; and I will show how the significance of the pulse that concerns me here has a prototype in rhythmic cinema. Rhythmic cinema acts on the perceptive capacities of the body, and we feel the pulse as rhythm on the skin. Affection is in the body in an experience of the image. This is where the pulse diverges from rhythm: the pulse is the affection that is Open or 'exposed' by the image/world. For the pulse, this means that the lived components of the body and the image/world are in energetic and material relation. That is, I will call the affection that is both in the body and in the image/world the pulse. I posit that the Open of the pulse goes both ways: not simply from the spectator to the image but also from the image to the spectator.

The Open in cinema occurs because the pulse in the body extends into, acts on, and is responsive to the image/world that extends into, acts on, and is responsive to the body, and comprises an affective relation. The Open receptiveness of the pulse supports considering the spectator in affective and energetic relation to the image. A cinema of the pulse and its affective character does not relay the effect upon a unified subjectivity; the pulse involves an energetic investment of the *dispositif*. The difference is one in which the spectator is a unified subject and the film is an object for interpretation based on signification and meaning, and one in which the body is a vital and living force by which the senses make sense, and by which the body is an energetic component in the *dispositif*. When Lyotard opens out and spreads the ephemeral body to produce the libidinal band/skin – a 'skin' that in its opening out shows how intensities are infinitely invested in the world – everything becomes organically embodied and energetically invested.[22] And yet, crucially, this embodiment is not fully formed – is not yet being – but is 'ephemeral' and 'heterogeneous', in a way that is 'becoming'.[23] The spectator subject is 'only a partial and momentary component' in the energetic flow that makes up the *dispositif* of the cinema experience.[24]

The Pulse: A Philosophical Enquiry

My purpose in identifying the pulse in spectatorship is to facilitate further inquiry into questions of operation and economy as energetic exchange and expenditure that precede any notion of the unified subject or subject positions. The movement of the force of intensities that is important in defining the pulse is best understood as the energetic investments that Lyotard uses the term *dispositif* to describe. The *dispositif* is different from the mechanical apparatus because even though the *dispositif* can be invested with energy in a way that indicates a stable structure, it is also open to change or new potentials. Insofar as the pulse suggests an Open relation between the body and the image/world, I am going to replace the notion of the cinematic apparatus with the more nuanced concept of the *dispositif*. The cinematic apparatus is characterised by the interpolation of the subject and ideology, as Jean-Louis Baudry writes:

> The ideological mechanism at work in the cinema seems . . . to be concentrated in the relationship between the camera and the subject. The question is whether the former will permit the latter to constitute and seize itself in a particular mode of specular reflection.[25]

The body is not separate from the cinematic image but Open in it because both act as components in the affective exchange that is film spectatorship. It is for this reason that we can also understand the cinematic apparatus not in the mechanistic sense but in the energetic sense as a *dispositif*. That is, although *dispositif* can be translated from the French to mean 'apparatus', it does not refer to the mechanical aspects of the apparatus but can, rather, be defined as an energetic arrangement that has a 'disposition to invest' and to be invested.[26] I understand the *dispositif* as a libidinal cathexis for the investment of components in an arrangement or set-up. By libidinal cathexis I mean the charge of energy that attaches desire to form. There is a need for conceiving the Open of spectator and image as a *dispositif* because it means we are not dealing with machines, the material filmstrip, film bodies, or objects, and their relation to a unified subjectivity, but rather the flow of energetic movements and displacements in the concatenation.[27] The pulse is a way of understanding the baseline of this energetic flow.

The *dispositif* operates in the libidinal economy. Lyotard's *dispositif*, or any set-up, including cinema, has or is, a 'disposition to invest'.[28] It is the libidinal economy of energies that invests the *dispositif* and subjects its components to 'economic movements and displacements'.[29] But it is also the *dispositif* that structures such libidinal energies. Lyotard defines the *dispositif* in relation to structure: 'every energetic configuration ... is a structure'.[30] This is the definition of the *dispositif*: as a set-up or arrangement where intensities are invested and energetically distributed. The libidinal economy is distinguished by an 'opening out' of the libidinal surface for intensities to exorbitantly invest, while the *dispositif* channels and exploits the intensities in the libidinal economy.

The pulse is a figure or concept that explains the way forces of intensity generated from energetic (but rhythmic) charges and discharges invest the set-up, arrangement or *dispositif*. Because of the operation of the *dispositif* in Freud's 'A Note upon the "Mystic Writing-Pad"' and in Lyotard's reading of Freud's 'A Child is Being Beaten', as well as in cinema, we can conceptualise the pulse as having the operation of investment. Rhythm is an acting upon – the charge of one surface and the discharge of another; the pulse is the force of intensity.

The pulse entails that rhythm is felt not as a series of beats, but as the force that arises from the energetic 'difference between a charge and a discharge'.[31] This pulse produced by energetic difference is another way of understanding the pulse in the *dispositif* besides the flow or investment of energy, but invests the *dispositif* nonetheless. In Freud's 'A Child is Being Beaten', the pulse is not the hand's charged and rhythmic contact with and release from the surface of the child's bottom but is instead the frictious pulse of *jouissance*, which cannot be suppressed and which occurs in the tension or difference between a charge and a discharge. The *jouissance* produced by difference is also that which libidinally invests the *dispositif*. These libidinal energies work to 'block' together pleasures, so that pleasures such as sadism and masochism are incompossible in the *dispositif*: they can be said to be one or the other of the pleasures, or even both.[32] The *dispositif* is the energetic arrangement of such libidinal investments.

While this book makes emphatic the appearance of ecstasy or *jouissance* produced, channelled, and exploited by the *dispositif*, what we see in Chapter 2 is that the pulse is the intensity invested in the set-up, arrangement, or *dispositif*. Significantly, the *dispositif* is not activated by unified subjects in its operation, but constitutes components, including subjects, as they are energetically activated in the flow of cathetic energy. The analysand is one such component in the *dispositif* of the phantasy, just as, in cinema, the spectator is a component in the *dispositif*. Characterised as passages of intensity, the pulse in cinema is a way to understand the Open relationship between the image and the spectator as an affective one as the pulse libidinally invests components in the *dispositif*.

The pulse will be understood as the intensities that invest (*positif*), while the *dispositif* is the 'disposition' of the arrangement to be invested.[33] In the quotidian sense, the pulse requires the architecture of the heart, arteries and veins to function – a kind of arrangement, set-up or *dispositif* – and blood has a 'disposition' to be invested or charged. It is the movement of blood that derives the economic exchange and expenditures associated with the pulse. It is blood that also has affective value. The *dispositif* is important for understanding the pulse then, because it is the economic arrangement in which the movement, exchange and expenditures, and affects of the pulse come about. Thus, from another point of view, the pulse is a 'libidinal operator' (*positif*) that is channelled or exploited by certain 'dispositions' or 'structures' (*dispositif*).[34]

As affect, the pulse is intensive or intensity. As economy, the behaviour of the pulse can be likened to the force of the charge and discharge in libidinal cathexis, which is how objects and images are invested with desire. As Open with the world, the pulse suggests a kind of erotics of spectatorship. This is because being open to communication with the world means opening oneself to the possibility of excitations and intensities. The body and the world are charged by excitations that are libidinal. And yet, in being open to the world, one also puts oneself at risk, much like in being open to an erotic encounter. Such an erotics distinguishes particular kinds of affective spectatorship because this is not an immediately cognised spectatorship but is the feeling before the brain organises feeling into thought.

This 'before' thought indicates a particular conceptualisation of aesthetics at play that heeds the sensations of the body, and that Lyotard describes as *aisthesis*.[35] In the sensory manifold of the body and the world *aisthetic* and originary sensation is a not-yet-being in the world. Sensation is not perception as such, which has more in common with (cognitive) recognition, but is 'prior to' perception as 'sensings'. *Aisthesis* is a good way of explaining the pulse because it entails an opening or 'exposing' of the originary sensations of the body.[36] What is 'exposed' of *aisthesis* by aesthetics is a sensory body that is Open and in communication with the world. This is sensation not as a recognised and cognised view of the world as given, but an encounter with the energetic and material qualities of the world 'sensed' in the act of 'sensing'.

The concept of *aisthesis* can be tracked through three thinkers of philosophy from Plato to Martin Heidegger to Lyotard. All describe an uncovering, revealing, or 'exposing' of *aisthesis*.[37] In his essay 'Prescription', Lyotard proposes that what is 'exposed' is an originary heterogeneity of the body prior to its formulation into an ego and its subordination to the language of the law.[38] *Aisthesis* is to 'be-there, here and now . . . before any concept or even any representation'.[39] *Aisthesis* is 'exposed' by the insensible 'touch': insensible because it is a touch that occurs before 'I' am constituted. And yet, the insensible touch that 'exposes' *aisthesis* must have a relation to the sensible touch. This, Lyotard continues, is the pursuit or 'obligation' of art: to 'absolve oneself for this insensible touch through the means of the sensible'.[40] The sensible touch is the 'touch' of aesthetics: a 'touch' that constitutes the subject at a distance and in thought, but that also 'exposes' what was 'before' as *aisthesis*. Thus, while in cinema, the erotic image is generally associated with the 'touch' or tactile cinema, horror is an aesthetic cinema that 'exposes' the originary sensations of *aisthesis*.

In the essay 'Prescription' Lyotard undertakes a reading of Franz Kafka's short story 'In the Penal Colony', by which the law enters the picture of his conception of *aisthesis*. The appearance of aesthetics as it relates to sensation is key. The law 'touches' the body by the threat of blood spilled. The 'touch' of the law seeks to mimic the 'first turn, this first *touch*' of *aisthesis* by acting on the body in a way that it will understand: the law 'touches' the body in a sensible way. At the 'touch of the law', what Lyotard writes is that 'aesthetics changes meaning'.[41] Aesthetics becomes associated with blood spilled, when before it was associated with the blood that circulates. This spilling of blood is pertinent for my conception of the pulse as it relates to a definition of *aisthesis* and of that which is 'exposed' by changed aesthetics: a freedom of the body that was 'before' and a cruelty done to the body, respectively. It is also pertinent to how I aesthetically describe the pulse's relation to the movement of blood, and how freedom and cruelty are made visible in this blood. That is, in the aesthetics of the blood spilled, what is 'exposed' is the originary sensation of *aisthesis* and the freedom of the blood that circulates by the force of the pulse. This book will go some way to exploring an *aesthetics* of the pulse 'exposed' by an aesthetics of the blood spilled in its horror film case studies.

An examination of the economy of the pulse transforms subjectivity into sovereign operations. The pulse is concerned with the energetic exchange and expenditures involved in cinema spectatorship, and gives rise to the operations of a sovereign spectatorship. The 'operation' of risking, 'putting at stake' of mastery or identity, expenditure, but also 'loss' – where, such 'loss', for Bataille, is an always on-going operation of risking or of 'putting at stake' oneself – is what defines sovereignty.[42] Sovereignty, in this sense, does not mean the reign of self either in terms of rights or freedom, or in terms of monarchy. Rather, in sovereignty one loses oneself by the operation of risking oneself.[43] The pulse is concerned with sovereign operations where one might enter the operation of putting oneself at risk for the films that I analyse. The putting oneself at risk in relation to the pulse is a putting oneself at risk to intensities 'felt'.

Sovereignty means a 'loss' of object and subject. As Bataille writes in *Inner Experience*: 'And above all *no more object*'.[44] Jacques Derrida writes:

> sovereignty has no identity, is not *self, for itself, toward itself, near itself*. In order not to govern, that is to say, in order not to be subjugated, it *must* subordinate nothing (direct object), that is to say, be subordinated to *nothing or no one* (servile mediation of the indirect object): it must expend itself without reserve, lose itself, lose consciousness, lose all memory of itself and all the interiority of itself.[45]

In fact, both Derrida and Allen S. Weiss say that the sovereignty that Bataille describes is an impossible sovereignty.[46] Such impossibility is derived from sovereignty's diacritical relation to the dialectic and also that sovereignty, in its relation to subjects and objects – 'to the destruction, without reserve, of meaning' – means that it cannot enter signification.[47] In this book I am not concerned with object or subject positions. An examination of the economy and aesthetics of the pulse requires a new way of understanding the cinema experience. With regard to spectatorship, mine is a different way of understanding the cinema experience as expenditure or 'loss', where what is lost is energy in the operation.

What is the freedom implied by sovereign operations? Certainly a freedom from object and subject positions. However, as I have noted, sovereignty itself is not defined by the rights of self as freedom, that is, by a freedom that has will and agency where there is no subject to have will or agency. Rather, sovereignty as a 'putting at stake' can be seen as the vulnerability or opening to possibilities. As Derrida writes: 'Freedom must go through the putting at stake of life (*Daransetzen des Lebens*).'[48] In this risking or opening to possibilities a savagery of the body is 'exposed': an *aisthesis*. As Lyotard notes, savagery is 'always there as a potentiality of the body'.[49] The savagery of the body is what is 'exposed' by the language of the law, where what is 'exposed' is the potential of the body for sensation.

Aisthesis is the potential of the body for sensation and sensation is in the realm of the possible. *Aisthesis*, like sovereign operations, cannot enter signification. The originary sensations that denote *aisthesis* may always be 'exposed' by the aesthetics of blood spilled. However, this is the crisis of *aisthesis*: that it can only ever be 'exposed' and never simply be 'for itself' in signification. The blood that circulates is thus a freedom that can only be 'exposed' by the blood that is spilled. And yet, this is a dire reflection on cinema that suggests that it is only by the cruelty that is done to the body that the freedoms of the body are 'exposed'. It would suggest that the film spectator is only free comparative to cruelty's prescription. Instead one should see freedom as an opening to possibilities: for film spectatorship, this is an opening to the possibilities of *aisthesis*'s sensation and to sovereign operations. This is not an infinite idea of the Open. One should see freedom not outside the bounds of desire's history, ground, specificity of self, and the world. That is, as Vivian Sobchack writes: 'Freedom is thus attained and lived within history and culture, not in impossible escape attempts from them.'[50] The freedom of *aisthesis* is a freedom to 'feel' the expressions of the world and is the potentiality of the body to be open to such 'sensings'. It is the freedom of a body (not yet) embodied, because it entails an *aisthesis* not yet inscribed by the language of the law and the ego.

Body Horror

While there is a potential for the cinematic pulse to be found in any and all cinema, the films through which I will theorise the operation of the pulse come from the horror genre. These films are William Castle's *The Tingler* (1959), George A. Romero's *Dawn of the Dead* (1978), Lucio Fulci's *L'aldilà/The Beyond* (1981), and Andrzej Żuławski's *Possession* (1981). Curiously, they are also all considered exploitation films. In them, horror begins in the body; horror has an intensive effect upon the cinematic body that becomes extensive through the visual and other aspects of film. The pulse's relationship to affect and blood all add up to ways of talking about horror film spectatorship. The exploitation of intensities by the *dispositif* of cinema is also a way of talking about the effects of these films as exploitation films.

Horror is not where this book begins, however. The images and films that I analyse in Chapter 1 include the protocinematic experiments of Étienne-Jules Marey, French Impressionist cinema, Dada cinema, and American avant-garde and Structuralist/Materialist cinema, and in Chapter 2, Georges Franju's slaughterhouse documentary *Le Sang des bêtes/Blood of the Beasts* from 1949. While such films focus on the body, their artistic intent is admittedly very different from 'body horror', even if they have affect in common. I begin my inquiry with protocinematic experiments, experimental, and avant-garde films because each of them makes distinctive use of rhythm without giving full expression to the pulse. That is, Marey's protocinematic experiments are concerned with capturing the gross motor functions of the body as snapshots in time on fixed plates in a process known as chronophotography, and capturing the interior movements of the body in graphical inscriptions. Rhythm is envisioned in these recordings as sequences in time or as inscribed recordings of interior movements that limit the full expression of the pulse. French Impressionist cinema, such as Jean Epstein's *La Chute de la maison Usher/ The Fall of the House of Usher* (1928), focuses on the capability of the camera lens to capture the rhythmic micro-movements of bodies that are otherwise unseen by the eye. Epstein's earlier film *Cœur fidèle/ The Faithful Heart* (1923) presents close-ups in succession to produce a rhythmic cinema. Marcel Duchamp's *Anémic Cinéma* (1926) enacts the desiring body of the spectator via an investment of the apparatus. Of the experimental and avant-garde films that I analyse, this film comes the closest to relaying the behaviour of the pulse in the movement of the image that pulls desire to the surface. Stan Brakhage's Structuralist/Materialist films interrogate what an 'act of seeing' the body entails. In his later work, Brakhage uses inks and dyes to paint the frames of the filmstrip while also scratching it and, by this hand-made method, depicts rhythm. The 'act of seeing' is also brought into question in Franju's *Le Sang des bêtes* where the rhythms of dissection in the slaughterhouse give way to intensities for a spectator.

I analyse experimental and avant-garde films as the rhythmic prototype for the pulsatile response developed in body genre films. Joan Hawkins writes of experimental and avant-garde films: 'Clearly designed to break the audience's aesthetic distance, the films [Peter Watkins's *The War Game* (1965) and Brakhage's *The Act of Seeing with One's Own Eyes* (1971)] encourage the kind of excessive physical response that we would generally attribute to horror.'[51] Hawkins also argues that these films 'use sensational material differently than many body genre movies do', and are deemed to have a 'higher cultural purpose' even if the differences are 'difficult to define'.[52] An important difference between experimental and avant-garde films and body genre films, I contend, can be attributed to a film's use of rhythm. Rhythm derives from the fact that a film focuses on the cinematic apparatus as mediating the capture of bodies. The movement of bodies is captured by the cinematic apparatus in inscriptions on the filmstrip, snapshots, or the cutting of film frames into sequences; or otherwise the experience of spectators is produced and captured by the cinematic apparatus as particular kinds of vision or desire. That is, they all rely on the rhythms of the cinematic apparatus as a way of understanding the movement of the body. The difference between these cinematic rhythms and the pulse is one in which the cinematic apparatus mediates experience versus one in which the *dispositif* is the cause for an Open relation between the image and viewer. But what does this difference between mediation and the Open really mean? Steven Shaviro helps us understand the difference between the two terms by contrasting mediation with the intensity of the image:

> film viewing offers an immediacy and violence of sensation that powerfully engages the eye and body of the spectator . . . The cinematic image is at once intense and impalpable . . . Images confront the viewer directly, without mediation . . . On the other hand, this literalness is empty and entirely ungrounded; it does not correspond to any sort of presence.[53]

Whereas mediation necessarily belongs to the realm of representation, what the Open is concerned with are intensities and operations. I understand the force of the pulse as the 'immediate', 'intense', and confrontational, yet 'impalpable' experience. The 'impalpable' experience of cinema means that sensations are 'felt' by the spectator, even when the virtual nature of the image is recognised. As Shaviro continues: 'The film is composed only of flickering lights, evanescent noises, and insubstantial figures.'[54] Just as the operations of the pulse in the body are largely unseen, the pulse in cinema is an energetic exchange and expenditure of intensities that has no real presence.

The importance of thinking about the pulse in relation to an Open spectatorship is that it operates in all film spectatorship. It enriches our understanding of particular genres of cinema, in this book horror, because it generates a mode of viewing in which the spectator experience is not mediated by the film. That is, the spectator cannot be understood as a unified subjectivity interpellated by film's apparatuses. The Open of the film spectator is a radical way of understanding horror film in particular, because the analytical and critical focus of the theorists of horror film to date has been on the identification of spectators with characters on the screen.

Because the pulse has a part to play in 'body horror' it is worth revisiting the work of the most prominent theorists of the genre to identify how my book intersects with their ideas and where it finds limitations in their work. I concur with Carol J. Clover's definition of body horror in her essay 'Her Body, Himself: Gender in the Slasher Film' as excessive portrayals of the body in pornography and horror that produce effects of sensation on the body of the spectator.[55] Each of the films that I analyse exploit, utilise, or eek out the body in some way, and some are remarkable for their combination of the horrific and the erotic. Clover assures us: 'But horror and pornography are the only two genres specifically devoted to the arousal of bodily sensation. They exist solely to horrify and stimulate, not always respectively, and their ability to do so is the sole measure of their success:

they "prove themselves upon our pulses.'"[56] While the genres of pornography and horror may have taken up different and attenuated names to describe themselves – erotica, exploitation, B-grade, 'splatter' – at base, it is in body genres that 'horrify and stimulate' that I seek to find the pulse. That is, not only do such films 'prove themselves upon our [the spectators'] pulses' inciting a physiological response, such films also exemplify ways of understanding the affective expenditures associated with the pulse in cinema.

Linda Williams takes up from Clover's 'body genres' in her essay 'Film Bodies: Gender, Genre, and Excess' describing three 'body genres' – horror, pornography, and melodrama.[57] These 'body genres' are characterised by films that produce 'ecstatic excesses' in the bodies on screen and in the viewer. And, as Williams writes: 'Visually, each of these ecstatic excesses could be said to share a quality of uncontrollable convulsion or spasm.'[58] Of the three 'body genres' described by Williams, I only analyse horror; nevertheless, the effects of which Williams speaks are found in my case studies in the intensive effects on bodies on the screen and on the body of the spectator.

My emphasis differs from Clover's on the issue of subjectivity. Where Clover speaks of the identification and cross-gender identification of the spectator with the characters of horror films, and specifically slasher film,[59] I speak of intensive affects that cause one to 'lose' oneself (one's subjectivity) and find communication or communion with one's fellow spectators. In other words, the effects of the horror film, as I analyse it, like *aisthesis*, is not a recognition of objects in the image/world and an identification with subjects in the image/world, but an encounter with the energetic and material qualities of the image/world – with the sensations therein. *Aisthesis* causes one to find oneself as part of, or Open with, the energetic and material qualities of the image/world. However, such an *aisthetic* encounter is often only 'exposed' by the exploitative mechanisms of the films and *dispositifs* themselves, which seek precisely to channel these effects, and specifically to channel desire. Clover's identification and cross-gender identification is in the realm of representation and predication. It is an aesthetic encounter rather than *aisthesis*. Her 'body horror' goes no further than a tautology of things that are done to the body; tautology because what is done to bodies on the screen produces identification or cross-gender identification in the bodies of spectators as a way of understanding what is done to spectators.

While Williams's 'body genres' register excess, she has a limited capacity to describe it. Bodily excess is found in the violence, sex, or emotion on screen: in the 'unseemly, "gratuitous" presence of the sexually ecstatic woman, the tortured woman, the weeping woman – and the accompanying presence of the sexual fluids, the blood and the tears that flow from her body'.[60] As Williams writes, this excessive movement and presence of fluids of bodies on screen has its analogue in the reciprocal movement and presence of fluids of the bodies of spectators. Indeed, the mimetic response of spectators to produce corresponding fluids stands as evidence of the bodily excess of these films.[61] Williams diagnoses this response as a perversion of film viewing best understood as sadism, sadomasochism, and masochism. In my analysis, I differentiate the mimetic response that Williams proffers from what I call automutilation. Instead of conceiving the spectator as mimicking what they see on screen, I argue that spectatorship involves a continuous energetics of expenditure between the image and the spectator that undoes subjectivity. Williams's spectatorship of excess does not advance the argument of excess beyond subject positions, which is my aim here.

My work nevertheless retains Williams's idea of the 'uncontrollable convulsions' of both the body on screen and the body of the spectator.[62] Her description of a 'quality of uncontrollable convulsion or spasm – of the body "beside itself" with sexual pleasure, fear and terror, or overpowering sadness' forms the basis of my notion of convulsive affect,[63] according to which I understand the movement of the pulse as pertaining to both the images on the screen and a particular kind of movement of the spectator. This movement is convulsive: jerky and elastic. This is because the movement of the pulse is not mechanically rhythmic in its beats but expands and contracts; extending outward and closing in on itself. To be convulsively affective, in this relationship, is thus to specify a body convulsively acting on the image/world and the image/world convulsively acting on the body in a way that gives rise to change. The jerky elasticity of the movement of the pulse as it beats and communicates with the world gives rise to change in each extension outward of the pulse. The communication between the body and the image/world happens in fits and starts.

Whereas Williams describes the body as 'beside itself' when gripped by these 'uncontrollable convulsion[s] or spasm[s]', I consider the implications of this condition of the body for subjectivity. I propose that a subject seized by convulsive affect and which, in being affected, is 'beside itself' or radically decentred.[64] Like the pulse, which in its extensions outward continually gives rise to something new – new freedoms – the spectator, in being seized by convulsive affect, at once loses themselves to this operation and puts themselves at risk to new freedoms. I will theorise spectatorship in relation to Bataille's concept of sovereignty to capture these aspects of the pulse.

The term 'body horror' is appropriate to the concept of the pulse in cinema that I formulate here. The body is foregrounded in different ways in each of the films that I have chosen to analyse. In fact, blood is also foregrounded in each of the films that I have chosen and in different ways, even as the pulse refers to movement and Open and affective expenditure rather than necessarily the material of blood that it propels. Each of my 'body horror' studies looks at different aspects of the pulse, whether it be the aesthetics, the economy, or the vectors of movement and affect that contribute to the behaviour of the pulse.

For William Castle's *The Tingler* (1959), spectators were literally 'tingled' in the cinema theatre in 1959, causing palpable excitation. *The Tingler* allows me to illustrate how the spectator body is a body prescribed by the aesthetic effects of the apparatus in ways that 'expose' him or her to *aisthesis*. Not only are the sensations of the spectator directly inspired by the apparatus in this film, the aesthetics of blood spilled 'exposes' *aisthesis* for the spectator. An aesthetics of the pulse will be conceptualised by the originary sensations of *aisthesis* that are 'exposed' for spectators in an image that spills blood. *The Tingler* also makes claim to 'The screen's first BLOOD BATH IN COLOR!' in this otherwise black and white film. My analysis of *The Tingler* will show how spilled blood changes *aisthesis* to aesthetics, and also how the function of the apparatus gives way to the investment of the *dispositif* in cinema spectatorship. George A. Romero's *Dawn of the Dead* (1978) is known as a 'splatter' film, and there is a focus on the splattering of blood in the automutilation that it depicts. Such automutilation allows for a discussion of the 'sustained' continuum of sensation that occurs between the characters and the spectators of the film. 'Splatter' also has the effect of intensities in this cinema of expenditures. Spectators, by this expenditure, take part in sovereign operations. This kind of cinema engages in the expenditure, channelling, and exploitation of energies that I understand as a function of the pulse. In Lucio Fulci's *L'aldilà/The Beyond* (1981), a tide of blood flows towards its victim, Jill (Maria Pia Marsala). The blood that flows towards Jill causes her to 'lose' herself in the operation. In my analysis of *L'aldilà*, I develop an idea of metonymy that is operative and that gives rise to an operation of the 'loss' of identity. Metonymic images work by 'contagion' for the operative movement of a continuing 'opening out' of identity. Metonymy also suggests a displacement of energies that occurs between images and spectators. Metonymy brings about a spectatorship involved in sovereign operations because identity 'loses' itself through the displacement of energies. Andrzej Żuławski's *Possession* (1981) has the female body on screen – a body always in movement – go into a vodoun-like trance. Blood also flows from the body of Anna (Isabelle Adjani) when she miscarries. I examine the movement and affect of blood as the incitement for dispossession by which characters and spectators 'lose' themselves to sovereign operations. In my analysis of this film I explore how the movement of bodies and blood – and the quantities of magnitude and direction that are the vectors of this movement – engenders convulsive affect. The visible movements of bodies and blood in this film gives me cause to analyse the movement of the pulse as convulsively affective, as a way of understanding the affective force of cinema.

Departing from commonly accepted ideas about the rhythm of the pulse, Chapter 1 asks, what is rhythm and what is the pulse? How can they be differentiated? Where do they intersect? To answer these questions this chapter analyses various prototypes of the pulse in cinematic rhythm, namely in the work of American avant-garde filmmaker Brakhage, Structuralist/Materialist filmmaker Peter Kubelka, French Impressionist filmmakers and theorists Epstein and Germaine Dulac, Dadaist filmmakers and artists Hans Richter and Duchamp, as well as the protocinematic experiments of Marey. In these prototypes we find that rhythm is concerned with 'perceived' movement, and the pulse, by contrast, is concerned with a response to the experience of a 'felt' time. I develop this conception of rhythm and the pulse by observing Freud's differentiation between the rhythmic action of stimuli upon the perceptual apparatus and the force of the investment of energies in the unconscious/drives. Using Freud's writings on 'A Note upon the "Mystic Writing-Pad"' and *Beyond the Pleasure Principle*, this chapter suggests that it is in the investment of libidinal energies in the image that we find the pulse. The pulse is thus theorised as a fact of the image inasmuch as the libido charges the image and attaches to it. Thus for cinema, I propose that it is by attending to the investment in libidinal energies that make up the forces of intensity that we find the pulse in the image.

Chapter 2 outlines the framework for understanding affective spectatorship as constituted in the pulse and its imbricated relation to rhythm. This chapter contrasts between what Lyotard calls '*surfaces of inscription*' and passages of intensity in the libidinal economy, whereby rhythm is understood as the energetic action inscribed on the Open surface of the body and the pulse as the passages of intensity.[65] Rhythm, because of its energetic action upon surfaces, is found in the memory and 'remains' of a past event,[66] and the pulse is the force of the intensities that are libidinally invested and which energetically open out the body in the arrangement, set-up, or *dispositif*. Because the pulse is Open on the world, in relation to cinema, the image and the spectator can also be thought of as Open. Whereas Deleuze writes that the rhythm of diastole–systole is a kind of envelopment in, or, what Deleuze calls, an Open of the self and the world, Lyotard describes an opening of the body to 'spread out all its surfaces'.[67] The literal pulse of the body and its movement in response to the world provides scope for arguing that the defining characteristic of an affective spectatorship must be the Open. Extending the Open to the conceptualisation of the pulse, we must also acknowledge its imbricated relation to rhythm. In Franju's *Le Sang des bêtes*, the rhythms of life encapsulate the shocks, bursts, or surges of energetic flow that connect and open the animals in the slaughterhouse to the 'felt' sensations of the spectator. The diastolic–systolic opening to sensation in Deleuze and the passages of intensity that travel the open 'libidinal skin' in Lyotard characterise the behaviour of the rhythm of life as a pulse.

Chapter 3 expands upon the notion from Chapter 1 that the pulse is 'felt' and claims that there is an originary aesthetics, or *aisthesis*, involved in this 'feeling'. Here I establish the parameters of *aisthesis* as sensibility in its most primitive state and as that which is 'exposed' by the capture of the subject by an apparatus. The concept of *aisthesis* that Lyotard develops to theorise the executing apparatus of Kafka's 'In the Penal Colony' permits a radical reinterpretation of the aesthetics associated with the pulse. The blood spilled by this apparatus exposes the 'felt' sensations of the originary body. In this chapter I show that *aisthesis* provides scope for defining the 'felt' spectatorship of the pulse, which can be differentiated from the aesthetic spectatorship concerned with the rhythms of the apparatus. By examining the viewing conditions established for Castle's *The Tingler*, which saw cinema seats wired with electric devices that would 'tingle' their occupants, I find that what this apparatus 'exposes' is the *aisthetic* sensations of the spectator.

The pulse entails a different kind of spectatorship than that seen in subject positions by which meaning is returned in value. The pulse entails a spectatorship of expenditure in which the spectator is 'put at stake' and 'loses' oneself to the experience. Chapter 4 examines the 'loss' of mastery and identity entailed in the energetic expenditure of the spectator of, particularly, horror or 'splatter' cinema as a sovereign operation of 'putting at stake'. Exploring an economy of the pulse in an analysis of two films, Romero's *Dawn of the Dead* and Fulci's *L'aldilà*, this chapter shows how 'splatter' images have the force of 'felt' intensities insofar as the pulse is a flexible and momentary intensity that suggests the flow and flexibility of a 'felt', but unseen, operation.

By this expenditure of intensities, it is not merely that the spectator is 'at stake' before the image, but that the force of intensities of the pulse constitutes the image as a sovereign one. In these films the characteristics of the pulse that we have previously understood as sensorial and libidinal intensities now express themselves in automutilation as the investment of energies in visceral fleshy appearances, and in the metonymic as the displacement of energies from image to image. Automutilation and metonymy are operations indebted to the consumption, expenditure, and the 'loss' in general economy that communicate through affective energies. For spectatorship, automutilation and metonymy ultimately generate a particular affective operation for a particular spectatorship: communication and communion.

Chapter 5 will conceptualise the vectors of the pulse as the quantities of magnitude and direction that communicate. The vector discloses the difficulty in isolating the place of the pulse, which in turn suggests the 'putting at stake' of self or sovereignty experienced in Bataille's general economy. What Bataille describes is sovereignty in the face of a spectatorship of violence and eroticism by which 'I' expend without return and sacrifice without reserve. Blood spilled is a visual encounter with expenditure and sacrifice, but also a visual encounter with vectors of the pulse.

I analyse the vector in relation to the form of spectatorship that Żuławski's film *Possession* gives rise to. The film is remarkable for the way it relates the magnitude and directional flow of blood to a frenzy of the body in a kind of convulsive affect. Blood points to the sacrificial expenditure, or dispossession, of the self, which nevertheless produces an intimate communication or communion between characters, film, and spectator. Spilled blood and the affective response in the spectator that attends it produces a material vector due to the magnitude of its directional flow. The appearance of the material vector of blood causes an affective operation amounting to a 'loss' of the subjective self in communication and communion.

Above all, the cinematic pulse can be found in affective intensities 'felt' by the spectator, and beyond this, makes up the energetic flow of intensities between the spectator and the image. The *dispositif* is the arrangement or structures that channel and exploit energies, and the pulse allows us to understand the behaviour of energies and the force of their investment. Lyotard writes about the opening of the libidinal band/skin as an energetic investment of 'folds, wrinkles, scars' and 'pubic fur, nipples, nails'.[68] It has even been said of Lyotard's libidinal body that it 'has no limits because various things such as books, food, images, as well as words, machines and even sounds can be charged with libidinal investment and therefore become areas of the body'.[69] This expression of a continuity of communication between the living being and the image/world as the living being and the image/world are invested energetically is aptly described by Bataille who writes about an 'ungraspable inner streaming' that 'opens' to an outside. Not only are things or objects invested in this energetic 'passage' from one thing to another, but 'individual beings' and their points of view 'matter little'.[70] Here, Bataille also writes of energetic investment as a kind of contagion: 'words, books, monuments, symbols, laughter are only so many paths of this contagion, of these passages'.[71] 'Contagion' is also the metonymic displacement of energies. We can thus see a similarity of interest in the investment of energies in Lyotard and Bataille's work. Both writers describe energetic investment, and we can say that there is an investment of energies in the *dispositif* of cinema. I advocate here for a conceptualisation of the cinematic pulse where the force of energies and their vectors – which comprise quantities of magnitude and direction – are key.

Notes

1. Deleuze, *Cinema 1*, p. 65.
2. Deleuze, *Francis Bacon*, pp. 42–3.
3. Deleuze, *Francis Bacon*, p. 42.
4. Deleuze, *Francis Bacon*, p. 42.
5. Krauss, 'The Im/Pulse to See', pp. 60–2.
6. Crary, 'Modernizing Vision', p. 43.
7. Crary, 'Modernizing Vision', p. 43; Krauss, 'The Im/Pulse to See', p. 51.
8. Krauss, 'The Im/Pulse to See', p. 51.
9. Krauss, 'The Im/Pulse to See', p. 60.
10. Krauss, 'The Im/Pulse to See', p. 62.
11. Krauss describes what Lyotard calls the phantasmatic matrix as a kind of 'block' of desire: 'For the matrix does not order and regulate difference, maintaining oppositions in a rule-governed system; rather, it courts the transformation of everything into its opposite, thereby undermining the productive work of the structure. So that its second feature is that the elements of the matrix "do not form a system but a block"' (Krauss, 'The Im/Pulse to See', p. 64).
12. Krauss writes: 'This form, which is that of on/off on/off on/off, is the alternating charge and discharge of pleasure, the oscillating presence and absence of contact, the rhythm "in whose regularity the subject's unconscious is, so to speak, 'caught', the formal matrix of both dreams and symptoms". It is onto this form that the matrix figure's fantasized gesture of a spanking that is also a caress can be mapped; for it is this form that can represent the rhythmic oppositions between contact and rupture' (Krauss, 'The Im/Pulse to See', pp. 66–7).
13. Krauss, 'The Im/Pulse to See', pp. 66–7.
14. Krauss, *The Optical Unconscious*, p. 202.
15. Krauss, *The Optical Unconscious*, p. 225.
16. Krauss, 'The Im/Pulse to See', pp. 51, 67.

17. Bois and Krauss, *Formless*, p. 165.
18. Bataille defines formless in his 'Critical Dictionary': 'A dictionary begins when it no longer gives the meaning of words, but their tasks. Thus *formless* is not only an adjective having a given meaning, but a term that serves to bring things down in the world, generally requiring that each thing have its form. What it designates has no rights in any sense and gets itself squashed everywhere, like a spider or an earthworm. In fact, for academic men to be happy, the universe would have to take shape. All of philosophy has no other goal: it is a matter of giving a frock coat to what is, a mathematical frock coat. On the other hand, affirming that the universe resembles nothing and is only *formless* amounts to saying that the universe is something like a spider or spit' (Bataille, 'Formless', p. 31).
19. Trahair, 'Jean-François Lyotard', p. 223.
20. The *Oxford Dictionary* defines the figurative use of the pulse as: 'denoting life, vitality, energy, feeling, sentiment, tendency, drift, indication, etc.; with *pl.*, a throb or thrill of life, emotion, etc.' (Waite, *Oxford Dictionary*, p. 1586).
21. Freud, *Beyond the Pleasure Principle*, p. 43; Lacan, *The Four Fundamental Concepts*, p. 31.
22. Lyotard, *Libidinal Economy*, p. 1.
23. Lyotard, *Libidinal Economy*, p. 17; Deleuze and Guattari, 'Oedipus at Last', p. 267.
24. Trahair, 'Jean-François Lyotard', p. 223.
25. Baudry, 'Ideological Effects', p. 295.
26. Grant, 'Glossary', p. x.
27. Grant, 'Glossary', p. x.
28. Grant, 'Glossary', p. x.
29. Grant, 'Glossary', p. x.
30. Lyotard, *Libidinal Economy*, p. 27.
31. Lyotard writes: 'The scansion + − + − has a meaning in terms of pleasure. This meaning, as Serge Leclaire appropriately recalls, consists, according to Freud, in the difference between a charge and a discharge. "The time of pleasure or *jouissance* is this time of difference (in this instance between a + and a −), in tension: a difference that is imperceptible in itself, the quick of pleasure, a difference that is not itself musical time, but its condition of possibility"' (Lyotard, 'Fiscourse Digure', p. 351; quoting from Leclaire, *Psychanalyser*, p. 67).
32. Lyotard writes: 'The unconscious . . . does not recognize negation; it does not know what contradiction is. The matrix does not consist in a series of fixed oppositions, and whatever "propositions" might be attributed to it that would combine the aim (to beat), the source (the anal zone) and the object (the father) of the drive in one sentence, are themselves condensed into a formula-product – "A child is being beaten" – whose apparent coherence conceals the fact that the life of the psyche contains a multitude of "sentences" that are mutually exclusive, that cannot possibly coexist. Of course it is only

word-presentations that are in question here, and we will study them more closely later on, but the same holds true for the impulsions of the drive they represent. The latter do not form a system but a block. By block I mean that in contradistinction to the propositions of a system, the impulsions occupy an identical position in (libidinal) space simultaneously . . . The investment is at once phallo-genital and anal-sadistic' (Lyotard, 'Fiscourse Digure', pp. 338–9).
33. Grant, 'Glossary', p. x.
34. Williams, *Lyotard*, p. 89.
35. Lyotard, 'Prescription', p. 184.
36. Curtis, 'The Body as Outlaw', pp. 256–7.
37. Available at <https://plato.stanford.edu/archives/win2013/entries/plato-theaetetus/> (last accessed 17 January 2020); Heidegger, 'Phenomenological Interpretations in Connection with Aristotle', p. 131; Lyotard, 'Prescription', p. 179.
38. Lyotard, 'Prescription', p. 179.
39. Lyotard, 'Prescription', p. 179.
40. Lyotard, 'Prescription', p. 179.
41. Lyotard, 'Prescription', p. 180.
42. Derrida describes Bataille's use of the terminology sovereign 'operation': 'Such an "operation" (this word, constantly employed by Bataille to designate the privileged moment or the act of sovereignty, was the current translation of the word *Tun*, which occurs so frequently in the chapter on the dialectic of the master and the slave) thus amounts to risking, putting at stake (*mettre en jeu, wagen, daransetzen*; *mettre en jeu* is one of Bataille's most fundamental and frequently used expressions) the entirety of one's own life' (Derrida, 'From Restricted to General Economy', p. 254).
43. Trahair, 'The Comedy of Philosophy', pp. 161–3.
44. Bataille, *Inner Experience*, p. 64.
45. Derrida, 'From Restricted to General Economy', p. 265.
46. Derrida writes: 'Sovereignty is the impossible, therefore it *is not*, it *is* – Bataille writes this word in italics – "this loss"' (Derrida, 'From Restricted to General Economy', p. 270).
Weiss titles his essay 'Impossible Sovereignty' and writes: 'The inner experience . . . being totally heterogeneous, is thus essentially incommunicable. Yet, insofar as this sovereign inner experience is insufficient unto itself, it becomes manifest in an excessive expression; it thus entails a type of communication, of community. The irony is that if such experience is to be fully heterogeneous, one must either fall into silence or else risk betraying it by communication' (Weiss, 'Impossible Sovereignty', p. 142).
47. Derrida writes: 'Sovereignty dissolves the values of meaning, truth and a *grasp-of-the-thing-itself*' (Derrida, 'From Restricted to General Economy', p. 270).
48. Derrida, 'From Restricted to General Economy', p. 254.

49. Lyotard, 'Prescription', p. 179.
50. Sobchack, *The Address of the Eye*, p. xix.
51. Hawkins, *Cutting Edge*, p. 6.
52. Hawkins, *Cutting Edge*, pp. 6–7.
53. Shaviro, 'Film Theory and Visual Fascination', pp. 25–6.
54. Shaviro, 'Film Theory and Visual Fascination', p. 26.
55. Clover, 'Her Body, Himself', p. 189.
56. Clover, 'Her Body, Himself', p. 189; quoting from Marcus, *The Other Victorians*, p. 278.
57. Williams, 'Film Bodies', pp. 3–6.
58. Williams, 'Film Bodies', p. 4.
59. Clover, *Men, Women and Chain Saws*, p. 43.
60. Williams, 'Film Bodies', pp. 5–6.
61. Williams writes: 'the success of these genres is often measured by the degree to which the audience sensation mimics what is seen on the screen. Whether this mimicry is exact, e.g., whether the spectator at the porn film actually orgasms, whether the spectator at the horror film actually shudders in fear, whether the spectator of the melodrama actually dissolves in tears, the success of these genres seems a self-evident matter of measuring bodily response' (Williams, 'Film Bodies', pp. 4–5).
62. Williams, 'Film Bodies', p. 4.
63. Williams, 'Film Bodies', p. 4.
64. Williams, 'Film Bodies', p. 4.
65. Lyotard, *Libidinal Economy*, pp. 16–17.
66. Lyotard, *Libidinal Economy*, p. 17.
67. Lyotard, *Libidinal Economy*, p. 1.
68. Lyotard, *Libidinal Economy*, p. 1.
69. Curtis, 'The Body as Outlaw', p. 260.
70. Bataille, *Inner Experience*, p. 97.
71. Bataille, *Inner Experience*, p. 97.

CHAPTER 1

The Rhythm of Life: The Pulse in the Image

From the nineteenth century onwards, experimental filmmakers and film theorists alike began to identify a cinematic rhythm that involved a representation of movement. Coinciding with early cinema technologies, theories of vision and the body, and the relation of vision and the body to technologies, what was emphasised were the rhythmic qualities embodied in the moving image. Simultaneously with theories of vision and the body, experimental film theorists and filmmakers explored the idea that movement enters the cinematic image through rhythm. While rhythm appears in cinematic forms as a way of understanding movement and even a movement of the body, a theory of the pulse has not been developed from these theories of rhythm.

Examples of work devoted to exploring the relationship between movement and rhythm include graphical prototypes of cinema, Dadaist cinema, French Impressionist cinema, American avant-garde cinema, and Structuralist/Materialist cinematic forms. Cinematic form's requirement of sequential space, material frames, inscriptive surfaces, abstract and metric measures of time, and series or sets of images produce cinematic rhythm. In addition to this, cinematic form is also capable of yielding the micro-movements of the physiological body on-screen that emphasise the perceptive capacities of the spectator body, as well as giving 'real movement' from which arises the unconscious time of the body.[1] The pulse is necessarily indivisible, irreducible to spatial or temporal fixtures, and even imperceptible. These aspects of the pulse suggest that the experiment with images or 'cinemas' that can be identified as pulsatile are particular kinds of moving images, namely images whose rhythms are circumscribed by the affects, even desire, that flows unconsciously in the body, and is pulled to the surface by movement. In comparison to cinematic rhythm, it is the intervention of the unconscious in cinematic rhythm that brings the pulse into play, and that makes its identification elusive.

The formulation of my argument is one that encounters cinematic rhythm, physiological rhythm, and psychical rhythm, and the forms they take, and works towards understanding how these rhythmic forms give expression to the pulse. Thus, while the articulations of rhythm in the cinematic, protocinematic, and psychoanalytic contribute to the pulse, they do not do so equally.

Rhythm and Pulse

We can begin to clarify the difference between rhythm and pulse by referring to the definition of rhythm derived from E. d'Eichtal by Jean Mitry, who contends that 'rhythm is in time what symmetry is in space'.[2] Elaborating on the definition of rhythm as 'order and proportion in space and time',[3] Mitry adds the quality of 'perceived periodicity' in consciousness.[4] Mitry writes: 'rhythm can be perceived only insofar as it is governed by our consciousness'.[5] Proportion is a natural measure of this periodicity. It is 'co-modulation' or 'harmonic proportion'.[6] Rhythm's perceived periodicity means it is that which occurs in consciousness as much as that which is necessarily 'seen' in cinema. And yet, it is not the twenty-four frames per second that we 'see' in cinema. Of course, the rhythm of film's twenty-four frames per second is a common misunderstanding about cinema because the rhythmic metre of frames is invisible to the spectator in the moving image. The rhythm of the filmstrip is not found in the transfer of the twenty-four frames to the spectator other than in our consciousness of it. Or rather, it is not the rhythm of the twenty-four frames per second that the spectator sees, because the 'persistence of vision' forestalls such rhythm in vision. Thus, Mitry writes: 'if rhythm is rhythm only insofar as it is perceived, its framework is inevitably the limits of our sensory capacities'.[7]

This rhythmic metre of frames does not mean that rhythm is the same as metre. Metre is defined by Mitry as 'static and completely regular'. It is a 'homogeneous rhythm' as a 'measure of time'.[8] Thus, metre is actually the sequence of images on the filmstrip, and rhythm is a sequence of events in intervals of time found in the film's diegesis and the cut of the film. Extending the limitations of the spectator's sensory capacities for metre to the rhythmic cut of the film, Mitry writes: 'Only relationships of time of the order of seconds or fractions of seconds relating to a whole lasting as much as thirty seconds can be perceived as rhythm.'[9]

'Perceived' rhythm, as Mitry defines it, is that which is sensed but must also be grasped by consciousness. Mitry writes: 'the notion of rhythm cannot be accepted as anything but an intellectual process which reconstructs mentally the perceived relationships in order to abstract an approximate general "idea"'.[10] What Mitry means by an 'intellectual process' is the process of perception that encapsulates the senses, consciousness, and memory. As Mitry describes the process, the relationships between beats in rhythm are the 'parts' perceived of what constitutes the 'whole' retained by memory.[11] Thus, perceived rhythm involves a consciousness of the relationship between beats as they are remembered. Mitry writes: 'this is possible only inasmuch as our memory is capable of doing this, by involving a process of "persistence of image" (auditory and visual), similar, as an effect of consciousness, to retinal persistence at the physiological level'.[12]

Equally, one must perceive the relationship between sounds to understand rhythm in music. We find a model of rhythmic cinema in music. Music relies on rhythm to ensure the *felt* movement of a piece, including 'where the climax occurs, how fast the harmony changes, where the music breathes at cadences, and how one section balances another in terms of time'.[13] Rhythm appears when the movement of the musician and the music are coupled. The manipulation of a musical device by the body means that the development of rhythm is often described in analogical relation to the body: rhythm is likened to the beating of the heart that speeds and slows, and musical phrasing is likened to breathing that can calm or quicken. Music is said to have 'life', and it is the physiological conditions of the body that suggest this 'expression' of rhythm. Recurrent patterns or stresses that break up the continuous action of the heartbeat and of breathing could be said to be their rhythm. Rhythm, in this instance, is close to a definition of the pulse, and certainly it can be said that the pulse has an organic rhythm. However, the difference remains that rhythm refers to 'perceived' and external movement as inscribed on a surface like the beats of a drum, whereas the pulse is movement 'felt' from within.

Speaking in quotidian terms we could say that the pulse is the beating or throbbing that results when the blood is pumped through the arteries from the heart muscle. The *Oxford Dictionary* defines the pulse as 'the "beating", throbbing, or rhythmically recurrent dilatation of the arteries as the blood is propelled along them by the contractions of the heart in the living body'.[14] This pulse is the rhythm that is 'felt' as an indication of a 'person's state of health'.[15] In *Black's Medical Dictionary*, a definition of the pulse propounds that the

> cause of the pulsation lies in the fact that, at each heart-beat, 80 to 90 millilitres of blood are driven into the aorta, and a fluid wave, distending the vessels as it passes, is transmitted along the arteries all over the body.[16]

Indeed, when we feel the pulse at the wrist, what we in fact feel is the wave of distension or the force of movement as blood passes through the arteries. The pulse, then, is this force of movement.

John Briggs and F. David Peat write that the heart displays the 'strange attractor behaviour' of a chaotic system in its pulsing rhythm.[17] This 'strangeness' is one that is not complicit with logico-temporal movement. The 'chaotic variations, microjolts, and tiny fluctuations' in cardiac rhythm give the heart a 'range of behaviour (degrees of freedom) that allows it to settle back into its rhythm even after it has been nudged away by some shock such as a fast run or a sudden step into subzero air'.[18] In fact, the heart is likely to go into defibrillation if its beat is too mechanical and regular.[19] The pulse thus entails a flexible beat that speeds and slows, extends and settles, dilates and contracts.

In her research project, 'Computational modelling to create a virtual map of arterial shape and blood flow', Dr Susann Beier at the University of New South Wales seeks to illustrate that the elasticity of the pulse's movement is dependent upon the wellbeing of the patient. Computational modelling from this research project shows that the pulse's movement is more elastic – maps as higher peaks – when the patient is well.

The pulse's movements of dilation and contraction are qualitatively changing as the wave of distension moves through the pliable blood vessels. But there is more to the definition than this. The pulse responds to causes, whereas rhythm is constituted by events. Rhythm refers to a sequence of events in time – not necessarily a structured or ordered sequence but a sequence nonetheless. The pulse entails an organic opening out in relations as a momentary force. The pulse in its verb form means also 'to drive, impel; to drive *forth*, expel'.[20] The movement of the pulse is pressure from within: movement that has the force of change and development.

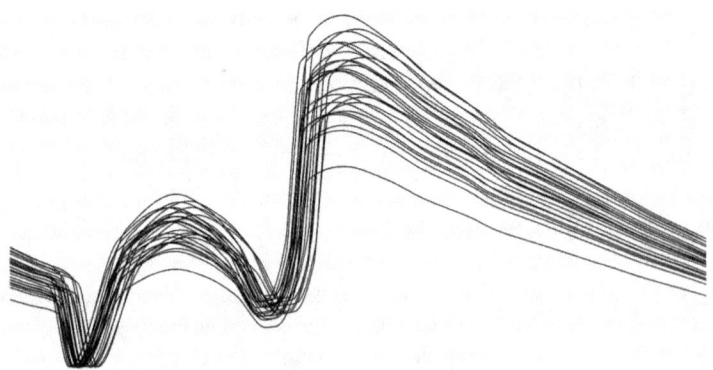

Figure 1.1 Mapping the pulse. Source: Dr Susann Beier, 'Computational modelling to create a virtual map of arterial shape and blood flow', University of New South Wales, 2020.

The pulse is 'felt', and in it we are carried along by the force of the vibrations of matter and the relationships of change and development. The pulse is different to 'perceived' rhythm because, as an expression of bodies and things, the pulse is movement 'felt' from within. As an initial way of thinking about the pulse we might simply refer to organic 'pulse beats'. The pulse can be likened to rhythm insofar as each entails a repetition of beats, but the pulse, in the first instance, differs from rhythm in its irregularity. The pulse suggests the flow and flexibility of the 'felt' beat where rhythm implies the pattern and regularity of the 'perceived' beat.

When rhythm has been previously taken up in relation to cinema, it has intersected with questions of visuality, the body, and form. The pulse also raises questions regarding visuality, the body, and form, but with vastly different consequences. Rhythm's involvement in visuality, the body, and form is derived from that which is perceived, thought, and inscribed. The pulse's involvement in visuality, the body, and form is derived from that which is felt, sensed in the body, and which moves qualitatively.

Even though a theory of the pulse may be developed from what we understand to be rhythm, what becomes apparent in definitions of the pulse is that when we talk about the pulse we talk about the rhythm of the pulse, thereby inextricably linking the two. We also tend to define rhythm and the pulse in our 'sensing' of them. Rhythm and the pulse are defined by our capacity to 'perceive' or 'feel' them. This makes rhythm and the pulse important for an analysis of cinema spectatorship and particular to affective cinema.

As something that is 'felt', the pulse is the image of affection and, as 'felt' sensation, seizes the body from within. In the nineteenth-century it was understood that the network of arteries communicate with one another in the body. Henry Gray writes in *Anatomy: Descriptive and Surgical*: 'The arteries, in their distribution, communicate freely with one another, forming what is called an *anastomosis* (ἀνὰ, *between*; στόμα, *mouth*), or inosculation . . . these inosculations become so numerous as to constitute a close network that pervades nearly every tissue of the body.'[21] However, it is not simply that the body communicates with itself. As we have seen in Briggs and Peat's description of the pulse's 'strange attractor behaviour', the pulse is 'attracted' to, or settles into a rhythm, but this rhythm is also 'open' to the conditions and changing developments of the world. Namely, this is a shift from a rhythmic mediation of an object and subject that are acted upon, towards a pulsatile opening of the affective body to the image/world.

Rhythm in Experimental Cinema

From the French Impressionist and Dadaist art movements in the first half of the nineteenth century to the American avant-garde filmmakers of the 1960s, rhythm in multifarious forms was regarded as a key site of aesthetic interrogation. The emphasis on rhythm in film frequently entailed a rejection of linear narrative and a reorganisation of the temporal experience of film viewing.

Rhythm takes different cinematic forms in American avant-garde and Structuralist/Materialist cinema, French Impressionist cinema, and Dadaist art cinema. What I will demonstrate in my examination of these filmmakers' concerns with rhythm is an underlying preoccupation with questions about the relation of energetics to opticality and form, and an interest in the unconscious dimension of the impact of rhythm that exceeds rhythm narrowly understood as a sequence of images in time. Taking Mitry's initial definition of rhythm as 'order and proportion in space and time',[22] what I show is a development from the simple terms of order and proportion to the various ways in which cinematic rhythm is 'perceived' in the image by the spectator. Different cinematic forms have different qualities that make them rhythmic, thereby illustrating both the way that spectators 'perceive' rhythm and the different relationships between the image and the spectator. The rhythmic movement of the image causes a particular movement of the spectator even at the micro-level of physiology. In rhythm's most pulsatile form, it is the movement that works on the unconscious and attracts desire and thereby gives form to this affective spectatorship.

American Avant-garde and the Structuralist/Materialists

American avant-garde filmmakers of the 1950s sought to incorporate a musical sense of rhythm into the aesthetic dimensions of the film they were exploring. This rhythm was located in the *visual* properties of cinema and in the material properties of cinematic technology, that is, film frames. This preoccupation comes to the fore in the filmmakers' interest in filming objects, painting or manipulating the filmstrip to leave shadows or shapes on the material film, which, when projected, generated abstractions.

Adopting both music and abstract form, Harry Smith melded the rhythms of live performance jazz to his cinematic work – a kind of visual music in the rhythmic appearances of colour and shape. In the 1960s, with the founding of the New York Filmmakers' Co-operative by Jonas Mekas, such ideas were developed to provide elements of a Structuralist/Materialist oeuvre that were later taken up by Peter Gidal and Malcolm LeGrice of the London Filmmakers' Co-operative.

In his work, Brakhage, one of the New York Co-operative filmmakers, shows similarity to the emphasis that the Structuralist/Materialists placed on the material form of the filmstrip and its manipulation. Brakhage speaks quite literally of film as a material extension of the physiological conditions of the body. In his response to Suranjan Ganguly he writes: 'Over the years I have come to believe that every machine people invent is nothing more than an extension of their innards. The base rhythm of film – 24 frames per second – is sort of centred in its pulse to our brain waves.'[23] When Annette Michelson, referring to Brakhage's work, insists that it brings to light the 'materiality of the filmic support', it is significant that the support here refers not simply to the filmstrip, nor indeed to the spectator's body's innards, but rather to rhythm itself.[24] That is, it is the condition of rhythm that we 'see' in viewing the film. Indeed, many of the Structuralist/Materialist filmmakers making film after Brakhage rely on the 'visibility' of cinema and its mechanisms to make rhythm meaningful.

Brakhage's intention in his films from the 1970s and 1980s was that the physiological conditions of vision – the 'act of seeing' – be envisioned in film. And it was Brakhage's inclusion in his definition of the 'act of seeing' of the many forms of vision such as 'open-eye, peripheral and hypnagogic vision, along with moving visual thinking, dream vision and memory feedback', which makes this visually interesting for the spectator, but also generates a link to the movements of the body through visual abstraction.[25] What is 'perceived' by the spectator is an abstracted image of the workings of the eye, or rather, of the perceptions seen in the 'act of seeing'. Brakhage's work intended an understanding of the consciousness of the filmmaker in a depiction of what is seen. However, it is not simply the innards of the eye and the physiological conditions of vision which are seen in Brakhage's films. Brakhage's *Window Water Baby Moving* (1959) and *Dog Star Man* (1961–1964) are earlier experimental films that show the birth of his children and which allow for a consideration of the movement of the pulse, blood and viscera, and what is seen in the 'act of seeing'.

Later, Brakhage scratched, defaced, and stained the filmstrip by hand. These marks on the filmstrip are continuous, and this continuity when viewed takes on a rhythmic appearance as scratches and colours come into being in the projection of the film. In Brakhage's *Vancouver Island Films* (1991–2000), for instance, these marks were intended to capture the rhythms of the sea. We could say that rhythm in light of Brakhage's work exceeds material alterations on the filmstrip to inscribe itself on the surface of the eye of the spectator.

Kubelka, in an interview with Mekas in 1966, uses the term 'metrical film', as a way of understanding film frames in relation to metrics:

> The projected frames hit the screen. For example, when you let the projector run empty, you hear the rhythm. There is a basic rhythm in cinema. I think very few filmmakers—if there ever was one, I don't know—have departed from making films from this feeling of the basic rhythm, these twenty-four impulses on the screen—brrhumm—it's a very metric rhythm.[26]

Kubelka's use of time in film operates like a formal musical time signature. He explains: 'I have no seventeenths and no thirteenths, but I have sixteen frames, and eight frames, and four frames, and six frames – it's a metric rhythm.'[27] Kubelka's interest in rhythm is thus derived from the material properties of the film itself – the ordering of twenty-four frames to generate a harmonious timepiece like the harmonious timepieces of music in duple and triple time.

Notably, P. Adams Sitney compares Kubelka's films to the 'graphic film' of the Futurist Fernand Léger: the intersecting point between the two being Hollis Frampton's *Zorns Lemma* (1970), which Sitney argues was influenced by both Kubelka and Léger.[28] His point here is that the order underlying Kubelka's films is hidden from the viewer rather than openly apparent to the viewer as it is in the case of other Structuralist/Materialist films. Another way of putting this would be to say that for graphic cinema the order is intellectually recognised by the viewer while the laws governing that order remain unperceived. A 'flicker film' like Kubelka's *Arnulf Rainer* (1960) relies on black and transparent photogrammes to beat out a rhythm on the screen. It is graphic because the photogrammes are an index of an unseen but metrical graphic arrangement. The Structuralist/Materialist film by contrast relies on the material filmstrip being acknowledged by the viewer as the site of inscription on which the film is constructed. We will see later in this chapter how graphic cinema comes close to the pulse in its indexation of unseen movement.

This distinction between the work of Kubelka and the Structuralist/Materialists also tallies with a musical distinction between metre or measure and metrics. This distinction opens up a more complex understanding of rhythm by pointing to the difference between 'points of reference' and 'periodicity'. Mitry's distinction between measure and metrics is helpful here in showing us how measure suggests an intellectually regulated rhythm because it gives rhythm 'points of reference', whereas metrics as a measure of rhythmic cadence, that is, 'proportions in time', expresses 'periodicity', even discontinuity.[29] By referring to his work as 'metrical', Kubelka indicates that he conceives of a specifically cinematic rhythm even though it is derived from a musical sense of time.[30] Metrics, however, is not a practical term for music.[31] Music has measures of rhythmic cadence in its quarter notes and half notes, and so on, but these are not expressions of time. The time signature gives the expression of time in music alongside the rhythmic measured length of notes, but time is not generated by rhythm alone. Metrics is adaptable to cinematic rhythm because of cinema's twenty-four frames per second, which gives time-based proportion to cadence. This is all as much to say that metric cinema, like the abstract cinema of the American avant-garde and Structuralist/Materialists, still demonstrates a concern with the filmstrip of cinema. The difference is that while the abstract cinema of the American avant-garde and Structuralist/Materialists worked with the filmstrip at the material level as a sequence of images, metric cinema worked with the filmstrip – constituted of the twenty-four frames per second – by cutting it to generate differences between continuity and discontinuity in proportional cadence. Both are concerned with rhythm but in different ways: the first in its material inscriptions, which once projected, constituted rhythmic form, the second in the order and proportion that cutting the filmstrip could provide.

The French Impressionists

The French Impressionists describe a cinema composed of perceptible movement in the body and the image. Impressionist cinema demonstrates that movement is not in the filmstrip but is rather embodied in the image. This is an important distinction for considering the theoretical aspects of rhythm as movement. As Tom Conley writes: 'From 1895 to 1945 cinema became the seventh art by embodying images not in movement but *as* movement.'[32]

The French Impressionist filmmaker and theorist Epstein, writing on cinema in the early twentieth century, makes an appeal for recognising rhythm as capable of capturing the inner lives of things by arguing that it is something more than the cut of the film. The cut of the film, he writes, produces a rhythm of images that acts like the laws of musical harmony where, for instance, 'in a rapid montage . . . segments of 2-4-8 frames create a rhythm which will inevitably be destroyed by the introduction of a 5 or 7 frame cut'.[33] This 'rhythm through images', he suggests, is only 'the most external aspect of cinematic rhythm'.[34] The psychological rhythm of the characters' lives and the rhythm of the scenario must also be acknowledged as rhythms that inscribe cinematic time:

> simultaneous mobility within the four dimensions of space–time – applies not only to the external aspects of things; it is also the key to the deeper soundings of cinematic dramaturgy, which are yet to be explored. Scenarios are lamentably poor mainly because they fail to recognise this basic rule: there are no inactive feelings which do not move in space, and there are no invariable feelings which do not move in time.[35]

Despite cinematic dramaturgy's attribution of 'feelings' and what should be an internal aspect of cinematic rhythm, Epstein clings to externally generated rhythm in the kind of image he describes. *Photogénie* is the mobility or rhythm of bodies that the close-up capability of the lens is able to capture. By capturing mobility, cinema reveals to its spectators the 'interior lives of things': what Epstein calls the 'cinematic property of things' or *photogénie*.[36] Thus, in Epstein's filmmaking, the close-up physiognomy of the face is a moving and quivering terrain that comprises a radical 'externality of relations'.[37] Epstein suggests that the close-up is devoid of thought and memory,[38] but full of gesture, personality, and space–time:

> In closeup, the eyelid with the lashes that you count, is a set remodelled by emotion at every instant. Beneath the lid appears the gaze which is the character of the drama—and which is even more than a character: it is a personality. Through imperceptible movements whose religious secret no emotional microscopy has yet been able to reveal, the circle of the iris spells out a soul. Between the tuft of the chin and the arc of the eyebrows an entire tragedy is won, then lost, is rewon and lost again. Lips still pressed together, a smile quivers off-stage, towards those wings which is the heart. When the mouth finally opens, joy itself flies out.[39]

The face is not always already realised (or even recognised) but is rather a development that involves complexity, turbulence, and conflict, which is emphasised by the movement of the image and the physiology that it depicts, from the 'tuft of the chin' to the 'arc of the eyebrows'. In the drama staged by Epstein's Impressionism, elements of the face are rhythmically cited in a way that makes up an entire face so that, in his words, 'an entire tragedy is won, then lost, is rewon and lost again'.[40] Moreover, the quivering terrain of the close-up physiognomy of the face and the quivering terrain of the image form an assemblage. The qualities of the eyelid and the lashes, the eye, the chin and eyebrow, lips and mouth – these elements are externally related to each other to create the quivering terrain of a face, and are coupled with the quivering terrain of the image. This is the radical 'externality of relations' in the movement of figures as they appear on the screen. And further, this movement is embodied in the movement of cinema itself. Cinema, in this sense, becomes a theatre of perceptible movements driven by the spectator's perception of objects and figures on the screen as much as by the perceptible movements of the image as it is driven by the mechanical apparatus.

The French Impressionist filmmaker and theorist Dulac, speaks similarly of the way the camera captures the rhythmic terrain of close-up physiognomy:

> The seventh art, that of the screen, is depth rendered perceptible, the depth that lies beneath that surface; it is the musical ungraspable.
>
> Whether it's a matter of a face, a geometrical form, an evolving line, it is movement, in all its richness, rendered by the rhythm of its curves, of its right angles, that creates the drama. A body that stretches out or contracts in a total movement. A grain of wheat that sprouts, the horse's leap, visual and silent movements of the same bearing, the same general lines. So it's not the extravagance of literary imagination that makes the film. The film is something much more simple. The expressiveness of a face, to have its full value, must not be divided between one shot and the next.
>
> A grain of wheat that sprouts does not change place, it rises up; a horse's leap is accomplished in a very limited space, and all the same, in all three situations, there is movement, more movement, believe me, than in a chase.[41]

By means of the mechanical camera, objects and bodies are 'rendered perceptible' in a way that goes beyond conventional seeing. Dulac suggests that the rhythms, movement, shape, and form of things and bodies, are revealed to vision by cinema – the 'stretch[ing] out or contract[ing]' of bodies provides a rhythm at the micro-level of movement itself. Bodies stretch and contract – a grain of wheat slowly sprouts, a horse leaps. Thus the French Impressionists describe a cinema composed of imperceptible movement in the body made perceptible by the image. Impressionist cinema further demonstrates that movement is not in the filmstrip but is rather embodied in the image. The 'radical externality' of such movement approaches the rhythm of the pulse because it exemplifies the way movement expressed in and by the image is simultaneously an expression of movement for the spectator. The physiognomy of movement that is captured by the close-up and seen by the spectator, brings focus to the movement of the spectator at the micro-level of physiology. Such movement approaches the rhythm of the pulse because it illustrates the way that spectators 'perceive' rhythm in the micro-movements of the image, and shows that the relationship between the image and the spectatorship is one of simultaneous perceptible movement.

Dada

The Dadaist filmmaker Richter proposes that 'abstract film' such as his *Rhythmus 21* (1921) uses the rhythmic qualities of cinema to void objects and bodies of their quotidian meaning. In Richter's *Rhythmus 21* the frame begins as a black frame, and is swept, from the left and the right, to become a white frame, and from the centre to the left and the right, to become a black frame. This sweep also occurs from the top and the bottom. There is an alternation of black and white shapes, which increase and decrease in size, and appear and disappear. Richter argues that the mechanism of movement creates an experience of rhythm as 'feeling' due to contrast, relationship and interaction. He writes:

> This film gives memory nothing to hang on. At the mercy of "feeling", reduced to going with the rhythm according to the successive rise and fall of the breath and the heartbeat, we are given a sense of what feeling and perceiving really is: a process—movement. This "movement" with its own organic structure is not tied to the power of association (sunsets, funerals), nor to emotions of pity (girl matchseller, once famous—now poor—violinist, betrayed love), nor indeed to "content" at all, but follows instead its own inevitable mechanical laws.[42]

Richter's films thus undertake a kind of 'abstraction' that transforms an object through movement by virtue of the mechanical laws that govern cinema, even though he himself argues that it is both abstraction and representation that is avoided.[43] That is, Richter does not call his films 'abstractions' in his essay 'The Badly Trained Sensibility', but says instead that by constructing a film by reducing it to its basic principles of movement, 'feeling' is produced. This emphasis on movement is important to the conception of rhythm that I am defining here because it implies that rhythm is not necessarily abstract form per se, but found in the 'idea' of structural form.[44] Expanding on this cognitive aspect, Richter himself says that this 'sensibility' of movement has a 'thinking power': 'This "thinking power" enables the sensibility to exercise its powers of judgement and of action.'[45] The 'sensibility' of which Richter speaks is thus a 'process' that is found in consciousness, and also in the 'successive rise and fall of the breath and the heartbeat' – a pulse.[46]

Rhythm, in Richter's sense, also has a close affiliation to the mechanical apparatus because the mechanical laws of movement in rhythmic cinema accentuate the sequential frames that make up the filmstrip. As Richter says, movement 'follows . . . its own inevitable mechanical laws'.[47] However, the sequential movement of the frames of cinema, as we will see in the case of Duchamp, is not the only movement in cinema.

The Dadaist Duchamp seized upon the possibilities of rhythm to break the hold of what he calls the retinal image. And although it could be said that Richter's *Rhythmus 21* (1921), and even Duchamp's *Anémic Cinéma* (1926), abstracts objects by taking objects from their context, Duchamp was quick to distinguish his ambitions from those of abstract art. In interviews with Pierre Cabanne, he exclaims: 'When you see what the Abstractionists have done since 1940, it's worse than ever, optical. They're really up to their necks in the retina!'[48] Sitney writes that the kind of 'abstraction' that Richter was working with entailed 'divesting itself of photographic objects' to reorient 'the work of "memory". The mind, free from associations which the sentimental cinema exploits, experiences time as feeling.'[49] Duchamp's work, on the other hand, reorients 'the work of "memory"' in a different way. While both Richter and Duchamp free objects and images from their associations and Richter argues that this frees the image of memory,[50] the work of Duchamp reinvests objects and images with memory traces by transference.

The use of movement for this purpose can be demonstrated in Léger's *Ballet mécanique* (1924) and Duchamp's *Anémic Cinéma* (1926) because they both use what Sitney calls 'shallow space' and 'deep space'. In Léger's *Ballet mécanique* the image generates a conflict between what Sitney calls 'shallow space', circumscribed by the limits of a two-dimensional field in the shot's focus on objects, and 'deep space' by which objects/bodies move back and forth in the image: an image that allows itself to be seen in depth in spite of the flat surface of the picture plane of the screen.[51] What is being seized upon is something more than simply 'deep space' – the space of renaissance perspective, for example – to a space that protrudes beyond the picture plane. Thus, more complexly, what can be said is that the 'shallow space' of the 'still' image produces a sensory effect, and the 'deep space' of the 'moving' image produces a memory imprint or unconscious image. Similarly the 'still' images, or discs, placed in movement in Duchamp's *Anémic Cinéma* are not read as formal signs or even objects. Set in motion, the discs generate an effect that undermines the formal system of these signs and their object-like status. The moving discs generate an illusion of three-dimensional space, from convex to concave cones and from vacuous spaces to focal-point protrusions. Such motion, Duchamp argues, does not generate an optical illusion, but a break with sensory perception inasmuch as the moving image produces a memory imprint or unconscious image.

Such images are different from those of Impressionist cinema, which is a sensory cinema generated in close-up terrains from which space–time relations unfold. Dadaist cinema breaks with the sensory image to generate what Duchamp calls a 'conceptual image' that moves away from the optical difficulties of abstraction because it constitutes a leap into the realm of desire. In the following note from *The Green Box*, Duchamp writes that to lose the possibility for recognising objects is to transfer a visual imprint to a memory imprint – to transform an insufficient retinal image into a conceptual image:

> Identifying
> *To lose* the po*ssibility of reco*gnizing *2 similar objects*—2 colors, 2 laces, 2 hats, 2 forms whatsoever to reach the Impossibility of sufficient *visual* memory, to transfer from one like object to another the *memory* imprint.
> —Same possibility with sounds; with brain facts.[52]

The work of rhythm demonstrates the way this mechanical movement, in subverting the object, incites a different kind of spectatorship that brings something conceptual into play. Duchamp's repudiation of the retinal and his advocacy of the conceptual does not necessarily avoid the somatic body, he simply argues that the image need not invest simply in a retinal (simply perceptual) image.

It is important to acknowledge the way that this relationship of movement to the mechanical, generated by the conflict between 'shallow space' and 'deep space', curiously incites a spectatorship bound to the non-sensory destructive space of the unconscious from which desire blossoms. In Léger's *Ballet mécanique*, the conflict between 'shallow' and 'deep space' is apparent in a mouth smiling, an eye blinking, a hat, a shoe, a shoe, a hat, which all suggest 'shallow space'; and the back and forth of the girl on the swing, the motion of gears and pistons, a washer-woman climbing and re-climbing the stairs, and the rotation of kaleidoscopic prisms, which all suggest 'deep space'. In Duchamp's *Anémic Cinéma* we see the conflict in the spiralling discs of the rotoreliefs that, when printed with the words of puns, suggest 'shallow space', and when printed with spirals move out of the two-dimensional plane of the picture to suggest 'deep space'. In *Ballet mécanique*, the back and forth movement of the girl on the swing (who is smiling) suggests the action of a penis thrusting towards the spectator, the girl's smiling mouth the slit-like opening of the urethra at the tip of the glans penis. In *Anémic Cinéma*, the sexual allusion in the spiralling text inclines the viewer to read the spirals as breasts, penises, vaginas, anuses, and faeces, disassociating the rotoreliefs from the optical. The mechanism of the still and moving, textual and pictorial rotoreliefs, demonstrates precisely the conflict that arises between 'shallow' and 'deep space'. The image is put in service of the primary processes that condense and displace meaning in a cathexis of energy stimulated by movement. Inaugurated by movement, desire extends beyond the optical image, even while the object of desire is grasped as a joke by consciousness. The optical image that calls forth the unconscious demonstrates at once the image that activates desire and the image that represses desire: the moving image is, in other words, a violence to – a negation of – the simply retinal image. Dadaist cinema demonstrates sensation in communication with the vicissitudes of the human nervous system, desire, and the unconscious, as if pulled to the surface by movement.

Dadaist cinema thus breaks with the aesthetics of Impressionist cinema by transitioning from an aesthetics grounded in phenomenology by which the sensory body is primary, to one that sets store in the non-sensory and destructive aesthetics of the unconscious. While the rhythm 'perceived' by consciousness in the work of the abstract cinema of the American avant-garde is focused upon the senses, specifically optics or the retina as the site for rhythm, in Duchamp's cinema, the rhythm 'perceived' by consciousness is rhythm perceived by thought or by the imprints of memory made up of unconscious traces, engendering the conceptual image. In making use of the flow of psychical energy, rhythmic images in Duchamp's work bring into operation another kind of movement that pulls desire to the surface. This pull is the force of the intensity of the pulse.

Figure 1.2 Spiralling discs in *Anémic Cinéma* (Marcel Duchamp, 1926)
© Association Marcel Duchamp/ADAGP. Copyright Agency, 2019.
Photo credit: George Eastman Museum.

Figure 1.3 Spiralling discs in *Anémic Cinéma* (Marcel Duchamp, 1926)
© Association Marcel Duchamp/ADAGP. Copyright Agency, 2019.
Photo credit: George Eastman Museum.

Protocinema: Étienne-Jules Marey

It is clear that well before Dada cinema of the 1920s the idea of rhythm was in evidence. Marey's studies in motion were produced in the latter half of the nineteenth century, and are concerned with physiological time and mapping the economy of the body, where the economy of the body is understood as the energetic system of movement and fatigue in the body's relation to the world. In effect, using chronometry, Marey's studies made chronological time the basis for analysing the continuous movement of the body.

The various methods that Marey developed to represent continuous movement can be grouped into three types: chronophotography; geometrical chronophotography; and graphic inscription. The term 'chronograph' is found in Marey's earlier work and refers to the graphic recording of time. It is superseded in his later work by the term 'chronophotograph', which refers to the photographic recording of time used in both chronophotography and geometrical chronophotography.[53] Marey calls the graphic depiction of the interior movements of the body and/or the forces at work in movement 'tracings' or 'notations' because of the use of a mechanical stylus that traced the results on a turning cylinder. These 'graphic notations' are now generally referred to as 'graphic inscriptions'. Indeed, the three methods – chronophotography, geometrical chronophotography, and graphic inscription – use different 'sensor' apparatuses to produce different kinds of inscriptive results.[54] The contrast in the methods is between chronophotographic inscriptions and graphic inscriptions; between inscriptions that rely on a camera at a distance and the 'sensing' of light to photograph an image, and those that rely on non-lens-based apparatuses that touch the body or 'sense' the movements of the body through effects such as the production of heat of the body, electrical nervous and muscular movement, and the force of air pressure in and around the body. The graphic inscriptions come closest to an inscription of the movement of the heart muscle and the literal pulse in a study of physiology in its unseen and 'interior' forms, while Marey's chronophotographic inscriptions move away from this concern to 'whole body' movement (a study of physiology in its seen and 'exterior' forms).

Marey's work studied physiology in its seen and 'exterior' forms, physiology in its unseen and 'interior' forms, and even gives evidence for the way both the seen and the unseen impinge on each other. Mapping both the seen and the unseen, Marey's recordings depict the force, duration, intensity, velocity and rhythm of physiological movement. Chronophotography and geometrical chronophotography provide a photographic image of the seen conditions of the body; graphic inscription provides a signature of the unseen conditions of the body. Marey's work records the economy of the body first as it relates to the interior movements of the body, including the movement of the heart muscle, the nerves, and air pressure in animal locomotion (graphic inscription), and second as a way of depicting animal locomotion as 'whole body' movement (chronophotography and geometrical chronophotography).

The results of these methods reveal the body's rhythms. Whether this rhythm is inscribed on fixed plates or paper, the results indicate the repetition of the movement of the body across time. These techniques, which are protocinematic in nature, play an important part in understanding rhythm in cinema. They also expose the limitations of chronometry as a way of analysing the movement of the body as far as we are trying to develop an understanding of the pulse. Marey's chronophotographic methods for envisaging continuity of movement in the living world, caught up as they were in the decomposition of movement into representative sections of time, end up hindering a demonstration of continuity. Marey's chronophotographic results were caught in the deficiency of the mechanism of their own making; they could not depict 'whole body' motion as continuous motion. Marey's earlier graphic inscriptions achieved this with greater success even as they generated mechanical notations that had to be deciphered to understand the movement of the body. Marey was unable to bring his graphic techniques to his chronophotographic work. Unable to transfer the dynamic continuity of graphic inscription to the image without deferring to the decomposition and recomposition of movement, Marey's chronophotographic images reveal the very discontinuity that cinema retains in its mechanism (most obviously in the frames of the celluloid). Such discontinuity extends to rhythm in cinema. What follows in this section is an analysis of Marey's chronophotographic images and graphic inscriptions – the products of which represent rhythm in some way.

In his later work of 1894, *Le Mouvement* (translated into English as *Movement* in 1895), Marey illustrates two techniques – chronophotography (Figure 1.4) and geometrical chronophotography (Figure 1.5) – for depicting a man running. In contrast to Eadweard Muybridge's chronophotographic work, which was comprised of single successive snapshots creating a series out of time, much of the chronophotographic work completed by Marey entailed superimposed photographic exposures on fixed plates. For Marey, fixed-plate presentation responded to a need to reference time as a continuous relation in the position of objects. The image demonstrates the trajectory of a moving object as it occupies various positions, and correlates to time and continuous motion in a manner that Marey believed Muybridge's set of successive images of framed 'snapshots' in time failed to achieve. Marey argued that between each 'snapshot' in Muybridge's work, time disappeared because it fell into the gap between 'snapshots'.[55] It is also in Marey's series of exposures on the fixed plate that the rhythm of movement is depicted. Each exposure captures a position in space and instant in time even as it breaks up the continuity of movement: the continuity of movement must be imagined as having taken place between each rhythmic 'beat' or exposure.

The chronophotographic process allows for a depiction of movement in its relation to time; movement is understood as physical and increasingly a fact of mechanical representation. Anson Rabinbach argues that: 'Marey's chronophotographs . . . challenged the notion of a static spatialization of time and motion by showing how the trajectory of any object was dependent on the ability of an apparatus to "decompose" it spatially and temporally.'[56] Chronophotography could break time into instants, decomposing it spatially and temporally into a totalising and abstract series of instants, but it could not demonstrate the lived experience of time. In other words, Marey's chronophotography could neither depict the perception of movement or what Henri Bergson calls 'absolute motion', nor its relation to dynamism.[57] In fact, Rabinbach also notes that Marey's work 'showed how distinct the mental processes of perception could be from the "objective" laws of objects in motion'.[58]

Figure 1.4 A man running (chronophotography). Source: Étienne-Jules Marey, 'Homme qui court. Chronophotographie sur plaque fixe/A man running. Chronophotography on a fixed plate', in *Le Mouvement*, 5th edn (Paris: G. Masson, 1894), p. 58.
Photo credit: Huntington Library.

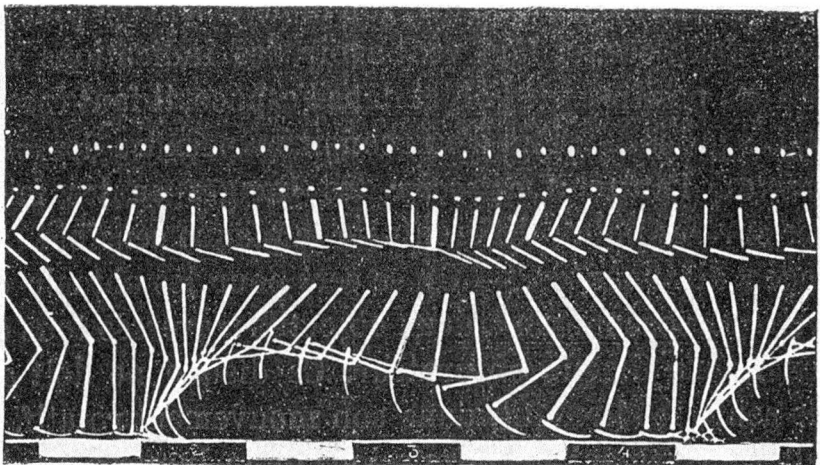

Figure 1.5 A man running (geometrical chronophotography). Source: Étienne-Jules Marey, 'Images d'un coureur réduite à des lignes brillantes qui représentent l'attitude de ses membres (Chronophotographie géométrique)/Images of a runner reduced to a system of bright lines for representing the position of the limbs (geometrical chronophotography)', in *Le Mouvement*, 5th edn (Paris: G. Masson, 1894), p. 61.
Photo credit: Huntington Library.

Geometrical chronophotography is a variety of fixed-plate chronophotography that was applied to reduce the blurring of space caused by closely superimposed objects. Geometrical chronophotographs require the photographic subject to wear a black suit with bright points or lines along the axes of his limbs. The posture of each limb is inscribed on the photographic surface at each filmed instant. The number of images taken over a period of time is greater than that achieved with chronophotography and the process of movement is captured without blurring. Geometrical chronophotography reduces the inscription of bodies in motion to the repetition of lines, and was intended, by Marey, to get rid of the 'noise' of space. The results of this method are that lines in space depict the trajectories of the movement of the body in time.

Marey's decomposition of movement into successive instants comes at the cost of the very continuity of movement he had sought to prove in the first place. This is because, as we see in Figures 1.4 and 1.5, while the capturing of time represents the continuity of movement, it also records time as a series of discontinuous instants. The gap between each exposure, which is based on shutter movement registering successive spatial positions, produces lost movement (as opposed to lost time). The method is caught up in time's infinite divisibility. The results of the chronophotographic plates emphasise movement in time captured as a series of instants in space. Rhythm is found in this series of instants, most remarkably in Marey's geometrical chronophotography experiments, because they depict the body's movement as definite beats in time where the effect is of abstract lines that staccato their way across the fixed plate.

Prior to his experiments with chronophotography, Marey experimented with the graphic method, publishing his results in *La Machine animale* in 1873 (translated into English as *Animal Mechanism* in 1874). The graphic method results in 'tracings' (otherwise called 'notations' by Marey) of the movement of the living body, including the effect and force of heat on gland and muscle action (thermodynamics); electrical nervous and muscular movement, including that of the heart; and terrestrial locomotion and aerial locomotion, often measured by air pressure. As noted, the graphic notations were designed to inscribe the force, duration, intensity, velocity, and rhythm of the movement of physiology, while also inscribing the relationship of the body to natural resistances.

The apparatuses that Marey invented or extended and applied in the graphic method took several forms. Graphic notation of muscle movement uses the myograph, which sends an electric current through muscle and traces the contraction and relaxation of the muscle movement on a turning cylinder. The sphygmograph (*sphygmos* meaning 'pulse') and later

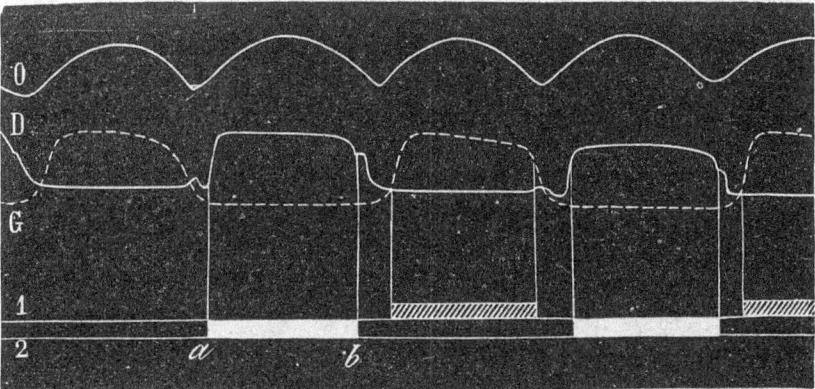

Figure 1.6 A man running (graphic inscription). Source: Étienne-Jules Marey, *Animal Mechanism: A Treatise on Terrestrial and Aerial Locomotion* (New York: D. Appleton and Co., 1874), p. 133. Photo credit: Huntington Library.

the cardiograph is used to measure the movement of the heart – the latter was the prototype for today's cardiogram.[59]

Graphic inscription could also notate a man running (Figure 1.6). A 'portable registering apparatus' that consists of specially adapted shoes and headgear is used to measure the 'ascending and descending oscillations' of the body. In this method, the current of air caused by pressure on the shoes and the oscillation of the head is 'traced'.[60] The line O is a tracing of the 'oscillations and vertical re-actions of the body' recorded by the headgear of the device. The line D is a tracing of the 'impact and rise of the right foot'. And the line G (dotted) is a tracing of the 'impact and rise' of the left foot.[61] Lines 1 and 2, Marey writes, 'form the *staff* on which will be written this simple music, consisting only of two notes, which we shall call right foot, left foot'.[62] Point a is the 'commencement of the pressure of the right foot'. Point b is the point at which the pressure of the right foot is released. The white line between points a and b expresses the 'duration of the pressure of the right foot'.[63] Rhythm can be read in this notated 'musical score'.

While his chronophotographic and geometrical chronophotographic experiments produced problems because of their dependence on the decomposition of movement into a series of instants, Marey's graphic apparatuses inscribed the rhythms of the body in linear notations. François Dagognet refers to Marey's graphic notations as 'direct writing' or 'direct inscription'.[64] Dagognet goes on to suggest that

> Marey's brilliance lay in the discovery of how to make recordings without recourse to the human hand or eye. Nature had to testify to itself, to translate

itself through the inflection of curves and subtle trajectories that were truly representative. Hidden, minute and fleeting, life's movement had to be captured (life is movement and nothing else).[65]

The graphic inscriptions enabled 'life's movement' to be 'captured', not by the 'human hand or eye', but by the mechanical apparatus.[66] Significantly, the body is not only revealed as physiologically subtle and able to be inscribed within a graphic language capable of registering the duration of the body's movements, but as polyrhythmic. Rabinbach writes, quoting from Marey, that the graphic inscriptions provide a '"graphic expression of the most fleeting, most delicate, and most complex movements that no language could ever express". These tracings reveal the "langue inconnue" [obscure language] of physiological time, the interior rhythms of the body.'[67] He argues further that, in tracing these interior rhythms, it could be acknowledged that: 'Each aspect of the body's rhythms was subject to its own discrete time, which could be traced.'[68]

The graphic notations are closer to a depiction of the rhythm of movement than a depiction of time, even given Marey's use of chronometry. Although the graphic inscriptions are mechanically produced, they represent continuous linear depictions of the interior movements of the body. The importance of rhythm in Marey's graphic inscriptions can be compared with the impact of rhythm in the Surrealists' automatic writing, although Marey's notations are different from the automatic writing of the Surrealists in that they reveal physiological movement rather than unconscious movement. The automatic writing of the Surrealists was

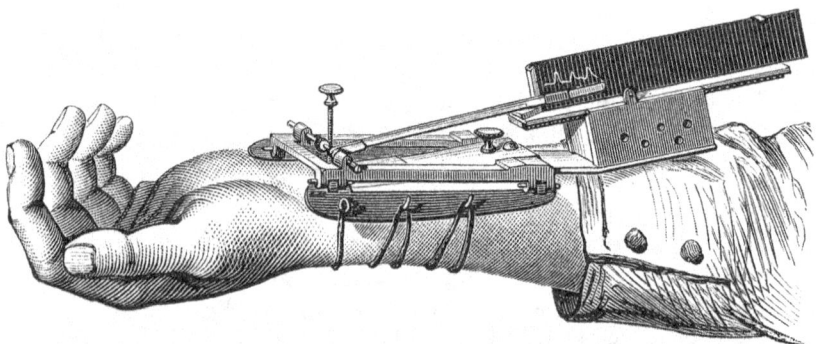

Figure 1.7 Recording the trace of the pulse. Source: Étienne-Jules Marey, '*Sphygmographe direct inscrivant le tracé du pouls*/Direct sphygmograph recording the trace of the pulse', in *La Méthode Graphique dans les Sciences Expérimentales et Principalement en Physiologie et en Médecine* (Paris: G. Masson, 1878), p. 560. Photo credit: Huntington Library.

produced with a sense of disconnection from the conscious mind such that it was thought that what was revealed on paper were elements from the unconscious. Rabinbach compares the production by Marey's graphic method to a kind of automatic writing which 'united the body's own signs (pulse, heart rate, gait, the flapping of wings) with a language of technical representation'.[69] The economy of the body was by this method 'notated' in a mechanical inscription, and likened to a motor in its demonstration of regularity and rhythm. Because they are mechanically produced, these graphic notations require deciphering because, like the difference between musical notation and music 'heard' and 'felt', they inscribe movement in a register that permits a distinction between mechanical notation and human experience.

To understand the limitations of Marey's work, if we take into account the ways that movement in time is inscribed, we need to ask how continuous time as duration can be inscribed. The continuous inscriptions that were produced by Marey's graphic methods still fall short of finding the pulse. The graphic inscriptions produced by Marey's cardiograph mechanically notated the movement of the rhythm of the pulse in the body, but inevitably show the difference between mechanical notation and 'felt' duration. The cardiograph inscribed the movement and rate of the pulse (in what is inevitably a mechanically inscribed rhythm, because it is inscribed by a machine) in a linear depiction, but could not capture the heterogeneous and mutually irreducible movements of the pulse. A machine cannot reproduce vital rhythms. Nevertheless, the cardiograph came closer to depicting a continuous trace in time than either chronophotography's or geometrical chronophotography's 'whole body' movements because the graphic notations that it produced stood as continuous and indexical equivalents of the rhythms of the heart. Such an indexical reference is necessary for thinking about the inscription of movement in time and of rhythm as an index of movement in both chronophotography (because of the index of light used in photography) and graphic inscription (because of the index of the 'wave of contraction' caused by muscle movement used in graphic notation[70]). Graphic inscription was an inscription that unfolded as a continuous movement – as Deleuze would say in *Cinema 1*, the 'act of covering'[71] – which, unlike the fixed-plate recordings of chronophotography or geometrical chronophotography, were less allied to a past position in space and instant in time.

Despite this continuous inscription, it is the signature of rhythm that is found in the graphic method because the movement of the organic pulse is not captured in its entirety in the indexical and graphical mark. Certainly, for Marey, it was enough to inscribe the interior rhythms of the body onto an external format on paper. It does, however, beg the question of how the pulse inscribes itself onto an external format outside the body, and how the methods of inscription and the conditions of the support alter the very understanding of the pulse.

My intention here is to locate a prototype of the pulse in rhythm in Marey's chronophotographic images, which I regard as a prototype of the rhythm of the pulse in cinema despite Marey's claims that cinema is incapable of precisely that. For Marey, the true potential of the scientific method over cinema is that it 'supplant[s] the insufficiency of our senses'. Cinema's focus upon 'what the eye can see', he argues, mistakes its abilities and limits our understanding because it limits us to phenomena seen by the eye.[72] We can infer from Marey's viewpoint that cinema, with its focus upon 'what the eye can see', cannot give us the pulse; however, the scientific techniques that he describes, including the instruments he used in his photographic inscriptions (chronophotography), intend, in their speed, frequency, and by superimposing movement onto a fixed frame, to give us something more than that which is seen by the eye and captured by the cinema camera alone. That is, with these scientific techniques, Marey gives more than rhythm or what is 'perceived'. Indeed, the use of the scientific technique to inscribe more than what is 'perceived' is in full effect in Marey's graphic inscriptions, where its purpose was to depict the unseen and interior movements of the body. Even though Marey's graphic inscriptions intend in one experiment to inscribe the movements of the heart muscle onto paper and, by this scientific method to give us the movement of the pulse, the same restrictions apply to his graphic method as to his photographic method. In recording the movement of the heart muscle, Marey's graphic inscriptions depict a mechanically inscribed rhythm, but do not give full expression to the movement of the pulse in the body.

Ultimately it is the relationship between the economy of the mechanical apparatus and the economy of the body – each demonstrating their own regularity and rhythm and balancing between duration and the expenditure of energy – that is of note for a conception of the pulse. The pulse is an unseen force, incapable of being fully inscribed by either chronophotographic or graphic inscription techniques. The limitations of Marey's work for an analysis of the pulse occur because of his focus on what the chronophotographs and inscriptions depict, whereas I am interested in what the relationship between the image and the spectator entails. That is, the pulse is as much found in the pull of desire and investment of the cinema spectator as it is in the movement of the image in cinema. I argue that it is the operation of the apparatus, rather than the legibility of the image, that is important. The operation of the cinematic and physiological apparatus suggests a 'felt' movement by which the pulse can be defined. The conceptualisation of the pulse, the *dispositif*, and the unconscious, will go some way to resolving the problems that Marey encountered with inscription, the mechanical apparatus and time.

The Pulse in Psychoanalysis: Sigmund Freud

Rhythm appears in the inscriptions made by the mechanical apparatus of the economy of the body in the work of Marey. In Marey's work, the rhythms of the body are 'notated' in a mechanically produced inscription. The 'writing' or inscription upon the Mystic Writing-Pad in Freud's work is a mechanical analogue for the rhythmic operation of stimuli on the psychical apparatus. Across Freud's two texts – 'A Note upon the "Mystic Writing-Pad"' and *Beyond the Pleasure Principle* – rhythm is found in three places: in perception, in the experience of pleasure (and unpleasure), and in the movement of the life (*Eros*) and death (*Thanatos*) instincts or drives. However, the force of the charge and the investment of libido in and to an object/image is better understood by the behaviour of the pulse than by rhythm. This will be crucial to how an argument of the pulse develops in this book in terms of the libidinal cathexis in the *dispositif* and for understanding how the force of libidinal cathexis gives us the pulse in the cinematic arrangement of image and spectator. In this chapter, however, I am concerned with a conceptualisation of the pulse as far as it pertains to the force of the charge of the libido by which the spectator invests the object/image.

The schemas where rhythm develops into the pulse relate to each other because Freud's models are economic. The behaviour of the pulse can be characterised by the charge, investment, or force of intensities in libidinal cathexis and in the libidinal distribution of energy in the *dispositif*. James Strachey translates Freud's *besetzung* as cathexis – which, in the German, means literally the 'state of being occupied'. *Besetzung* also has connotations of the 'charges' of energy (as of electricity) that build up and require release, thus implying the 'discharge' of energy.[73] Cathexis refers to the process of investment of the libido or to the excitatory processes in the mental apparatus. With 'occupation' and 'charge' in mind, it is possible to see how libido cathects objects and attaches to form, comprising life-affirming connections for the bound and binding form of *Eros*.[74] In this way libidinal cathexis allows desire to flourish in the object/image. It is by understanding the force of intensities in libidinal cathexis that we can understand how the rhythm of the perception of stimuli, the rhythm of the charge and discharge of pleasure, and the rhythm of the life and death drives diverge into the behaviour of the pulse.

Freud's essay 'A Note upon the "Mystic Writing-Pad"' provides a meta-psychological reading of the action of stimuli on the perceptual apparatus and the impressions that are retained by the unconscious, which I take up here in my quest to understand how rhythmic inscription becomes pulsatile. Freud's Mystic Writing-Pad is an analogue for the 'mnemic apparatus',[75] whereby the unconscious serves as the site of receptivity for energetic impressions that are apprehended rhythmically. In addition to providing an analogue for the sensory apprehension of stimuli by the 'mnemic apparatus', the inscriptions on the Mystic Writing-Pad are more generally applicable to the operations of rhythm and meaning, and assist our understanding of the pulsating images that emanate from the flickering of the frames of film and how they generate a receptive continuity between the spectator and the moving image.

Freud's writing apparatus is comprised of three layers: a resin or wax slab; a thin translucent paper layer; and a protective transparent celluloid layer. Writing is done with a stylus on the protective celluloid layer, which allows the thin paper layer between the celluloid and the slab to adhere to the solid resin or wax slab at the point of writing. After writing is complete the protective celluloid can be lifted to reveal the writing below. When the message is no longer needed the thin paper may be lifted to erase the writing and to produce a blank sheet on which to write again. An impression of the writing is retained on the resin or wax slab where the wax has been scratched, effectively displaced, by the stylus.[76] For Freud, the writing apparatus provides the perfect model for the perceptual apparatus: the resin or wax slab corresponds to the unconscious ($Ucs.$); the thin, translucent waxed paper layer corresponds to perception-consciousness ($Pcpt.-Cs.$), which is the layer that 'receives perceptions but retains no permanent trace of them'[77]; and the protective celluloid layer to the 'protective shield against stimuli'.[78] Freud writes on the comparison between the writing apparatus and the 'mnemic apparatus':

> I do not think it is too far-fetched to compare the celluloid and waxed paper cover with the system $Pcpt.-Cs.$ and its protective shield, the wax slab with the unconscious behind them, and the appearance and disappearance of the writing with the flickering-up and passing-away of consciousness in the process of perception.[79]

What becomes apparent in Freud's unfolding of the analogy between this rudimentary machine and the conscious and unconscious is that the appearance and disappearance of the writing on the Mystic Writing-Pad is a discontinuous process, precisely because writing is done and then the layers are lifted to write again. As analogue for the process of perception in consciousness the rhythmic excitation and enervation happens in fits and starts, with breaks in contact between discrete recordings of excitations:

> It is as though the unconscious stretches out feelers, through the medium of the system *Pcpt.-Cs.*, towards the external world and hastily withdraws them as soon as they have sampled the excitations coming from it. Thus the interruptions, which in the case of the Mystic Pad have an external origin, were attributed by my hypothesis to the discontinuity in the current of innervation; and the actual breaking of contact which occurs in the Mystic Pad was replaced in my theory by the periodic non-excitability of the perceptual system. I further had a suspicion that this discontinuous method of functioning of the system *Pcpt.-Cs.* lies at the bottom of the origin of the concept of time.
>
> If we imagine one hand writing upon the surface of the Mystic Writing-Pad while another periodically raises its covering-sheet from the wax slab, we shall have a concrete representation of the way in which I tried to picture the functioning of the perceptual apparatus of our mind.[80]

This discontinuous functioning of perception-consciousness (*Pcpt.-Cs.*) – that is, the rhythmic action of stimuli reception – is comparable to a sequence of events inscribed in intervals of time, and evidenced in the 'writing' or impressions.

What is significant here is that the rhythm of inscription taking place on the Mystic Writing-Pad is in fact confined to the middle layer of the apparatus, namely the thin translucent paper layer as it is written upon and lifted to write again. The apparatus accommodates two kinds of writing: rhythmic and erasable inscription (which occurs on the thin paper layer), and deep and lasting impressions that are permanent yet subject to transformation by further action (on the wax slab). The two kinds of writing differ in that the first is a kind of neutral writing, while the second is a physical deformation; the first is representative, while the second has the intensive force of change. On the one hand, the writing on the thin paper surface is not legible at the site of the wax slab; and on the other, the 'writing' that is generated appears as scratches or grooves – 'cavities' or 'lumps'[81] – on the wax slab. On this second kind of 'writing', more 'writing' will be inscribed in a way that retraces cavities, bisects grooves already made, and is resisted and forced awry by previously constituted lumps. Thus, this rhythmic action of inscription on a surface gives way to the 'impressions' made by the intensive force (or operation) of stimuli.[82] Freud describes the action of the stylus on the surface of the Mystic Writing-Pad as performing a (violent) displacement of the wax surface: the 'pointed stilus [sic] scratches the surface, the depressions upon which constitute the "writing"'.[83] However, the two kinds of writing, or surfaces for writing, differ also in their continuity. The thin paper layer exists in a discontinuous present because it is subject to the rhythms of inscription upon it – of writing being done and the sheet being lifted to erase the writing and to write again. The wax slab is an atemporal entity. And although the unconscious stands as a continuous surface it is not continuously 'open'.[84] That is, while the unconscious is a continuous surface, it is the action of rhythmic excitation that 'opens' the unconscious for impressions to be made.

It is arguable, however, that Freud's conceptualisation of the psychical apparatus in this way limits the possible understanding of the unconscious to a surface of inscription. The topography of the wax slab and its relation to writing emphasises the inscriptions made upon surfaces by, in the 'mnemic' analogue, the rhythmic action of stimuli. The functioning of the perceptual processes here is reduced to the rhythmic action of stimuli on perception-consciousness. The 'flickering-up and passing-away of consciousness in the process of perception' is, in Freud's analogy, likened to the inscription and erasure of the writing on the thin paper surface.[85] As in Marey's graphic inscriptions, rhythm is found in this writing. Whether the surface is the wax slab or the unconscious, what is produced is a 'writing' upon the surface that is the result of the rhythmic action of stimuli, but is also rhythmic in its signature. What the senses sample of the world is not a complete and continuous picture, but is dictated by the rhythmic excitability and enervation of the perceptual system: the perceptual system does not want to overload itself with sensations. The 'impressions' left on the unconscious are the signature of this rhythmic action of stimuli.

In the Mystic Writing-Pad, the periodicity of the system has 'an external origin', which is the lifting of the page to write again, and the inscription on the surface can be likened to the action of stimuli from the world onto perception-consciousness. In the perceptual system, periodicity is caused internally by the 'periodic non-excitability of the perceptual system'.[86] The external and internal origins of rhythm mean that the relation of the unconscious to the world directs the periodic excitation and enervation of the perceptual system. As Freud writes and as I have noted above, 'It is as though the unconscious stretches out feelers, through the medium of the system *Pcpt.-Cs.*, towards the external world and hastily withdraws them as soon as they have sampled the excitations coming from it.'[87]

In this action of the unconscious we begin to see the relation of rhythm to the pulse. While rhythm entails the periodic excitation and enervation of the perceptual system as well as the action of stimuli upon a surface, thus bringing emphasis to the topography of the surface of perception-consciousness as the site for inscription, the pulse refers to the charge of intensities in the relationship between the unconscious and the world. This charge of intensities is the investment of desire or libidinality in the system; an investment that not only produces but also results from the accumulation and repression of intensities in the unconscious because of the rhythmic inscription of stimuli. The unconscious may be inscribed by stimuli, but it is the arrangement of 'impressions' upon the unconscious that are invested or charged. If the action of stimuli inscribing the unconscious to produce 'impressions' is rhythmic, the force of the sensible in the grooves or passages that are inscribed on the wax slab is better understood by the behaviour of the pulse. The pulse has force and, like the arrangement of 'impressions' on the unconscious, the force of the pulse is directed into grooves or passages: in the body, the arrangement of arteries and veins. But the pulse also has affective or libidinal value because, like the unconscious, the pulse has impetus or drive that corresponds to its 'felt' relation to the world. And like the 'impressions' on the unconscious that are charged or invested, the pulse's libidinal value is found in its response to the world but is not necessarily a response that is in direct correspondence with the action of the world upon it. The 'impressions' made on the unconscious do not produce direct and legible meaning in the unconscious. Instead, they correspond to the arrangements of accumulations and repressions: they are 'impressions' through which charges and investments travel in the unconscious. This is how I understand the behaviour of the pulse in cinema: as the force of the charge or investment in the arrangement between the image and the spectator that does not produce the exchange value of signification, but has libidinal value.

Laplanche notes about rhythm in Freud's work, that while external stimuli are perceived rhythmically by perception, such rhythm 'is encountered again in internal perception with respect to pleasure and unpleasure'.[88] The salient point for us here is that Freud's work in the later text shifts from an analysis of perceptual stimulus and reaction to the most 'obscure and inaccessible region of the mind'.[89] In the unconscious, pleasure and unpleasure are 'more primordial, more elementary, than perceptions arising externally'.[90] Like the rhythm of the action of stimuli in the perceptual system, the rhythm of pleasure and unpleasure in the unconscious can also be understood to diverge into something that we can call the pulse.

Beyond the Pleasure Principle presents an 'economic' point of view in the rhythm of pleasure and unpleasure.[91] The pleasure principle is an energetic model of charge and discharge that describes a particular economy of the charge, investment and release of energies. The psychical apparatus discharges energy with the aim of remaining constant. This is G. T. Fechner's principle of the 'tendency towards stability'.[92] Unpleasure is understood here as an '*increase* in the quantity of excitation' or charge, and pleasure is felt as a '*diminution*' or discharge, and the management of pleasure and unpleasure points to a rhythmic series.[93] To put it another way, any psycho-physical movement that works towards stability is attended by pleasure, and any psycho-physical movement that works towards instability is attended by unpleasure. For this reason, the organism cathects energy into zones of the psychical system to discharge energy and to find pleasure in stability.[94] My point here is that it is a stability or homeostasis achieved through rhythmic excitation and enervation.

The pleasure principle, thus understood, entails a rhythm. Moreover, the focus on the rhythmic charge and discharge of stimuli that generate either pleasure or unpleasure misses the intensities in the libidinal cathexis. No longer tied to surface as the rhythmic inscriptions of stimuli are, libidinal cathexis is the force of the charge or investment of desire in the arrangement of the rhythmically produced inscriptions upon the unconscious, but also the force of the charge or investment of desire in the arrangement between the psychical system and the world. These arrangements for libidinal cathexis are a way of defining the *dispositif*. The force of this charge or investment of desire can be better understood by the behaviour of the pulse, even as rhythm is found in the action of excitation and enervation, charge and discharge, which produces the pleasure/unpleasure series. The operation of the pulse is in fact the best descriptor we have available to us for comprehending the force of libidinal cathexis, where charge and discharge are its organically rhythmic beats.

Hence my endeavour to affiliate the psychoanalytic unconscious and the pulse: the investment or flow of libidinal cathexis in the unconscious, which has the impetus or force of the instincts or drives, demonstrates the behaviour of the pulse. This aspect of the pulse as it relates to the instincts or drives clarifies how libidinal cathexis happens in the *dispositif*. The cathexis of energy in the *dispositif* characterises the charge and attachment of libido that attaches to or cathects objects/images. Freud's economic perspective as it relates to the pleasure principle is important inasmuch as the impetus or *force* of energy can be better understood by the behaviour of the pulse.

In *Beyond the Pleasure Principle* rhythm is derived from the management of pleasure and unpleasure in the psychical system which seeks to master or 'bind' the excitations that come from within.[95] Unpleasure is worked through, repeated, mastered, so that pleasure can be derived from it. At the same time, the 'beyond' of this pleasure principle is the unpleasure that cannot be worked through and in this case the analysand is caught in the automatic, pathologically inspired movement of repetition.

The 'beyond' of the pleasure principle can also be described as rhythmic on the basis of discontinuity and that something is missing. For Freud, what is missing is nothing other than the site of trauma, which must be returned to again and again. Accordingly, in this inaccessible region Freud hears the beat of another 'rhythm' – the life and death instincts – which together work to conserve life, even while the death instincts seek to 'lead organic life back into the inanimate state'.[96] It is necessary to go on and describe Freud's analysis of the life and death drives in the 'beyond' of the pleasure principle to see whether a pulse can also be identified there.

Just as the unconscious samples the outside world in rhythmic bursts so as not to overburden itself with stimulation, so too do the instincts (that is, the death instincts and life instincts) relay each other in a way that produces rhythm. Freud's theorisation of the death drive in *Beyond the Pleasure Principle* is a theory of life (*élan vital*) that heeds the organic elasticity that is found in the instincts or drives. However, it concerns death – a force that seeks to return organic matter to an inorganic past. As an instinctual desire to return to an inorganic heredity, the death drive seeks to restore the organism to 'an earlier state of things'.[97] As Freud writes:

> *It seems, then, that an instinct is an urge inherent in organic life to restore an earlier state of things* which the living entity has been obliged to abandon under the pressure of external disturbing forces; that is, it is a kind of organic elasticity, or, to put it another way, the expression of the inertia inherent in organic life.[98]

What is pertinent in understanding a theorisation of the instinct or drive as distinct from the pleasure principle is that the life drive (*Eros*) and the death drive (*Thanatos*) appear to work in opposition, as Freud writes, 'struggling with each other from the very first'.[99] That is, while the life drive works to a coalescing of cell bodies – 'seeks to force together and hold together the portions of living substance'[100] – the death drive, on the other hand, tends to a return to a 'pre-conscious', chaotic past. For Freud, the life drive is 'constructive or assimilatory', the death drive, 'destructive or dissimilatory'.[101] Economically, the life instinct (*Eros*) represents change and differentiation in response to the outside world, even if the goal of that differentiation cannot be distinguished from a return to an earlier, or primary, state of things. The death instinct (*Thanatos*) represents a conservative outlook, invested in a return to 'an earlier state of things', as opposed to change or progress.[102] As conditions change so too is the organism forced from its course of return, to make *détours* in its final goal to death. Freud writes: 'These circuitous paths to death, faithfully kept to by the conservative instincts, would thus present us to-day with the picture of the phenomenon of life.'[103] This is the rhythm supplied by the life and death drives, as Freud writes:

> It is as though the life of the organism moved with a vacillating rhythm. One group of instincts rushes forward so as to reach the final aim of life as swiftly as possible; but when a particular stage in the advance has been reached, the other group jerks back to a certain point to make a fresh start and so prolong the journey.[104]

Rhythm is found in the stages of development of the organism as one group of instincts rush to their goal and are jerked back by the other group of instincts. Once again, rhythm is conceived as a sequence of events in intervals of time. And yet, the life and death drives cannot be said to be in opposition as such, but, because of the kinds of energetic forces at work, the life and death drives are imbricated in their tendency to an earlier, or primary, state. That is, both the life instinct (*Eros*) and the death instinct (*Thanatos*) 'tend towards the restoration of an earlier state of things'.[105] The 'vacillating rhythm' between the life and death drives is made against the generative tension that impels the organism; is made against the impetus or force of the instincts or drives in the life of the organism. The pulse, I want to argue, is the force or drive of the libidinal cathexis, or the condition that precedes the distinction between the life and death drives.

The recursion to rhythm in both 'A Note upon the "Mystic Writing-Pad"' and in *Beyond the Pleasure Principle* overlooks the force of the libidinal cathexis by which intensities, desires, or affections even, are pathologically inspired. In Freud's description, rhythm is in the reception of stimuli, in the charge and discharge of excitations that produce pleasure and unpleasure (in the pleasure principle), and in the stages of development produced by the relay of the life and death drives (in the 'beyond' of the pleasure principle). The rhythm of life, as such, is conceived first as perceptual or experiential events in time, and second, as developmental periods that make up events in time. Although Freud gestures towards time as a possible way of thinking about both 'A Note upon the "Mystic Writing-Pad"' and *Beyond the Pleasure Principle*,[106] time is depicted as rhythmically experiential, chronological, and even unchronological, as in the compulsive repetition of traumatic events. What is absent from such descriptions is the very force of the intensities that produce the movement in the unconscious. Such intensities can only be accommodated by the libidinal intensities of the pulse as I understand it. Chronological time is infinitely divisible and sequential – like rhythm. The pulse strikes at the lived force of time in the unconscious: it is made up of indivisible singularities and is, in the sense Freud uses it, 'timeless'.[107]

The way in which the intensities or forces of the instincts or drives operate is understood better by the behaviour of the pulse than by rhythm. The return to an earlier, or primary, state that the force of the instincts or drives have as their trajectory are met by the resistances that maintain repression.[108] With respect to the Mystic Writing-Pad, these resistances are the impressions made on the wax slab: the scratching that the stylus produces, can be retraced, bisected or met as resistance in subsequent scratchings, but the wax slab cannot be returned to its smooth, or blank, origins. The 'impressions' on the unconscious are libidinally invested. *Beyond the Pleasure Principle* exemplifies a rhythm of the life and death drives, which are themselves forces tending towards an earlier, or primary, state. Such forces are organically elastic in their trajectory, in that 'there is no alternative but to advance in the direction in which growth is still free', thus demonstrating the '*dynamic* conditions for its [the instinct's] development'.[109] The pulse is at once an organically elastic force, while also the force of the wave directed into passages. The pulse is a more vital model for the operation of these psychical exchanges than rhythm is, although rhythm still exists in the functioning of the psychical apparatus. The unconscious stands as a continuous surface that is 'opened' by rhythm, but is described by Freud as 'timeless'. The unconscious, in other words, is atemporal, having no sequence of events in the past or present. The pulse may be marked or 'opened' by rhythm, but the force of the pulse is itself 'timeless'.

From physiology to the psyche, what we find is that to capture the pulse is to capture the operation of the 'felt' relation. Rhythm is 'perceived' in its periodicity or series, and even the inscription of stimuli on the psychical apparatus is rhythmic. The pulse is a deep, unseen and vital force, unconscious even, which charges and invests desire. By understanding rhythm, I have sought to describe how the pulse also operates in the image, most closely aligned with the libidinal cathexis of the image as the desires of the spectator are pulled to the surface by movement. Such libidinal forces are important for how I go on to envisage the Open of the image and the viewer in the arrangement, set up, or *dispositif* that gives affective spectatorship.

Notes

1. Deleuze, *Cinema 1*, p. 1.
2. Mitry, *The Aesthetics and Psychology of the Cinema*, p. 104.
3. Mitry, *The Aesthetics and Psychology of the Cinema*, p. 104.
4. Mitry, *The Aesthetics and Psychology of the Cinema*, p. 104.

5. Mitry, *The Aesthetics and Psychology of the Cinema*, p. 104.
6. Mitry, *The Aesthetics and Psychology of the Cinema*, p. 104.
7. Mitry, *The Aesthetics and Psychology of the Cinema*, p. 104.
8. Mitry, *The Aesthetics and Psychology of the Cinema*, pp. 105–6.
9. Mitry, *The Aesthetics and Psychology of the Cinema*, p. 104.
10. Mitry, *The Aesthetics and Psychology of the Cinema*, p. 105.
11. Mitry, *The Aesthetics and Psychology of the Cinema*, p. 104.
12. Mitry, *The Aesthetics and Psychology of the Cinema*, p. 104.
13. Lloyd, *The Golden Encyclopedia of Music*, p. 472.
14. Waite, *Oxford Dictionary*, p. 1586.
15. Waite, *Oxford Dictionary*, p. 1586.
16. Macpherson, *Black's Medical Dictionary*, p. 523.
17. Briggs and Peat give the name 'strange attractor behaviour' to the activity of a collective chaotic system. Plotting the system reveals a pattern of behaviour to which the system is 'attracted', and to which it has the tendency to return even when it is nudged from this behaviour. This 'strange attractor behaviour' is unpredictable and non-mechanical. That is, because 'the system is open to its external environment, it is capable of many nuances of movement'. The 'strange attractor behaviour' is what defines the behaviour and thus the movement of the collective chaotic system: a constantly unfolding creative system that is dynamic and complexly interwoven with individual elements on many different scales (Briggs and Peat, *Seven Life Lessons of Chaos*, pp. 63–4).
18. Briggs and Peat, *Seven Life Lessons of Chaos*, pp. 64–5.
19. Briggs and Peat, *Seven Life Lessons of Chaos*, p. 65.
20. Waite, *Oxford Dictionary*, p. 1587.
21. Gray, *Anatomy*, pp. 327–8.
22. Mitry, *The Aesthetics and Psychology of the Cinema*, p. 104.
23. Ganguly, 'All that is Light', p. 21.
24. Michelson, 'Paul Sharits and the Critique of Illusionism', p. 25.
25. Ganguly, 'All that is Light', p. 21.
26. Kubelka, 'The Theory of Metrical Film', pp. 139–40.
27. Kubelka, 'The Theory of Metrical Film', p. 140.
28. Sitney, 'Introduction', pp. xlii–xliii.
29. Mitry, *The Aesthetics and Psychology of the Cinema*, pp. 106–7.
30. Kubelka, 'The Theory of Metrical Film', p. 140.
31. Mitry, *The Aesthetics and Psychology of the Cinema*, p. 107.
32. Conley, 'Movement-Image', p. 179.
33. Epstein, '*Bonjour cinéma*', p. 16.
34. Epstein, '*Bonjour cinéma*', p. 17.
35. Epstein, '*Bonjour cinéma*', p. 17.
36. Epstein, '*Bonjour cinéma*', p. 21.
37. Deleuze, *Empiricism and Subjectivity*, p. 7.
38. Epstein, '*Bonjour cinéma*', p. 19.

39. Epstein, 'For a New Avant-Garde', p. 28.
40. Epstein, 'For a New Avant-Garde', p. 28.
41. Dulac, 'From "Visual and Anti-Visual Films"', p. 34.
42. Richter, 'The Badly Trained Sensibility', p. 22.
43. Richter writes: 'The single "sensuous shape", the "form", whether abstract or representational is avoided. This film is concentrated on the process of movement.
    – and □ (1/1, 1/2, 1/3,) serve as the simplest, most economical formal means by which movement is defined spatially; the essential elements of the set of relations horizontal–vertical are made dominants as the □ are built up. So the form is not arrived at arbitrarily, and improvisation is ruled out. Both rhythm and formal content are built up stage by stage within a definite frame-work' (Richter, 'The Badly Trained Sensibility', p. 22).
44. Richter writes: 'Whatever kind of film ("abstract", adventure, or some form yet unknown) is produced is unimportant compared to the SOUND STRUCTURAL BASIS OF OUR GENERAL IDEA, upon which depend the coherence and intensity of our feelings' (Richter, 'The Badly Trained Sensibility', p. 23).
45. Richter, 'The Badly Trained Sensibility', p. 23.
46. Richter, 'The Badly Trained Sensibility', p. 22.
47. Richter, 'The Badly Trained Sensibility', p. 22.
48. Cabanne, *Dialogues with Marcel Duchamp*, p. 43.
49. Sitney, 'Introduction', p. xi.
50. Richter, 'The Badly Trained Sensibility', p. 22.
51. Sitney, 'Introduction', p. xii.
52. Duchamp's emphasis. Sanouillet and Peterson, *The Writings of Marcel Duchamp*, p. 31.
53. Marey, *Animal Mechanism*, p. 122; Marey, *Movement*, p. 17.
54. Dagognet, *Étienne-Jules Marey*, p. 56.
55. Marey's chronophotographic fixed plates were photographed using a rotating shutter. The rotating shutter was an important means of capturing solid bodies in short intervals of time in a series. The fixed plate was exposed for a duration of $\frac{1}{500}$ of a second at intervals of $\frac{1}{10}$ of a second, causing superimposition (Marey, *Movement*, pp. 55–6). Filming with Marey's rotating shutter at intervals too close together meant creating overlap that blurred any one position of the object. In time, a photographic gun designed by Marey replaced the static camera and reduced the problem of blurring, allowing birds to be captured in flight in successive and short intervals of time. To capture continuous movement, Marey, like M. Demeny before him, also experimented with a slow shutter speed. However, these bodies captured during movement are less open to analysis because, although the start and finish positions of the moving object were brought into relief, the movement between the two positions was blurred.
56. Rabinbach, 'Time and Motion', p. 110.

57. Bergson writes in *Matter and Memory* that 'absolute movement' is movement expressed as a totality. In this respect, absolute movement would be nothing other than a 'change of place' as 'absolute positions in an absolute space' (Bergson, *Matter and Memory*, pp. 255–6). However, Bergson goes on to write that the perception of movement differs little from what would entail absolute movement (as opposed to relative movement): 'muscular sensations within me, the sensible qualities of matter without me, and neither in the one case nor in the other do I see movement, if there be movement, as a mere relation: it is an absolute'. According to Bergson, what we perceive as movement are changes in '*state* or of *quality*', but these changes can be expressed as much as absolute changes as 'real' changes (Bergson, *Matter and Memory*, p. 258).
58. Rabinbach, 'Time and Motion', p. 110.
59. Dagognet, *Étienne-Jules Marey*, p. 29.
60. Marey, *Animal Mechanism*, pp. 124–7.
61. Marey, *Animal Mechanism*, p. 128.
62. Marey, *Animal Mechanism*, p. 133.
63. Marey, *Animal Mechanism*, p. 133.
64. Dagognet, *Étienne-Jules Marey*, p. 20.
65. Dagognet, *Étienne-Jules Marey*, p. 30.
66. Dagognet, *Étienne-Jules Marey*, p. 30.
67. Rabinbach, 'Time and Motion', p. 95.
68. Rabinbach, 'Time and Motion', p. 95.
69. Rabinbach, 'Time and Motion', p. 97.
70. Dagognet, *Étienne-Jules Marey*, p. 47.
71. Space covered belongs to a divisible space made up of identical, homogeneous, immobile sections. Movement, on the other hand, is an irreducible heterogeneity. Deleuze explains: 'Space covered is past, movement is present, the act of covering. The space covered is divisible, indeed infinitely divisible, whilst movement is indivisible, or cannot be divided without changing qualitatively each time it is divided' (Deleuze, *Cinema 1*, p. 1).
72. For Marey, 'cinema produces only what the eye can see in any case. It adds nothing to the power of our sight, nor does it remove its illusions, and the real character of a scientific method is to supplant the insufficiency of our senses and correct their errors. To get to this point [Marey claims], chronophotography should renounce the representation of phenomena as they are seen by the eye' (Braun, *Picturing Time*, p. 255).
73. Richter, 'Translator's Note', pp. 39–40.
74. Laplanche, 'Economic Paradox of the Death Drive', p. 264.
75. Freud, 'A Note upon the "Mystic Writing-Pad"', p. 227.
76. Freud, 'A Note upon the "Mystic Writing-Pad"', p. 229.
77. Freud, 'A Note upon the "Mystic Writing-Pad"', p. 228.
78. Freud, 'A Note upon the "Mystic Writing-Pad"', p. 230.
79. Freud, 'A Note upon the "Mystic Writing-Pad"', pp. 230–1.

80. Freud, 'A Note upon the "Mystic Writing-Pad"', pp. 231–2.
81. Lyotard, *Libidinal Economy*, p. 3.
82. Freud, 'A Note upon the "Mystic Writing-Pad"', p. 230.
83. Freud, 'A Note upon the "Mystic Writing-Pad"', p. 229.
84. Freud writes in his essay 'The Unconscious' quite clearly on the atemporality of the unconscious (Freud, 'The Unconscious', p. 187). While this atemporality suggests that the unconscious is continuously 'open' (by its timelessness), I argue instead that, along with Freud's description of cathexis, that it is a matter of the 'withdrawal' of cathexis even as the unconscious retains cathexis. As Freud writes: 'It must be a matter of a *withdrawal* of cathexis; but the question is, in which system does the withdrawal take place and to which system does the cathexis that is withdrawn belong? The repressed idea remains capable of action in the *Ucs.*, and it must therefore have retained its cathexis. What has been withdrawn must be something else.' He continues: 'Thus there is a withdrawal of the preconscious cathexis, retention of the unconscious cathexis, or replacement of the preconscious cathexis by an unconscious one' (Freud, 'The Unconscious', p. 180).
85. Freud, 'A Note upon the "Mystic Writing-Pad"', p. 231.
86. Freud, 'A Note upon the "Mystic Writing-Pad"', p. 231.
87. Freud, 'A Note upon the "Mystic Writing-Pad"', p. 231.
88. Fletcher and Stanton, *Jean Laplanche*, p. 165.
89. Freud, *Beyond the Pleasure Principle*, p. 4.
90. Freud, 'The Ego and the Id', p. 22.
91. Freud, *Beyond the Pleasure Principle*, p. 3.
92. Freud, *Beyond the Pleasure Principle*, p. 6.
93. Freud, *Beyond the Pleasure Principle*, p. 4; Lyotard, 'The Connivances of Desire with the Figural', p. 58.
94. Freud, *Beyond the Pleasure Principle*, p. 5; quoting from Fechner, *Einige Ideen*, p. 94.
95. Freud, *Beyond the Pleasure Principle*, pp. 32–3.
96. Freud, 'The Ego and the Id', p. 40.
97. Freud, *Beyond the Pleasure Principle*, p. 45.
98. Freud, *Beyond the Pleasure Principle*, p. 43 (emphasis in original).
99. Freud, *Beyond the Pleasure Principle*, footnote 21, p. 73.
100. Freud, *Beyond the Pleasure Principle*, footnote 21, p. 73.
101. Freud, *Beyond the Pleasure Principle*, p. 59.
102. Freud, 'The Ego and the Id', pp. 40–1.
103. Freud, *Beyond the Pleasure Principle*, p. 46.
104. Freud, *Beyond the Pleasure Principle*, p. 49.
105. Freud, *Beyond the Pleasure Principle*, p. 45.
106. In 'A Note upon the "Mystic Writing-Pad"' Freud writes: 'I further had the suspicion that this discontinuous method of functioning of the system *Pcpt.-Cs.* lies at the bottom of the origin of the concept of time' (Freud, 'A Note upon the "Mystic Writing-Pad"', p. 231). In *Beyond the Pleasure*

Principle Freud writes that 'our abstract idea of time seems to be wholly derived from the method of working of the system *Pcpt.-Cs.* and to correspond to a perception on its own part of that method of working' (Freud, *Beyond the Pleasure Principle*, p. 32).
107. Freud, 'The Unconscious', p. 187; Freud, *Beyond the Pleasure Principle*, pp. 31–2.
108. Freud, *Beyond the Pleasure Principle*, p. 51.
109. Freud, *Beyond the Pleasure Principle*, p. 51.

CHAPTER 2

The Rhythm of Life: The Pulse in the Spectator

The shock of repeated blows, the dissection of body parts into segments, the micro-movements of the nervous response – these actions are characteristic of the rhythms of life (and death) in the slaughterhouse in Georges Franju's *Le Sang des bêtes/Blood of the Beasts* (1949). In *Le Sang des bêtes*, the violence of displacement is seen in the juxtaposition of out-of-place curios in the vacant lot and the dismemberment of bodies in the slaughterhouse. In the slaughterhouse, a horse's head is cleaved with a mallet. The prosthetic right leg of Ernest Bruyet has a foot like the hoof of the horse he has just skinned, his leg amputated, the narrator tells us, after he severed his femoral artery. A cow wears its flayed skin like a huge floppy coat, the arms too big. The stomach of a cow skitters like a blob of mercury across the floor. Intestines are threaded out of an animal cavity by hand, string by string. Calves on racks drip blood from their open necks; headless, their bodies twitch with the micro-movements of the nervous response. With their hooves cut off, the bodies of the calves look like filled jumpers with no occupants. And once these jumpers are stripped off, the bodies underneath are revealed as white and naked. Sheep are lined up on a rack, their legs kick rhythmically like a crazy centipede until these limbs are also lopped off. The rhythm of life is key to the sensorial opening out of bodies in the slaughterhouse in *Le Sang des bêtes*, as well as the sensorial opening out of spectator bodies in cinema.

My aim is to consider cinema in its energetic terms as an 'opening out' for the libidinal investment of image and spectator. I examine two texts by Lyotard with regard to the opening of the body – his book *Libidinal Economy* and his essay 'Anamnesis of the Visible, or Candour'. *Libidinal Economy* deals with the opening of the surfaces of the body to produce the libidinal band/skin. By understanding the operation of intensities in the opening of the libidinal band/skin, and the way this 'skin' composed of intensities can be differentiated from 'pellicule "in the technical sense", meaning "film"',[1] I advance the argument that the pulse can be conceived as the force of intensities, channelled into 'passages', that makes up the *dispositif* in film spectatorship. 'Anamnesis of the Visible, or Candour' describes a certain

Figure 2.1 *Le Sang des bêtes/ Blood of the Beasts* (Georges Franju, 1949)

Figure 2.2 *Le Sang des bêtes/ Blood of the Beasts* (Georges Franju, 1949)

Figure 2.3 *Le Sang des bêtes/ Blood of the Beasts* (Georges Franju, 1949)

Figure 2.4 *Le Sang des bêtes/ Blood of the Beasts* (Georges Franju, 1949)

'open' receptiveness,[2] and is important because it talks about the body's openness to an outside. The pulse, I contend, can be understood as the sensibility of this 'open' receptiveness in film spectatorship because of the rhythmic movement between image and spectator. For my argument, 'passages of intensity' is what occurs in film spectatorship. Intensities travel between the image and the spectator, charging and investing both as components of the *dispositif*. As charges in the *dispositif*, passages of intensity turn individual film experiences into privileged sites for the opening out of image and spectator. Passages of intensity also exemplify the possibility for the libidinal investiture of every surface in its opening out, distinguishing the spectator as one libidinally charged component.

If the behaviour of the pulse is found in the passage of intensities that constitute an energetic 'opening out' in the cinematic arrangement or *dispositif*, then the status of the Open needs to be understood for the operations of the pulse in cinema to be articulated. Deleuze is important here, because he articulates a more complex notion of movement that will be utilised to define the Open of the pulse. In the course of this chapter I will show that he does so in two places, in his books *Cinema 1: The Movement-Image* and *Francis Bacon: The Logic of Sensation*. Deleuze's model shows that what the film is Open to is the movement of the universe (percepts, affects, action) and the possibility of thought; Lyotard's model comprises libidinal openings. Lyotard's work supplements the work of Deleuze on the Open because *Libidinal Economy* never loses the intense libidinal and energetic exchanges of the matter of bodies in the *dispositif*. Deleuze, as in his essay 'The Body without Organs', takes away the organic aspects of the subject.[3] Even though Lyotard's opening of the libidinal band/skin is psychical, the opening of the libidinal band/skin is conceived of as an opening and spreading of 'the so-called body' in which the 'skin' becomes everything and everything becomes a site for libidinal investment.[4] This organic element is important for defining the pulse, because the moving and vibratory effect of the pulse is that it seizes matter – blood – in its wave of distension.[5] The pulse is the energetic system that creates and retains the life of the body, even while the pulse is open to relations in its responsiveness to the world.

Such an opening also highlights 'skin' and offers a way to consider the opening out of the skin of the animals in the slaughterhouse in Franju's *Le Sang des bêtes* as the provocation for the spectator's opening to sensation. The Open that I describe is compelling in that it is not concerned with viewing positions, but with the passage and flow of intensities. The concept of the Open extends the rhythms of life to encapsulate the shocks, bursts, or surges of energetic flow that connect and open the animals in the slaughterhouse to the 'felt' sensations of the spectator.

Surfaces of Inscription and Passages of Intensity

Lyotard takes the concept of '*surfaces of inscription*' from the works of Freud, in which the 'discourse of the patient' is generated from their symptom or surface.[6] In 'A Note upon the "Mystic Writing-Pad"', there are two kinds of surface for writing: perception-consciousness is the surface that encounters stimuli and upon which 'inscriptions' are made, but these 'inscriptions' give way to 'impressions' on the unconscious. The surface of the unconscious is like a geological terrain of 'impressions' which intensities course through, but in Lyotard's conceptual development of the libidinal skin, the 'surface' is a libidinal skin that is itself composed of the '*track* of intensities, ephemeral work'.[7] The libidinal skin is made up of passages of intensities, but also, the quasi-physical residue of intensities is a semi-permeable 'skin' upon which more intensities will be invested. Furthermore, the libidinal skin is not just in the unconscious, but the passages of intensities and the 'opening out' of 'skin' is the libidinal 'opening out' and attachment of the unconscious to objects and images in the world.

Thus, moving away from surfaces for rhythmic inscription, Lyotard 'forge[s] the idea of an intensity' – passages or tracks of intensity – of which the libidinal band/skin is comprised.[8] In such passages of intensity one can see the energetic movements, investments, and expenditures in the opening of the libidinal band/skin. Passages of intensity illustrate how the libidinal economy invests components in the arrangement, set-up, or *dispositif* as these components open out into libidinal surfaces. The passages of intensity that seize movement from within will entail the seizing of components in the arrangement, set-up, or *dispositif* by opening-out.

Although this 'opening out' of the libidinal skin is 'ephemeral work', the preservation of the passage of intensities in the libidinal skin necessarily locks down, channels and regulates desire. 'These surfaces' are not empty canvases or blank pages whose neutrality supports the production of figures, but as Lyotard writes,

> are themselves flows of stabilized quiescent libidinal energy, functioning as locks, canals, regulators of desire, as its figure-producing figures. No goal, no cause, no reason: a formation of Eros that brings to a halt the nomadism of the death drive, that reduces the intensities.[9]

The passages are the force and trajectory of intensities, however, in such passages one can also see the formations, structures, or *dispositifs* that seek to 'channel and exploit' these intensities. As James Williams writes of intensities on the libidinal band/skin: 'According to Lyotard, dispositions [arrangements that structure a particular *dispositif*] or structures channel and exploit feelings and desires, but they also limit them and miss something of their original intensity.'[10] The challenge for Lyotard is how to account for such intensities without recursion to the structures that limit and miss their force. Williams thus observes the paradox of the methodology of libidinal economy: 'when it takes account of intensity, it only does so through dispositions, and hence it only captures a cold, residual intensity'.[11] Thus, a problem Lyotard faces in his conception of the intensities that traverse the libidinal band/skin, is one of determining the limits of the surfaces of inscription (the dispositions or structures that limit intensity). That is, how to capture intensity without limiting intensity.

Surfaces of inscription are the dispositions or structures that both channel and limit intensity. We could likewise say that the structures of intelligibility that capture and limit the pulse are those of rhythm. The cardiograph's rhythmic inscription is a way of understanding the movement of the pulse that is intelligible to us. In the psychical apparatus, the action of stimuli on sensitive surfaces is rhythmic,[12] and rhythm is in the structures that make movement and intensities intelligible when they are inscribed. The sensitive surfaces of the body upon which rhythmic stimuli act are the eye and perception-consciousness. In cinema, sensitive surfaces are not just those of the psychical apparatus, but also include the emulsive surface of the filmstrip.

In the body, the arteries and veins that channel the force of the pulse make up a formation or arrangement in the body. This arrangement of arteries and veins is a necessary system for the body's function, whereby the vibratory wave of the pulse in the arrangement propels blood to various organs and to the extremities of the body. The pulse is also part of an arrangement of energetic components that responds to the world. The movement of the pulse in the body is responsive to stimuli in the world, and thus the pulse is one component in the body's energetic relation with the world. In the psychical apparatus, the pulse supplements the rhythmic impressions of stimuli made on sensitive surfaces by giving them the force of intensities. The pulse can be conceived as the force of intensities channelled by the passages or arrangements of 'impressions' on the unconscious. However, these passages of intensities on the unconscious also extend to the world, whereby the unconscious invests components in the world (images and objects) with libidinality and desire. In the energetic arrangement of film spectatorship, the pulse can be found in the force of intensities, channelled into passages, which flow between the spectator and the film.

Surfaces of inscription thus constitute the topography that apprehends the rhythmic and energetic excitations. Passages of intensity by contrast are the passages caused by the force of intensities. Intensities constitute and invest the libidinal band/skin. In these forces of intensity, we can find the behaviour of the pulse. This way of understanding rhythm (as the action on surfaces of inscription) and the pulse (as the forces of intensity that are channelled into passages) refines my definition of rhythm and the pulse, and demonstrates the ways we can speak about the relationship between rhythm and the pulse as they relate to the inscriptions and intensities of cinema respectively. In Chapter 1, we understood rhythm as the representation of form in time (often found in abstraction as movement inscribed on the filmstrip). The filmstrip is one surface of inscription, the eye and the unconscious of the spectator are others. But this does not give us a full definition of what comprises cinema. Cinema is also in experience. Lyotard's surfaces of inscription, so closely allied with rhythm, are a negative definition of the pulse's relation to passages of intensity. According to Lyotard, intensities and the passages they create or follow by their force are 'ephemeral work', 'useless', 'heterogeneous', but also those that initially 'produce' the libidinal band/skin.[13] The experience of cinema is this 'ephemeral work', 'useless' and 'heterogeneous'. Cinema is comprised both of an energetic and intensive opening out of libidinal surfaces, and of arrangements, set-ups, or *dispositifs* that structure these energies. The pulse in cinema can be understood as this energetic flow of energies structured into arrangements. The spectator can be understood not simply as 'symptom, surface',[14] of inscription, but as a component for the investment of intensities in the opening out of the libidinal band/skin. The spectator is another component in the cinematic arrangement, set-up, or *dispositif*.

This move away from surfaces of inscription to passages of intensity is indicative of Lyotard's departure from Freud:

> we will no longer speak of *surfaces of inscription* (except inadvertently, count on it), of regions to invest, and other similar things. We are suspicious of the separation allowed between inscription and its site . . . Therefore not a surface first, then a writing or inscription over it. But the libidinal skin of which, *after the event*, one will be able to say that it is made up of a patchwork of organs, of elements from organic and social bodies, the libidinal skin initially like the *track* of intensities, ephemeral work, useless like a jet trail in the thin air at an altitude of 10,000, with the exception that it be, as opposed to the trail, completely heterogeneous.[15]

The issue that arises when speaking of surfaces of inscription is that of a separation between inscription and its site, or rather, a separation between the action of inscription on the surface and the site where 'writing' is produced, where 'writing' is understood as the 'impressions' made on the unconscious. In the psychical apparatus, this is a separation between the rhythmic action of stimuli on perception-consciousness and the transformations of the unconscious that occur as a result of it retaining these intensities. With respect to the cinematic apparatus, the separation between inscription and its site amounts to a separation between the film's flickering action upon the spectator and the formations of intensity and desire that are produced and retained in the unconscious. In a reading of cinema, such a separation is untenable, precisely because it separates the action of the film from the site of the spectator. The film and the spectator are hence separated by the surface.

Lyotard also acknowledges that the inscription on a surface is a compromising position precisely because of the representation by which the libidinal band/skin is itself produced:

> Between the libidinal skin and a register of inscription, confusion will always be possible, as between Christ and the Antichrist, between matter and anti-matter. We haven't the *power*, thank god, to dissociate them, to isolate a region, precisely, a domain, precisely! which would be a good representation, precisely, of the libidinal band and would escape the management of the concept, its hard scepticism and its nihilism. There is no *affirmative region*, words which cancel each other out.

> Freud said, marvellously: the death drives work in silence in the uproar of Eros. Eros and the death drives, incompossibles, are indissociable. And so it is, all things being equal, for the passage of intensities and the surface of inscription.[16]

Thus according to Lyotard, the necessity for surfaces of inscription cannot be limited, as such. This is the compromise that we make in defining the libidinal band/skin: that it must be defined by intensity's inscriptive traces, and in defining intensity in this way we 'miss something of [its] original intensity'.[17] As Lyotard writes, 'We haven't the *power*' to make a 'good representation' of the libidinal skin.[18] Equally, the pulse must be defined by rhythm because the pulse makes its appearance via rhythmic beats felt on the skin or in its recorded rhythmic inscriptions such as those produced by the cardiograph. In recording the pulse in this way we 'miss something of [its] original intensity'.[19] Like the libidinal band/skin that is reliant on a representation of it, the pulse is reliant on rhythm by which its movement is revealed. Rhythm and the pulse are 'indissociables', just as in Lyotard 'the passage of intensities and the surface of inscription' are 'indissociables'.[20] Such indissociability is also an imbrication. Where the intensities meet the structures and limits of the 'surface' that makes recordings is the point at which intensities and surfaces are imbricated.

One of the constitutive moments between surfaces of inscription and passages of intensity is that inscription 'preserves' intensity. While there is a delineation made between the surfaces of inscription and the passages of intensities, Lyotard, making a concession with inscription, suggests that the relationship between the two is that surfaces of inscription operate like memory, 'preserving the passage, it is that by means of which effervescence is recorded and conserved . . . The surface of inscription is then the means of recording.'[21] It is also notable that in preserving passages of intensity, intensities are in fact transformed into what Lyotard calls 'terms of presence/absence' by which their value is assigned a place in a 'form, Gestalt, or composition'.[22] In other words, preservation is the means by which recording transforms intensity into what I define as rhythm; rhythm having all the qualities of 'presence/absence' that speak to 'form, *Gestalt*, or composition'.[23] The transformation of intensities is also into, Lyotard writes, 'the form of *lists*, of words, of registery offices, of notebooks, of indexes, under the double law of paradigm and syntagm, of the column and the line, where what remains of intensity is recorded, its trace, its writing'.[24] That is, the transformation of intensities is into things that are charged with libidinal investment, even as this transformation of intensities limits the intensities themselves.

In the libidinal economy there is an imbricating relationship which suggests that while passages of intensity are 'preserved' by the surfaces of inscription, these surfaces of inscription also generate new intensities. Thus, preservation also involves intensification in that, although Lyotard writes that initially the libidinal band/skin is 'like the *track* of intensities' – 'ephemeral', 'useless', and 'heterogeneous' – it is only '*after the event*' that the libidinal band/skin is formulated from the passages of intensity.[25] For this reason, the libidinal band/skin is the passage for as well as the result of intensities, which makes passage for new intensities. Based on the reading that I made of Freud in Chapter 1, the passages for intensity can be described by the scratches or grooves made on the wax slab of the Mystic Writing-Pad causing 'cavities' and 'lumps', and which can be retraced but also cause resistances.[26] This arrangement of grooves is demonstrative of the accumulation and repression of intensities in the unconscious. The libidinal band/skin is 'like' the '*tracks* of intensity', Lyotard writes: 'being at the same time the surface crossed and the crossing'.[27] And continues:

> You will say: 'crossed' is a past, it is not the passage which produces the skin, but the past of the passage, not the intensity, but what it will have been (*son après coup*); and the surface, the libidinal skin is thus already a memory of intensities, a capitalization, a localization of their passages, there is the intensity and what *remains* of it, and your comparison doesn't count since there is a *caput*, a surface of inscription, a register, when its function was to render the acephalus visible.[28]

Thus, what remains is in the register of inscription with the potential for new intensities. The register of inscription is rhythmic, and is the action as well as the remains of intensities, with the potential for new intensities. Williams writes about the relationship between inscription and intensities exactly thus; that

> structure, language, and the dream-narrative function because they are the aftermath of intensity but also because they are the source of new intensities. To deprive them of all the energy born of intensities would be to render them inoperative: a useless structure, a dead language and a narrative without a story to tell.[29]

I argue that cinema, like 'structure, language and the dream-narrative', functions because recorded films are the 'aftermath of intensity but also ... the source of new intensities'.[30] The recorded film (the inscribed filmstrip) is the source of intensities – intensities that have been channelled and exploited by the filmmaker. The film's inscription (projection) on the spectator surface is the source of new intensities; that is, derives from it the appearance of new discourses that will be produced about the film by the spectator. The spectator surface also retains the 'memory of intensities' that will inform new intensities.[31]

In this register of inscription Lyotard describes the activity of the signifying record produced by the mechanical apparatus (by which I define rhythm), as that which remains:

> The fact remains that they *remain*, that the marks of variations are inscribed on these objects and transform them into monuments of a past activity, into means of determining an activity to come, they thus open the space of an upstream and a downstream in production, of a cumulative diachronic time, of a capitalizing history.[32]

Rhythm can be viewed in this light: as signifying marks that have the activity and temporality of capital. That is, of that which has charge and discharge, profit and return. If rhythm determines an activity in expectance which then passes, the pulse is the force of that activity. The libidinal band/skin thus gives rise to a way of thinking about a particular kind of economy for the pulse: a libidinal economy, to be precise. And that libidinal economy has a very particular relationship to the secondary sphere of theatre, discourse, representation (marks, monuments, capital): in a literal sense, the inscriptions made on the filmstrip.

With this function of the surfaces of inscription in mind, and taking into account the signification of intensity in film viewing/spectatorship, we can thus say that there are two (inextricable) films in any one viewing. The first film is 'recorded and conserved' on the filmstrip by the filmmaker, and in turn inscribes itself on the sensitive surface of the spectator, and is 'recorded and conserved' in memory (and 'is the means of transforming the singular sign of nothing, which is intensity, into terms of presence/absence',[33] or, indeed, rhythm). The other film is the experience of the film itself – a libidinal economy that is described by the passage of intensities that make up the investment of the image by the spectator, and which engenders the behaviour of the pulse. And yet, the differentiation between inscription and intensities, rhythm and the pulse, is not a static one, but rather an imbricating relationship: not one without the other.

However, from a certain perspective the cinema 'machine' may be only said to produce intensity; that is, singularity. To take up Lyotard's note of care:

> And beware, because with the instrument, the machine, you are already right in the zero. When the whirls of the disjunctive segment in its libidinal journey, being singular, produce no memory, this segment only ever being where it is in an ungraspable time, *a tense*, and therefore what was 'previously' journeyed through does not exist: acephalia, time of the unconscious.[34]

It is not the apparatus, or even the effects of the apparatus, that differentiate what Lyotard calls the 'theatre' of inscription from the libidinal band/skin; in my terminology, rhythm from the pulse. Rather, it is the signifying record ('"printout" (*sortie*)'[35]) produced by the apparatus machine that differentiates the two. That is, if we have previously identified rhythm as the inscription that makes a recording of presence/absence, and further, which generates memory and I add, monument (the filmstrip), then the pulse produces no memory – is 'acephalia'[36] (from the Greek *akephalos*, literally 'headless'). That is, film can only be said to be found in the intensities and expenditures (the acephalia) that are generated. When the filmstrip lies in its canister, it is only an inactive, or deactivated, film. The filmstrip is not cinema, per se.

The difference is one of movement. Lyotard accepts that the unconscious is structured like a language, but only when 'intensities are in decline';[37] that is, when libidinal economy is exchanged for what Lyotard calls the theatre of inscription: the 'theatrical "volume"'.[38] Williams describes the libidinal band/skin and the 'disintensification' of the libidinal band/skin that produces the 'theatrical "volume"':

> when a propeller on an aircraft is at full speed it gives the appearance of a disk. At any given time, it is impossible to tell whether a point on the disk is closer to the leading edge or the trailing edge of the propeller. The distinction between the two edges only makes sense when the propeller has slowed down. This is also true of events or intensities on the libidinal band: they can only be distinguished from one another when their energy has been diminished.[39]

We can read the movement of the propeller on an aircraft like the movement of the filmstrip. That is, when the filmstrip is being pulled at full speed through the projector by its sprockets, it is impossible to tell the leading edge and the trailing edge of each photogramme. Instead, at this speed, what one sees of the film is emerging intensities in the real movement of the *dispositif*.

In another sense, the intensity of the libidinal economy means that there is no negation – it does not grasp the conceptual opposition of the 'this' and the 'not-this' found in discursive (linguistic) inscriptions – and because of this does, in fact, embrace figural difference. There is no 'this' and 'not-this' of the photogramme in experience other than in thought. In other words, a libidinal economy is an incompossible realm, where there is no conceptual opposition but 'this' and 'this', and 'this', ad infinitum. This incompossibility of the 'this' and 'this', and 'this', Iain Hamilton Grant notes, affords Lyotard's libidinal economy 'a logical violation, but an expensive and metamorphic economics'.[40]

And yet, in the 'disintensification' of a segment of the libidinal band/ skin – the slowed aircraft propeller, the photogramme on a filmstrip, or indeed, the transformation of the film into discourses about it – a conceptual and 'theatrical "volume"' arises – a 'this' and a 'not-this'.[41] As Grant writes: 'It is through procedures of exclusion (notably negation and exteriorization) that the bar gives birth to the conceptual process, twisting the band into what Lyotard calls the 'theatrical "volume"'.[42] What is revealed by the 'disintensification' of the libidinal band/skin to the 'theatrical "volume"' are the precepts for defining inscription in relation to the libidinal economy. The presence/absence of the beat of rhythm on an exterior surface marks it as a 'this' and a 'not-this' in the procedure of conceptual exclusion. This procedure of conceptual exclusion is also the premise by which we might say that passages of intensity can be defined by the pulse. The pulse is as unrepresentable as the force of the intensities that come into presence via the analogue of the libidinal band/skin.

The inscriptive sign is only a substitution for intensities; rhythm a substitution for the pulse. In this way, Williams writes of the: 'substitution of intensities, which in themselves have no fixed meaning and depend on no perceivable differences, by systems of signicative signs, carrying meaning and therefore dependent on differences that can be recognized'.[43] If the pulse is fundamentally unrepresentative, then rhythm is the way by which the pulse can be recognised. Rhythm thus defined is a substitution for the force of intensities that makes up the pulse. Rhythm is also an inscription of the pulse's movement. At this point it is enough to reiterate that both the libidinal and discursive are formations (*Gestaltungen*).[44] Thus, what was noted at the outset was the way that surfaces of inscription were a way of preserving intensity as figures or formations. Such figures or formations were found to be a consequence of the action of rhythm. What is of particular interest to me is the way rhythm is imbricated with the pulse in this characterisation; and further, in cinema, the way that the recording mechanisms of cinema are imbricated with the intensities of cinema. If both the libidinal and the discursive are formations, intensities in the libidinal formation are simply energetic de/formations.

Passages of intensity are constituted by the force of libidinal energies exorbitantly invested in the opening of the libidinal band/skin. They witness the de/formation of the *dispositif*. Grant writes about intensities:

> Lyotard considers intensities as unbound excitations of force which are characterized by their displaceability, their instantaneity and their resistance to the temporal syntheses of memory ... It is through an organizing and regulatory central instance (e.g. the great Zero) that the singularity of an intensity becomes a communicable and exchangeable sign.[45]

Intensities are thereby the 'unbound excitations of force' that can be organised into communicable formations or arrangements.

According to Deleuze and Claire Parnet in *Dialogues*, it is possible to conceive intensities as the sounds, colours, or images in the movement-image.[46] Deleuze and Parnet write: 'Movement does not go from one point to another – rather it happens between two levels as a difference of potential. A difference of intensity produces a phenomenon, releases or ejects it, sends it into space.'[47] In Deleuze's *Cinema 1* intensities are defined by real movement in the movement-image, which can be differentiated from the abstract movement of an object through space and time.[48] Lyotard, for his part, does not dismiss the relation of intensities to movement but describes in *Libidinal Economy* a 'turning' of a segment of the libidinal band/skin (what he calls the 'turning of the bar'): 'the more quickly it turns on itself, the more energy it employs and expends, and heats the travelled zone'.[49] The spinning bar has an 'aleatory rotation'; an 'incandescence'.[50] The spinning bar can also be likened to the movement of the propeller on an aircraft described by Williams.[51] What Lyotard means by this spinning of the segment of the libidinal band/skin is that, while the bar 'draws distinction between things on the libidinal band',[52] in the high-speed spinning of the bar it cannot be discerned which side of the libidinal band singularities fall on. In other words, intensities can only be captured in the slowing and cooling of the bar. In Lyotard's image of the 'turning of the bar', movement makes the distinction between singularities that can be discriminated by structures in the slowed bar and, in the high-speed bar, intensities are too intense to distinguish. This latter is, Lyotard writes: 'Not a matter of separation, but on the contrary, of movement, of displaceability on the spot.'[53] Intensities, for Lyotard then, are defined by the movement that makes distinction impossible, because only the energy – the incandescence of the spinning bar – can be recognised.

Movement, and an Opening

Evidence of the pulse as real movement can be seen in the conception of cinema that Deleuze develops through recourse to Bergson's work on duration.[54] In *Cinema 1* Deleuze insists on the difference between movement understood as the decomposition and recomposition of immobile sections in space and the movement-image, which conceives real movement as a 'concrete' and 'qualitative duration'.[55] Real movement is different from space covered. The latter is divisible and made up of 'single, identical, homogeneous', 'immobile sections'. The movements of this space, on the other hand, are of an irreducible heterogeneity.[56] Deleuze explains: 'Space covered is past, movement is present, the act of covering. The space covered is divisible, indeed infinitely divisible, whilst movement is indivisible, or cannot be divided without changing qualitatively each time it is divided.'[57] The movement-image is the movement of matter-flux, as Deleuze writes, 'beyond the conditions of natural perception'.[58] Such movement is Open on the world and is open to change.

Movement thus understood inspires an Open spectatorship for cinema. Things become complicated, however, when one attempts to attribute duration to the pulse. For the pulse is better described as shocks, bursts or surges of energetic flow, even as duration describes the Open state of change that is the chaotic behaviour of the pulse.[59] Nonetheless, the 'movement-image' requires a concept of the Open that will be useful in describing the pulse. The pulse can only be adequately understood when it is seen to be part and parcel of the spectator's openness to the image/world, and this is because the pulse in the body, by its movement and affective response, is also open to the world.

Deleuze's concept of the movement-image is deliberately devised to shift the terrain that Bergson establishes to expose the limitations of the representation of movement. In *Matter and Memory*, Bergson demonstrates that real movement is not the transfer of a thing from one place to another but the 'transference of a state'.[60] This state, which involves the quality of internal vibration, can be defined as 'duration'.[61] Similarly, the pulse must be understood in terms of real movements that are 'heterogeneous' and 'irreducible amongst themselves'.[62]

Deleuze argues for cinema as real movement by producing three commentaries on Bergson's philosophy of time. Each of these commentaries is important for our thinking about the transition of the movement of rhythm to that of the pulse. The first is important because, as we will see, in the decomposition and recomposition of immobile sections in space, what is described are the sequences of space in succession of which rhythm is composed. The significance of the second commentary lies in the fact that the accumulation of 'privileged instants' is a quantitative process that describes the succession of closed sets that are rhythm's instants. And the value of the third commentary rests in the way the opening of the whole to relations specifies a way to approach the movement of the pulse as it responds to the world.

In his first commentary, Deleuze demonstrates simply that movement has two formulas. In the first formula, movement is divided into immobile sections of space supplemented by abstract time. In the second, real movement occurs as a concrete duration. The first formula suggests that when the space between two points is decomposed into immobile sections and recomposed into movement, what follows is an abstract conception of time. Abstract time is comprised of a mechanical succession of 'homogeneous', 'universal', 'identical' positions in space.[63] Deleuze stands alongside Bergson in his insistence that the decomposition and recomposition of movement is false movement. Thus, photography, like modern science, 'always isolates moments'.[64] But Deleuze also argues that Bergson errs when he names this false movement 'cinematographic'. Deleuze writes: 'In short, cinema does not give us an image to which movement is added, it immediately gives us a movement-image. It does give us a section, but a section which is mobile, not an immobile section + abstract movement.'[65]

Significantly Deleuze's movement-image conceives movement in reality. Movement thus understood implies a qualitative change in state. This is denoted by Deleuze's second formula 'real movement → concrete duration'.[66] The movement-image is therefore a mobile section of duration, rather than an immobile section of space to which abstract time is added. This description of movement is important because it allows Bergson, and Deleuze after him, to focus on qualitative changes in the state of things, rather than simply quantitative transitions brought about by sections of space in succession.

In his second commentary on Bergson's philosophy of time, Deleuze describes 'privileged instants' and 'any-instant-whatevers'. The error of the illusion of movement is the same for this commentary in that movement is reconstituted 'from instants or positions'.[67] 'Privileged instants' designate the ancient form of taking intelligible elements – 'Forms and Ideas' – from movement, and making them 'eternal and immobile'.[68] Bergson writes, for example, that the 'multitudinous successive positions of a runner are contracted into a single symbolic attitude, which our eyes perceive, which art reproduces, and which becomes for us all the image of a man running'.[69] Consciousness synthesises a pose from movement and attributes it with a qualitative (hence singular) status. Deleuze calls these 'single symbolic attitudes', 'poses', or 'privileged instants', and writes that in the modern era of the cinematic 'any-instant-whatever', singularities are the qualitative instants plucked from the accumulation of 'any-whatever': 'Now this production of singularities (the qualitative leap) is achieved by the accumulation of banalities (quantitative process), so that the singular is taken from the any-whatever, and is itself an any-whatever which is simply non-ordinary and non-regular.'[70]

The production of singularities is thus derived from the corpus of cinema's accumulated instants. Or, to put it another way, movement produces singularities as qualities of change or transformation, and it is consciousness that captures these singularities in the movement of the whole. However, singularities, whether 'privileged instants' or 'any-instant-whatevers', are a consequence of closed sets. As Deleuze writes:

> to recompose movement with *eternal poses* or with *immobile sections* comes to the same thing: in both cases, one misses the movement because one constructs a Whole, one assumes that 'all is given', whilst movement only occurs if the whole is neither given nor giveable. As soon as a whole is given to one in the eternal order of forms or poses, or in the set of any-instant-whatevers, then either time is no more than the image of eternity, or it is the consequence of the set; there is no longer room for real movement.[71]

Consciousness does two separate things between the whole and the Open (the second and third commentary). In the second commentary Deleuze writes that one assumes a whole that is 'given', even though, if the whole is 'given' movement is missed and time is conceived as either eternal because it is found in *'eternal poses'* or as a 'consequence of the set'.[72] In the third commentary the whole is Open and changing. The Open whole is privileged because it preserves real movement, in turn enabling movement to open up the world. This openness is a state of consciousness that is 'becoming'. Thus Deleuze writes in his third commentary: 'The whole creates itself, and constantly creates itself in another dimension without parts – like that which carries along the set of one qualitative state to another, like the pure ceaseless becoming which passes through these states.'[73]

Thus Deleuze's third commentary on Bergson's philosophy of time is that movement as a change or transformation in state is Open: 'if the whole is not giveable, it is because it is the Open, and because its nature is to change constantly, or to give rise to something new, in short, to endure'.[74] Duration is defined as the coincidence of the opening of consciousness to the whole and the whole opening itself to consciousness. Bergson conceives duration as identical to consciousness. Consciousness is an opening upon the whole.[75] As Deleuze writes: 'For, if the living being is a whole and, therefore, comparable to the whole of the universe, this is . . . because it is open upon a world, and the world, the universe, is itself the Open.'[76]

In this openness Deleuze refers time, or duration, to *relations*: 'We can say of duration itself or of time, that it is the whole of relations.'[77] Deleuze's third commentary, I want to argue, therefore allows for the Open between the consciousness and the world to be conceived in relations, and gives us an insight into how consciousness is conceptualised in the last two commentaries. The identifying point for this Open is that relations are not of a thing, but that 'through relations, the whole is transformed or changes qualitatively'.[78]

Literally, the closing of the pulse is the movement of the valves as the blood passes through the ventricles of the heart and is what gives the pulse rhythm. The rhythmic action of the valves results in the inscriptive traces of 'beats' that are made in the recording by the cardiograph. The closing also circumscribes the closed set of objects of the heart and the circulation system as a whole – the left and right atriums, the left and right ventricles, and the various valves that open and close to various arteries and veins. The circulation system is a closed set or system. The opening, on the other hand, indicates the responsiveness of the pulse to the world. The movement of the pulse changes and, by its elasticity, gives, as Deleuze writes of the whole, 'rise to something new'.[79]

Furthermore, the whole is defined by relations. Relations refer either to a property of the closed set of objects of a system or to the whole that is transformed or changed qualitatively through relations and its relation to the world.[80] Likewise, the pulse is defined by the force of the movement of the blood in the circulatory system of the body, even while the movement of the pulse changes qualitatively or is transformed through relations and its relation to the world. What the pulse adds to the concept of the Open in cinema then, is that it makes relations.

The pulse and the world are in an Open relation. The pulse by its Open relation to the world shows us that the behaviour of the pulse is also found in the opening of consciousness to the image of cinema. This relation is what Deleuze means by the Open. To explicate duration in terms of the pulse is to conceive of the whole as the whole of consciousness and the image of cinema in Open relation. In fact, the pulse exists in the Open relationship between the film and the viewer that forms one of many relations in the *dispositif*.

The Logic of Sensation as a Diastolic–Systolic Opening

In Deleuze's earlier work *Francis Bacon*, a diastolic–systolic rhythm opens the self to the world. This diastolic–systolic rhythm is the closest Deleuze gets to describing the movement of the pulse, where diastole and systole characterise the dilation and contraction of the heart muscle felt in the rhythm of the pulse. The pulse can be conceived not simply as the Open movement of matter-flux, but an openness of the subject or spectator to sensation. The pulse is responsive to the world and the movement of the pulse is also determined by its affective response to stimuli. The movement of the diastolic–systolic rhythm that comprises the sensorial relation between self and image/world is thus an expression of the pulse in film spectatorship.

In this text, Deleuze shows how a single image of a work of art that comprises the whole reflects a state of change and duration. Rather than understanding the work of art as a static section of framed space, the single image is a movement-image that involves the Open heterogeneity of change effectuated by intensive forces. Francis Bacon's works demonstrate 'a movement "in-place", a spasm', which reveals '*the action of invisible forces on the body*'.[81] The whole, and the opening of the whole, does not simply relate to movement, relations of movement, and responses to change between consciousness and the world, but to a Figure of sensation. This Figure of sensation gives us a way to conceptualise the force of intensities in the energetic circuit of spectator and image, like the force of intensities in the energetic circuit of pulse and world.

The Figure is bound up in a 'logic of the senses', 'which is neither rational nor cerebral', as Cézanne says.[82] Such Figures do not go through the brain, but through the nervous system, defining a particular kind of Figure as sensation.[83] The spasmodic movement of sensation ('*the action of invisible forces on the body*'[84]) leads Deleuze to a phenomenological hypothesis. The domain of sensation is made visible by Bacon in a single visual unity. In order to explain the painter's capacity to unify the multiplicity of the senses in a single visual unity, Deleuze summons rhythm as the 'vital power' and unifying function. This 'vital power' is the movement of diastole–systole, which Deleuze describes as the Open:

> What is ultimate is thus the relation between sensation and rhythm, which places in each sensation the levels and domains through which it passes. This rhythm runs through a painting just as it runs through a piece of music. It is diastole-systole: the world that seizes me by closing in around me, the self that opens to the world and opens the world itself. Cézanne, it is said, is the painter who put a vital rhythm into the visual sensation.[85]

Both seizing the self and opening the self to the world, this rhythm of diastole–systole is a kind of opening and envelopment of self and world. Such openness implies that the self is in a state of change, and the work of art changes in state. The diastole–systole allows Deleuze to articulate a more complex notion of rhythm than that which might be defined as immobile sections in succession. This complex notion of rhythm is the pulse. The diastole–systole – the rhythm of the pulse – goes beyond the closed sets of beats that group distinct objects or parts, towards an Open state of duration in which self and image are continuous in the sensorial relation. The pulse is found in the internal change of 'felt' relations.

Francis Bacon's *Figure with Meat* (1954) is a good example of the force of intensities that open out the single image. In an interpretation of Diego Velázquez's *Portrait of Pope Innocent X* (c. 1650), Bacon's painting depicts the seated Pope, flanked by meat carcasses on either side, his mouth open in a silent scream. The silent scream of the Pope signals '*the action of invisible forces on the body*' and opens the spectator to the 'felt' vibrations of the image.[86] In a rhythmic diastole–systole, the vibratory intensities of the scream seize the self and open the self to the world. The energetic circuit of image and spectator is an intensive 'arrangement'.

Figure 2.5 The 'felt' vibrations of the image. *Figure with Meat* (Francis Bacon, 1954)
© The Art Institute of Chicago / Art Resource, NY

The rhythm of diastole–systole is understood by Deleuze in relation to aesthetic experience – this is the experience that the spectator has of the music or painting invested at the auditory or visual level, as much as it is an experience of the work itself, whether music, painting, or film. The 'vital power' of rhythm is that it takes sensation from a particular domain (auditory or visual) and opens the self to the world.[87] The rhythm of diastole–systole, or what I call the pulse, is here envisaged as a kind of back and forth between myself and the world. As 'I' am seized by the world closing in around me, 'I' open to the world and in so doing open the world itself. In other words, the world encompasses me and insofar as 'I' am open to its embrace, 'I' open it with my response. In the Open relation of self and world there is no certainty as to which moment the development and change occurs, for it is as if the possibility of invention is always already there, and 'I' am always already Open.

This Open relation of spectator and image is an alternative model for spectatorship outside the more conventional way of thinking about the subject–object relation, where subject and object are independent of each other and thus assumed to be closed and distinct entities (closed sets). Simply put, the Open relation of spectator and image is what we might call a continuum of communication in the network of relations. However, at the same time that this Openness and envelopment enfolds spectator and image, the spectator also makes a bid for freedom. This freedom is a 'becoming other' – an invention of the new that is found in being 'open to an infinite number of possibilities'[88] as Maurice Merleau-Ponty writes in *Phenomenology of Perception*; or in the 'strange attractor behaviour' of the cardiac rhythm that occurs because the 'system is open to its external environment, [and thus must be] capable of many nuances of movement',[89] as Briggs and Peat write of the movement of the heart. This freedom is also expenditure: a force of intensity outward. As Bergson writes in *Creative Evolution*: 'vital properties are never entirely realized, though always on the way to become so'.[90] By this definition, the 'vital properties' of the pulse that make up the Figure of sensation are 'never entirely realized'.[91] This is what I am describing as the Open of the pulse because it reflects the creative unfolding dynamic that is at the origin of life: a dynamic that works both to open and relate, to connect in relations and to extend to new possibilities.

The Figure of sensation is nonrepresentative and, as such, vision is itself a 'multisensible Figure' promoted by rhythm. As Deleuze writes: 'Between a color, a taste, a touch, a smell, a noise, a weight, there would be an existential communication that would constitute the "pathic" (nonrepresentative) moment of *the* sensation.'[92] Deleuze goes on to write that: 'Rhythm appears as music when it invests the auditory level, and as painting when it invests the visual level',[93] and we begin to see how cinema has a unique position in relation to the rhythm of the pulse in its inclusion of both the auditory and the visual. Moreover, in cinema, the *dispositif*, defined not simply by the image but by the spectator of the image (in other words, by the movement-image), is itself an opening onto a world that is Open. The Figure does not represent; it relates via the diastolic–systolic opening to sensation that is the pulse.

The significance of the pulse lies in its capacity to define the film spectator in relation to the Open. Defining cinema as an Open relation of image and spectator signals a contrariness to notions of inscription where inscription implies the action of beats made on the sensitive emulsive surface of film or on the sensitive surface of the spectator in which a subject–object relation figures. The movement-image works against closed sets of beats towards an Open state of duration that makes cinema less about an inscriptive spectatorship in which an enclosed subject figures. The diastolic–systolic rhythm that Deleuze describes as the impetus for the sensorial opening of the self to the world means that forces of intensity create a continuous circuit. The pulse in cinema demonstrates the Open relation of image and spectator – a continuum of communication in the network of energetic relations that is the *dispositif*.

The Aesthetics of the Open: Georges Franju's *Le Sang des bêtes/Blood of the Beasts* (1949)

Franju's *Le Sang des bêtes* is a documentary made in 1949 of Paris's Vaugirard and La Villette slaughterhouses. The imagery of *Le Sang des bêtes* is a forerunner to the fictional horror seen in Franju's later film *Les Yeux sans visage/Eyes without a Face* (1959) in its inclusion of dissection. *Le Sang des bêtes* acts like the dissection tools it envisages, opening out, dislocating and isolating the body. In their dissected form, body parts in *Le Sang des bêtes* contribute to a rhythmic tableau. Rhythm extends to the shock of repeated blows upon skin and the micro-movements of the nervous response in the slaughterhouse, which comprise, for the cinema spectator: 'a movement "in-place", a spasm'.[94] It is thus in the shock effect of the beat that the force of intensity arises. As the narrator of *Le Sang des bêtes* exclaims: '"I shall strike you without anger and without hate, like a butcher" wrote Baudelaire – without anger and without hate, with the simple cheerfulness of killers who whistle or sing as they slit throats.'

Figure 2.6 Sheep lined up on a rack their legs kicking like a crazy centipede. *Le Sang des bêtes/Blood of the Beasts* (Georges Franju, 1949)

In an interview for *Cinéma de notre temps*, a television series created by André Bazin's widow, Janine Bazin, and André S. Labarthe, which showcased contemporary filmmakers, the director Georges Franju, speaks of the aesthetics of *Le Sang des bêtes* as forestalling an ethics of violence:

> As I always say, violence isn't the end. Violence is the means. I believe there's nothing but the truth, whether it's beautiful or not, and consequently, only the truth matters. Nothing else counts. I don't see any way to express that which is intrinsically beautiful – and all things are beautiful – other than by the truth. But the way to express it if you're a realist – if you're a documentary filmmaker, as I was – is by stripping the object of its frills. To express it as a surrealist, but remaining a realist is by displacing the object, situating it in another context. In a new setting, the object rediscovers its quality as an object.

By the surrealist act of displacement to which Franju refers, objects open out to a new space. In *Le Sang des bêtes*, the qualities of objects are rediscovered in the displacement of curios in the vacant lot and body parts in the slaughterhouse. This latter displacement promotes sensation by the rhythm of dissecting bodies and the rhythmic tableaux of dissected bodies. Such sensation is not inspired by colour (specifically, the red of blood), but by the movement and rhythm of bodies. Franju goes on to say:

> When I made my film *Blood of the Beasts* I was often told, 'If only it were in colour!' If it were in colour, it'd be repulsive. Period. The sensation people would get would be a physical one. But since it's not in colour – I chose black and white for this film – the emotion people get – at least I hope – is an aesthetic one.

Franju's film, through black-and-white images, and shock, rhythm and displacement, does away with the spectator's ability for anthropomorphising. For this film, it is not the affectivity of red blood but the shocks, bursts or surges of energetic flow that connect and open the animals in the slaughterhouse to the 'felt' sensations of the spectator. That is, it is the rhythm of life as an opening to sensation that generates an investment of intensities in film and viewer, for these body-populated, rhythmic tableaux promote an 'opening out' of intensities that also 'open out' the viewer.

Figure 2.7 The heads of calves: a rhythmic tableau. *Le Sang des bêtes/Blood of the Beasts* (Georges Franju, 1949)

A Libidinal Economy, and an Opening

Lyotard begins *Libidinal Economy* with a call to action to 'open' the libidinal band/skin:

> Open the so-called body and spread out all its surfaces: not only the skin with each of its folds, wrinkles, scars, with its great velvety planes, and contiguous to that, the scalp and its mane of hair, the tender pubic fur, nipples, nails, hard transparent skin under the heel, the light frills of the eyelids, set with lashes – but open and spread, expose the labia majora, so also the labia minora with their blue network bathed in mucus, dilate the diaphragm of the anal sphincter, longitudinally cut and flatten out the black conduit of the rectum, then the colon, then the caecum, now a ribbon with its surface all striated and polluted with shit; as though your dressmaker's scissors were opening the leg of an old pair of trousers.[95]

Lyotard's call to 'open the so-called body' generates a contradiction. It is a libidinal description of the very act of the separating of surfaces that Lyotard will later reject. It is an opening or exposure of surfaces that Lyotard calls for, and yet he disregards the surface as something that transforms the sign into presence/absence and functions as a means of 'recording'.[96]

To take apart the 'surface' of the libidinal band/skin as site and to describe its formulation by passages of intensity is to describe it as 'skin' (*pellicule*). Passages of intensity are both the passage that intensities make and their product, which produce the energetic arrangement in which image and spectator are Open. The production of passages can be understood as an 'opening out' of the libidinal band/skin for the investment of intensities. Grant's translation note points out that Lyotard also 'refers to the pellicule "in the technical sense", meaning "film"'.[97] In cinema, the technical sense of film (*pellicule*) is different from the intensities produced in the cinema experience that make up 'skin' (*pellicule*). In the Open relation between the image and the spectator, the 'opening out' of libidinal surfaces – which is an 'opening out' of the 'skin' of the spectator that extends to images and objects – is an 'exorbitant' investment of intensities in 'skin'.[98]

Rhythm in *Le Sang des bêtes* is produced by a beating upon skin from which intensities arise. The shock effect of the beat causes rhythm by its action or inscription upon a surface, like the skin of drum. Rhythm is also found in the action of dissection and the rhythmic tableaux of dissected bodies in *Le Sang des bêtes*. However, rhythm can be distinguished from the pulse, even as the shock effect of the beat causes rhythm's imbrication with the pulse's 'opening out' of intensities. That is, in *Le Sang des bêtes* the 'opening' is at once an opening out of skin by and for rhythm's beats, and an opening out of 'the great ephemeral skin' as an investment of intensities.[99]

Lyotard differentiates the 'real images inscribed on the film (*pellicule*)' from the 'skin' of *The great ephemeral skin* (*La grande pellicule éphémère*).[100] We can use this difference to differentiate the rhythm of the ordered sequence of images on the filmstrip from the forces of intensity produced in the cinema experience, which I argue are pulsatile. For Lyotard, the 'real images inscribed on the film' are a monument to memory.[101] The 'skin' – that 'has no outside' – is, as Lyotard writes, 'some kind of monstrous beast whose constitutive parts would change according to unforeseeable modulations, would appear and disappear with the same terrifying ease as virtual images on a screen'.[102] Lyotard continues that these 'virtual images on a screen' are 'not determined by real images inscribed on the film (*pellicule*) (in a technical sense)'.[103] What Lyotard describes in this 'skin' is the 'ease' by which the passages of intensity will be transformed into appearance and disappearance. That is, in the appearance and disappearance – the flicking up and passing away – of intensities in the libidinal band/skin, intensity is transformed into the virtual image. The intensities that constitute this 'monstrous beast' give way to the action of rhythmic appearance and disappearance as 'virtual images on a screen';[104] the intensities of the pulse are transformed into the action of rhythm but of a difference in kind than that which is inscribed on the material filmstrip.

Does this 'virtuality' drive Lyotard away from the 'skin' that he sets out when opening the body to 'spread out all its surfaces' in the first place or is it an appropriate descriptor for these 'ephemeral' and 'heterogeneous' tracks of intensity? And what does this 'virtuality' mean for cinema in terms of 'film (*pellicule*) (in a technical sense)'? In fact, the following passage in which Lyotard describes 'film (*pellicule*) (in a technical sense)' anaesthetises the 'skin' opened of the body. Lyotard writes:

> More generally, let's imagine that neither the so-called contents nor the technical procedures permit the synthesis into a story, into a doctrine, into a style, of the fragments of the film joined end to end; it would then be impossible to construct a single time to contain and organize the monster of images; even the recurrences suggested by certain schemes would remain ignored, each occurrence would be experienced as a present and innocent effect. And there would be nothing monstrous about this assemblage, which would exist for neither a mind nor an eye.[105]

The film and 'skin' appear substantially different. At a technical level, the film(strip) of images that constructs a linear or temporal narrative, an ideology or aesthetics, is not of kind with the monstrous opening of the 'skin':

'there would be nothing monstrous about this assemblage'.[106] In the 'skin', the body no longer has narrative, ideology, or aesthetics constructed in an 'ordered series' in time.[107] The 'monstrous beast', made up of intensities to produce 'skin', is the disturbing link between the rhythmic 'recurrence' of images and its disruption as infinite invagination. The opening of the body to 'spread out all its surfaces' is the work of intensification as an energetic de/formation of 'difference' and 'opposition'. As Grant describes it: 'The great ephemeral skin is the libidinal materialist (dis)solution of figural difference and conceptual opposition as polymorphous (hence "ephemeral"), material (hence "skin") intensity.'[108] The call to 'open out' the 'so-called body' monstrously deforms the body into an openness in which organs – the intestine, the labia, the tongue – no longer exist within the surface than describe their function. The 'opening out' of the 'skin', analogous to the 'opening out' of the image and spectator in cinema, I contend, is attacked through intensification. And yet, the 'monstrous beast' is made innocuous by its recording, which turns the 'occurrence' and 'recurrence' of images into 'present and innocent effect'.[109] Thus, we can understand the 'opening out' of the film and the spectator *as* intensities opened out in 'skin'. And yet, the film and the 'skin' are another unavoidable imbrication. The better course here is not to distinguish between film and 'skin' – since they are materially the same (witness the opening out of the libidinal band/skin in the call to action) – but to outline the relationship between them. The 'film (*pellicule*) (in a technical sense)' would simply be the inscriptive trace of what remains.[110]

By 'opening out' the 'skin', Lyotard describes the body as having neither inside nor outside, but constituting a continuous surface for libidinal cathexis. In this way, Lyotard goes about reconceptualising a body that is caught by the necessity of an inside and an outside (a closed-ness in boundaries), or as Geoffrey Bennington puts it, 'an inside representing an outside (the Real, the Absent)'.[111] The 'opening out' of 'skin' is constructed of the passages and investments of intensities. The libidinal band/skin is a Moebius strip that is inscribed with the ceaseless signification of corporeality; a 'polymorphous diversity'.[112] The folding of 'skin' upon itself produces invaginations and pockets.[113] In this sense, the libidinal band/skin is continuous and made up of energetic investments, trajectories, or relations. While its 'opening out' is like the ceaseless signification that paper and celluloid layers afford the wax slab of the Mystic Writing-Pad, the Moebius strip suggests a heterogeneous and libidinal band/skin that does not delineate a surface and the inscription on that surface (between 'a surface first, then a writing or inscription over it'[114]). Lyotard instead argues that the libidinal band/skin is itself determined by the passage of intensities that are a '*track* of intensities, ephemeral work'.[115] This is a different way of conceiving of the subject, and for my argument the spectator, which allows for the spectator to be conceived of as a component in the energetic arrangement of cinema determined by the intensities that are invested in the open and 'polymorphous' 'skin'.[116]

This 'opening out' and 'exorbitant' investment of energy in 'skin' also allows a different way of conceiving of desire as the force for libidinal cathexis. The libidinal economy is Lyotard's name for an economy's investment and release of desires and feelings.[117] Lyotard calls these desires and feelings 'intensities'.[118] In *Libidinal Economy*, Lyotard describes the 'opening' of the body as an economy that finds no closed volume, no 'representative cube', no 'lack': 'intensities run in it without meeting a terminus, without ever crashing into the wall of an absence, into a limit which would be the mark of a lack, there is nothing the libido lacks in reality, nor does it lack regions to invest'.[119] Lyotard's libidinal band/skin on which the libido invests, invests interminably. Lyotard's libidinal band/skin is, it must be noted, 'ephemeral', and thus in itself could be said to be in the order of the '*non-realized*'.[120] Nevertheless, the force of desire that is 'of the death drive, or of libido under the "regime" of zero or infinite' is '*positive* and *affirmative*'.[121] As Bennington writes, it is only if we are to differentiate 'desire-as-wish' (*Wunsch*) and 'desire-as-force (libido)', that negativity ('object, absence, lost object' – and the fulfilment of the wish) can be distinguished from 'desire-libido, desire-process, primary process'.[122] The libidinal economy is on the side of 'desire-as-force (libido)', and in this way we can understand the forces of intensity that invest the 'skin' as '*positive* and *affirmative*'.[123] The forces of intensity in Lyotard's libidinal economy are important in determining the force of the pulse in cinema and the spectator's position in the *dispositif*. It is the forces of intensity that arise in the spectator that suggest an erotic encounter.

Surfaces of inscription are the topography, or place of implementation, of the intensities of the libidinal economy, but, as Williams writes, the libidinal band/skin 'knows no boundaries, and has no recognizable stable features, other than its critical role as the place where the energy in the economy meets the structures that exploit it'.[124] Thus, on the one hand, Lyotard's answer to '*surfaces of inscription*', at least in part, is to relinquish the concept of 'surface'. Instead of bounded surfaces implying, through the very imposition of boundaries, transgression, for Lyotard's conception of the libidinal band/skin, 'there is no need to begin with transgression'.[125] Instead, for the libidinal band/skin, boundaries should be interleaved, dissected: 'we must go immediately to the very limits of cruelty, perform the dissection of polymorphous perversion, spread out the immense membrane of the libidinal "body" which is quite different to a frame'.[126] While the 'immense membrane of the libidinal "body" . . . is quite different' to the frame of a painted canvas, it is also quite different to the frame of a photogramme and quite different to the frame of the projected film screen. At the site of the 'immense membrane of the libidinal "body"'[127] surfaces open out into continuous zones in an economy of intensities:

> All these zones are joined end to end in a band which has no back to it, a Moebius band which interests us not because it is closed, but because it is one-sided, a Moebian skin which, rather than being smooth, is on the contrary (is this topologically possible?) covered with roughness, corners, creases, cavities which when it passes on the 'first' turn will be cavities, but perhaps on the 'second', lumps.[128]

In this description Lyotard extends the terrain of the wax slab in Freud's 'A Note upon the "Mystic Writing-Pad"'. The libidinal band/skin has an inside (on the 'first' turn) and an outside (on the 'second'), even while it has 'cavities' and 'lumps'.[129] And yet, in Lyotard's libidinal economy intensities emerge on the libidinal band/skin. Such intensities, locked down, channelled, and regulated by passages on the surfaces of inscription, are forces – feelings and desires – that are themselves singular events. In this way, instead of an endlessly interleaved reconception of surface as such, the pulse will be understood as a force undermining any sense of the location or place of implementation: the libidinal band/skin is itself defined as having no location or place of implementation. Working with the substantial argument made in Lyotard's *Libidinal Economy*, which is that libido is not set against representation but that representation is itself libidinal,[130] the libidinal band/skin will see passages of intensity emerge in the energetic investment of components in the arrangement, set-up, or *dispositif*. Moving away from 'surfaces' then, the intensities that invest the libidinal band/skin have no 'stable features' but are structured and exploited by the energetic arrangement.[131]

In a literal sense, the pulse is the force of movement that emanates from the heart. But the heart could not be said to be the 'place' of the pulse. Rather the heart has a critical role as the place where the energetic movement of the pulse meets the structures of the heart. The pulse itself is an energetic movement to be channelled and exploited by these structures. This is the argument I make for film spectatorship: that the pulse be understood as the intensities as they are energetically invested in the open components of film spectatorship, and are structured by the arrangement, set-up, or *dispositif*. In this sense the spectator is comprised of 'no recognizable stable features' but is a component in the flow of energy of the libidinal economy that 'meets the structures that exploit it' in cinema.[132]

Candour as the Body's Openness to an Outside

Between Lyotard's text *Libidinal Economy*, written in 1974, and his essay 'Anamnesis of the Visible, or Candour', written in 1989, it is possible to see the development of Lyotard's thought regarding a different kind of Open. This second Open is more phenomenological than libidinal, more sentimental than organic; it concerns the soul more than it concerns libidinal desire. For this reason, it comes closer to Deleuze's opening of the consciousness and the world in its theorisation of an Open receptiveness of the artist/spectator to the world.

In his essay 'Anamnesis of the Visible, or Candour', Lyotard describes the apprehension of form, and particularly the form of beauty: 'There is no boundary to be crossed between an object and a subject existing in a mode of respective closure, but an instantaneous openness. Landscapes have no need of exposition; they exist as states of the soul.'[133] 'States of the soul', or feelings, are here depicted in a reading of Immanuel Kant's third moment of the *Analytic of the Beautiful* as free forms not yet objectified. As Lyotard writes: 'Before thought determines objects, it is gripped by free forms which it does not initially objectify. Susceptibility to forms is a constituent element of the sensibility which creates sentiment, and not a world.'[134] Anamnesis, Lyotard writes, 'tries to recapture the childhood of a thought dedicated to the world'.[135] Such sensibility as thought can be characterised by consciousness opening to the world.

In relation to painting Lyotard writes in this essay that only by withdrawing – by 'turning away' – is there the possibility that a painter may turn to desire in absence with the memory of presence.[136] This is what Lyotard describes as an opening to form: 'When the painter withdraws from the world, turns his gaze away from the intrigue and from motion, he abandons himself to forms, opens his hand to them.'[137] Candour describes this openness to the 'susceptibility to forms':

> Feeling, or rather sentiment, is not a matter for the ego; it is matter taking on a form, and its hold is neither active nor passive, as it exists before the act and before subjectification. Affinity rather than precision. By moving through the intrigue, by reaching a point in advance of any intrigue, he may be moving towards candour.[138]

Lyotard writes here of feelings as 'matter taking on form'. However, I contend that form, in this sense, can also be called a 'virtuality' in that it is the opening of the subject to a sensibility that is described: 'a direct affinity between a form and our "inner" receptiveness'.[139] The 'felt' experience opens the viewer to a network of relations:

> the field of the visible, the world, is, by its very constitution, transitive through and through. Woven like a network of ever-possible, incessant transactions between here and over there, between him or you and me. Stretched between a thousand positions which any existent, myself included, can occupy for an instant.[140]

A prototype of the kind of subjectivity being posited can be seen in Lyotard's reference to Merleau-Ponty's notion of 'chiasmus'.[141] Lyotard writes of the experience of looking at a painting that is also the reading of a text, by which 'the immanence of the seer to the field of the visible is the lot of any seer'.[142] 'Chiasmus' is a 'crossing [of] subject and object, in which the world is of the same "flesh" as my body, and that body of the same "objecthood" as the world it sees'.[143] Like the rhythms of the unconscious that work in two ways and two directions – stimuli 'beat' on the unconscious from the outside causing 'impressions' and the unconscious 'stretches out feelers, through the medium of the system *Pcpt.-Cs.*, towards the external world' from the inside[144] – rhythms, as Bennington writes of the kind of spectatorship that Lyotard puts forward for the artwork, 'solicit an answering rhythm in the body of the viewer'.[145] It is likewise for cinema. While rhythm is the movement of communication and response between the subject and the object, the pulse is the opening of the subject and the image/world that refers back to the sensory body. It is by the energetic impetus and connections, of and between the body and the image/world that openness is described.

There is a problem with the Open, however, as indicated above. It is the question of whether the Open, specifically Lyotard's idea of the Open, allows for an idea of the infinite. Such an opening to the infinite must be refuted because of the passages that channel and regulate desire. I have characterised the Opening of spectator and image as the formulation of a network of relations in the *dispositif*. Returning to *Libidinal Economy*, Lyotard's idea of the Open describes a heterogeneous '*track* of intensities, ephemeral work'[146]: 'ephemeral' in the sense that it 'offers nothing to hold onto or secure'.[147] If cinema demonstrates an Open relation between the spectator and the image, an opening such as the continuum of communication found in the network of relations suggests an Open direction in the desire to communicate. It suggests that the opening of the spectator to the image makes of desire a free-flowing energy that moves into whichever space it likes. There are constraints on subjectivity and on desire: history, ground, specificity of self, and the world in which a reading takes place. Such a conception of desire is imperative to this book in that it complicates the ways that the libidinal economy – the passages of intensities that retrace cavities, bisect grooves already made, and are resisted and forced awry by previously constituted lumps – can be understood. The concept of the pulse transforms the unconscious into a place where something happens in the dynamism of the drives. This means that the pulse can be characterised by an economy of the movement of intensities in passages and their arrangement in the *dispositif*. As I have noted, desire is locked down, channelled and regulated by that which seeks to bind it.[148] Another way of contrasting rhythm and the pulse is in terms of escape and capture. The pulse is the movement of diastole and systole that, in its action of dilation and contraction, engenders the escaping of the force of movement imbricated with the rhythmic 'beats' that capture the force of movement.

Rhythm is found in the inscription upon a surface. The Open characterises the pulse as an investment of intensities in Open relation with the world. The pulse is described by its Open relation: an opening of consciousness to the image of cinema; an opening of the body and the world. Openness allows for a model for film spectatorship that is intense, libidinal and sensorial. Cinema is unable to do without the surfaces of inscription (the filmstrip and the spectator surface) – the technical aspects of film (*pellicule*) – from a certain point of view, but is defined by the passages of intensities in the investment of components in the *dispositif*. Spectators are no longer conceived as unified subjectivities, and subject and object positions are no longer binaries. Instead they become Open in the *dispositif*. The cinematic *dispositif* is therefore an energetic and intensive experience that is found in the charged relationship between the spectator and the image. There are no limits to this experience other than those that arise from the channelling and exploitation of feelings and desires that take place within a particular *dispositif*: it is Open. That is, cinema is found in the opening of the 'skin' of the film.

Notes

Copyright © 2020 Johns Hopkins University Press and Substance, Inc. This article first appeared in *SubStance*, Volume 49, Issue 3, November 2020, pages 54–70.

1. Lyotard, *Libidinal Economy*, footnote, p. 1.
2. Lyotard, 'Anamnesis of the Visible', p. 235.
3. Deleuze and Guattari, 'The Body without Organs', pp. 9–16.
4. Lyotard, *Libidinal Economy*, p. 1.

5. The relation of blood to the pulse is an interesting one, and is revealed by Marey in his recording of the movement of the pulse. Dagognet writes: 'He [Marey] realized immediately that the pulse did not correspond to the passage of blood in the artery but to that of an independent and faster-moving wave (a vibratory effect)' (Dagognet, *Étienne-Jules Marey*, p. 51).
6. Lyotard, 'Several Silences', p. 98.
7. Lyotard, *Libidinal Economy*, p. 17.
8. Lyotard, *Libidinal Economy*, pp. 16–17.
9. Lyotard, 'Several Silences', p. 98.
10. Williams, *Lyotard*, p. 89.
11. Williams, *Lyotard*, p. 89.
12. A topographical separation or division of the 'layers' of the psychical apparatus to be inscribed suggests rhythm in two ways and two directions. First, the action of rhythm from the outside; that is, the rhythm of stimuli on the site of reception. Second, the action of rhythm from the inside; that is, the rhythm of the 'current of innervation' as the unconscious reaches out to the external world through perception-consciousness (Freud, 'A Note upon the "Mystic Writing-Pad"', p. 231).
13. Lyotard, *Libidinal Economy*, p. 17.
14. Lyotard, 'Several Silences', p. 98.
15. Lyotard, *Libidinal Economy*, pp. 16–17.
16. Lyotard, *Libidinal Economy*, p. 17.
17. Williams, *Lyotard*, p. 89.
18. Lyotard, *Libidinal Economy*, p. 17.
19. Williams, *Lyotard*, p. 89.
20. Lyotard, *Libidinal Economy*, p. 17.
21. Lyotard, *Libidinal Economy*, pp. 17–18.
22. Lyotard, *Libidinal Economy*, pp. 17–18.
23. Lyotard, *Libidinal Economy*, p. 17.
24. Lyotard, *Libidinal Economy*, p. 18.
25. Lyotard, *Libidinal Economy*, p. 17.
26. Lyotard, *Libidinal Economy*, p. 3.
27. Lyotard, *Libidinal Economy*, p. 17.
28. Lyotard, *Libidinal Economy*, p. 17.
29. Williams, *Lyotard*, p. 92.
30. Williams, *Lyotard*, p. 92.
31. Lyotard, *Libidinal Economy*, p. 17.
32. Lyotard, *Libidinal Economy*, p. 16.
33. Lyotard, *Libidinal Economy*, p. 17.
34. Lyotard, *Libidinal Economy*, p. 16.
35. Lyotard, *Libidinal Economy*, p. 16.
36. Lyotard, *Libidinal Economy*, p. 16.
37. Lyotard, *Libidinal Economy*, p. 27.
38. Grant, 'Glossary', p. xii.

39. Williams, *Lyotard*, p. 91.
40. Grant, 'Glossary', p. xi.
41. Grant, 'Glossary', p. xii.
42. Grant, 'Glossary', p. xii.
43. Williams, *Lyotard*, p. 90.
44. Lyotard, *Libidinal Economy*, p. 25.
45. Grant, 'Glossary', p. xiii.
46. Deleuze and Parnet, *Dialogues*, p. 4.
47. Deleuze and Parnet, *Dialogues*, p. 31.
48. Deleuze, *Cinema 1*, pp. 1–2.
49. Lyotard, *Libidinal Economy*, p. 15.
50. Lyotard, *Libidinal Economy*, pp. 16, 27.
51. Williams, *Lyotard*, p. 91.
52. Williams, *Lyotard*, p. 91.
53. Lyotard, *Libidinal Economy*, p. 16.
54. Deleuze, *Cinema 1*, p. 1.
55. Deleuze, *Cinema 1*, p. 1.
56. Deleuze, *Cinema 1*, p. 1.
57. Deleuze, *Cinema 1*, p. 1.
58. Deleuze, *Cinema 1*, p. 2.
59. Briggs and Peat, *Seven Life Lessons of Chaos*, pp. 63–4.
60. Bergson, *Matter and Memory*, p. 267.
61. Bergson, *Creative Evolution*, p. 201; Bergson, *Matter and Memory*, p. 268.
62. Deleuze, *Cinema 1*, p. 1.
63. Deleuze, *Cinema 1*, p. 1.
64. Bergson, *Creative Evolution*, pp. 330, 332.
65. Deleuze, *Cinema 1*, p. 2.
66. Deleuze, *Cinema 1*, p. 1.
67. Deleuze, *Cinema 1*, p. 3.
68. Deleuze, *Cinema 1*, p. 4.
69. Bergson, *Matter and Memory*, p. 277.
70. Deleuze, *Cinema 1*, p. 6.
71. Deleuze, *Cinema 1*, p. 7.
72. Deleuze, *Cinema 1*, p. 7.
73. Deleuze, *Cinema 1*, p. 10.
74. Deleuze, *Cinema 1*, p. 9.
75. Deleuze, *Cinema 1*, pp. 9–10.
76. Deleuze, *Cinema 1*, p. 10.
77. Deleuze, *Cinema 1*, p. 10.
78. Deleuze, *Cinema 1*, p. 10.
79. Deleuze, *Cinema 1*, p. 9.
80. Deleuze, *Cinema 1*, p. 10.
81. Deleuze, *Francis Bacon*, p. 41.
82. Deleuze, *Francis Bacon*, p. 42.

83. Deleuze, *Francis Bacon*, p. 34.
84. Deleuze, *Francis Bacon*, p. 41.
85. Deleuze, *Francis Bacon*, pp. 42–3.
86. Deleuze, *Francis Bacon*, p. 41.
87. Deleuze, *Francis Bacon*, pp. 42–3.
88. Merleau-Ponty, *Phenomenology of Perception*, pp. 453–4.
89. Briggs and Peat, *Seven Life Lessons of Chaos*, p. 64.
90. Bergson, *Creative Evolution*, p. 13.
91. Bergson, *Creative Evolution*, p. 13.
92. Deleuze, *Francis Bacon*, p. 42.
93. Deleuze, *Francis Bacon*, p. 42.
94. Deleuze, *Francis Bacon*, p. 41.
95. Lyotard, *Libidinal Economy*, p. 1.
96. Lyotard, *Libidinal Economy*, pp. 17–18.
97. Lyotard, *Libidinal Economy*, footnote, p. 1.
98. Grant, 'Glossary', p. xvi.
99. Lyotard, *Libidinal Economy*, p. 1.
100. Lyotard, *Libidinal Economy*, footnote, pp. 1, 36.
101. Lyotard, *Libidinal Economy*, p. 36.
102. Lyotard, *Libidinal Economy*, pp. 35–6.
103. Lyotard, *Libidinal Economy*, p. 36.
104. Lyotard, *Libidinal Economy*, p. 36.
105. Lyotard, *Libidinal Economy*, p. 36.
106. Lyotard, *Libidinal Economy*, p. 36.
107. Lyotard, *Libidinal Economy*, p. 36.
108. Grant, 'Glossary', p. xv.
109. Lyotard, *Libidinal Economy*, p. 36.
110. Lyotard, *Libidinal Economy*, p. 36.
111. Bennington, *Lyotard*, p. 27.
112. Bennington, *Lyotard*, p. 19.
113. Lyotard, *Libidinal Economy*, pp. 21–2.
114. Lyotard, *Libidinal Economy*, p. 17.
115. Lyotard, *Libidinal Economy*, p. 17.
116. Bennington, *Lyotard*, p. 19; quoting from Lyotard, *Économie libidinale*, pp. 31–2.
117. Williams, *Lyotard*, p. 10.
118. Williams, *Lyotard*, p. 40.
119. Lyotard, *Libidinal Economy*, p. 4.
120. Lacan, *The Four Fundamental Concepts*, p. 22.
121. Bennington, *Lyotard*, pp. 24–5.
122. Bennington, *Lyotard*, pp. 15–17; quoting from Lyotard, *Des dispositifs pulsionnels*, p. 238.
123. Bennington, *Lyotard*, p. 25.
124. Williams, *Lyotard*, p. 40.

125. Lyotard, *Libidinal Economy*, p. 2.
126. Lyotard, *Libidinal Economy*, p. 2.
127. Lyotard, *Libidinal Economy*, p. 2.
128. Lyotard, *Libidinal Economy*, pp. 2–3.
129. Lyotard, *Libidinal Economy*, p. 3.
130. Bennington, *Lyotard*, p. 25.
131. Williams, *Lyotard*, p. 40.
132. Williams, *Lyotard*, p. 40.
133. Lyotard, 'Anamnesis of the Visible', p. 235.
134. Lyotard, 'Anamnesis of the Visible', p. 235.
135. Lyotard, 'Anamnesis of the Visible', p. 235.
136. Lyotard, 'Anamnesis of the Visible', p. 228.
137. Lyotard, 'Anamnesis of the Visible', p. 236.
138. Lyotard, 'Anamnesis of the Visible', p. 226.
139. Lyotard, 'Anamnesis of the Visible', p. 235.
140. Lyotard, 'Anamnesis of the Visible', p. 232.
141. Lyotard, 'Anamnesis of the Visible', p. 232.
142. Lyotard, 'Anamnesis of the Visible', p. 232.
143. Bennington, *Lyotard*, p. 57.
144. Freud, 'A Note upon the "Mystic Writing-Pad"', p. 231.
145. Bennington, *Lyotard*, p. 57.
146. Lyotard, *Libidinal Economy*, p. 17.
147. Lyotard, *Libidinal Economy*, p. 241.
148. Lyotard, 'Several Silences', p. 98.

CHAPTER 3

Aisthesis and *Dispositif*: The Pulse and Its Analogues

I am William Castle, director of the motion picture you are about to see. I feel obligated to warn you that some of the sensations – some of the physical reactions which the actors on the screen will feel – will also be experienced, for the first time in motion picture history, by certain members of this audience. I say certain members because some people are more sensitive to these mysterious electronic impulses than others. These unfortunate, sensitive people will at times feel a strange, tingling sensation; other people will feel it less strongly. But don't be alarmed – you can protect yourself. At any time you are conscious of a tingling sensation you may obtain immediate relief by screaming. Don't be embarrassed about opening your mouth and letting rip with all you've got, because the person right next to you will probably be screaming too. And remember, a scream at the right time may save your life.[1]

William Castle

To produce the effect of which Castle speaks, the release of *The Tingler* saw cinema seats wired with electric devices that would 'tingle' the occupant of the seat. Such a prescribed spectatorial experience was prescribed in another sense. The opening sequence of the film shows the execution by electric chair of the brother-in-law of cinema theatre owner Oliver 'Ollie' Higgins (Philip Coolidge). For the original release of the film, this execution was supported by promotional posters that asked: 'Do you have the GUTS to sit in this chair?' This made the 'tingling' an electrocution in which the spectator became the executed. The electric chair of the film's opening sequence and the cinema seat were, in this move, conflated. A second meaning of the 'tingling' is found in the narrative of the film, which describes the formation of an organism along the spine – 'the Tingler' – produced by spine-tingling fear. The organism dissipates when a person screams. Screaming is demanded of the spectator by the narrative when an extracted Tingler organism escapes into Ollie's cinema theatre. Even though a Tingler organism is not produced in the actual cinema theatre of the spectator (as were some of Castle's gimmicks, such as the 'Emergo' skeleton of *House on Haunted Hill* (1959)), the 'tingling' and subsequent tingling of the spine prescribes a metaphorical extension.

In this chapter, I will explore an aesthetics of the pulse found in the effect of the prescriptive and mechanical manipulation of the body of the spectator. For the film *The Tingler*, Castle prescribes the spectator's response and provokes this response through the mechanical manipulation of the body. Not only does the director's use of the apparatus, in its prescriptive inscription upon the body, open the body to sensation, the apparatus 'exposes' the originary sensations of the body, which I argue is an exposure of *aisthesis*.[2] The beating of the heart and thus, the pulse, is the originary sensation of the body. The beating of the heart, the tingling sensation in the spine, and the scream are the products of *aisthesis* 'exposed' by the apparatus. This chapter undertakes to revise existing philosophical, fictional and film theoretical conceptions of aesthetics, by relating *aisthesis* to an understanding of the pulse that I have developed in Chapter 2: a pulse that is Open rather than 'inscriptive'. *Aisthesis* is the sensation which is 'exposed' or opened by aesthetics.[3] This situates the pulse aesthetically as *aisthesis* for this chapter: the sensation which is 'exposed' or opened by aesthetics.

This argument is necessary to my conception of the pulse because it demonstrates that the pulse is aesthetic, but that this aesthetics is found in proximity to the body and the sensations therein. That is, *aisthetic* spectatorship does not involve critical reflection or even judgement in recognition of an object or subject, but rather refers to sensation. This is not a distanced contemplation but an energetic way of thinking about aesthetics that is found to be in operation: a 'seeing' in the act of 'seeing'. Such energetics also characterise an Open relation between the world and the interior workings of the body. Sensation refers not simply to what is 'seen' without, but also what is 'felt' within. The film *The Tingler* perfectly emblematises that which is 'exposed' or opened by aesthetics. Not just an aesthetic film, *The Tingler* engages the spectator directly in sensation, and 'exposes' *aisthesis*.

Extracting the Fear that Tingles the Spine: The Hype, the Buzz of the Gimmick and the Bottom Line

William Castle is known as the King of Gimmicks, the P. T. Barnum of filmmaking, the director who led John Waters to exclaim in reminiscence of his childhood experience of *The Tingler*: 'As I sat there experiencing the miracle of Percepto, I realized that there could be such a thing as Art in the cinema.'[4] He also inspired Waters to create his own gimmick 'Odorama' for the film *Polyester* (1981).[5] Thus, as a filmmaker, Castle plays a greater role in film history than purely as a creator of spectacle cinema. Castle's contribution to cinema is one that engages in spectacle as an experience that refigures what is meant by aesthetics.

Following *Macabre* (1958) and *House on Haunted Hill* (1959), *The Tingler* is the third of Castle's films to use a gimmick to contribute to the cinematic experience. In *Macabre*, Castle's voiceover announces to his audience that after the clock has struck sixty seconds the spectator will be insured by Lloyd's of London for $1,000 in case they die of fright. The gimmick came complete with nurses stationed in the lobby and ambulances parked out the front of cinemas to tend to faint-hearted patrons. In special guest appearances Castle himself would leap out of a coffin delivered by a hearse.[6] *House on Haunted Hill*'s gimmick was 'Emergo'. It included a rigged pulley system that flew an inflatable skeleton over the audience to extend, not only figuratively but also literally, the moment in the narrative in which a skeleton rises from a vat of acid to terrorise Annabelle Loren (Carol Ohmart), the iniquitous wife of Frederick Loren (Vincent Price). *The Tingler*'s gimmick was 'Percepto'. 'Percepto' saw a selected number of cinema seats rigged with electric devices (similar to handshake gag 'joy' buzzers) that when activated by the film projectionist would 'tingle' the occupant of the seat. The intention was to make the spectator share in experiencing the 'Tingler': an 'organism' that, according to the film's narrative, is a solidified form of the fear that develops in, and tingles, the spine. Promotional posters claimed: 'The first motion picture in PERCEPTO! You will experience the emotions of the characters on the screen. Guaranteed: The Tingler will break loose while YOU are in the audience!' The electric 'tingling' of the spectator also doubled as a simulated electric chair gimmick. A further gimmick for *The Tingler* can be found in the blood filmed in red Technicolor in this otherwise black-and-white film, the film poster exclaiming: 'SEE – The screen's first BLOOD BATH IN COLOR!'

Castle's cycle of films intended, in their use of gimmicks, to produce 'felt' sensations. They were distinct from the identification of the spectator at a distance from the image. As David J. Skal writes in *The Monster Show: A Cultural History of Horror*: 'Horror gimmicks provided audiences with a needed sense of contact, engagement, and recognition. Even if the dominant sensation was gooseflesh, at least it was a feeling.'[7]

Most notably, Castle's films contributed to a disciplining of spectatorship practices. Linda Williams reflects in her essay 'Learning to Scream' that the first screenings of Alfred Hitchcock's *Psycho* (1960), released just a year after *The Tingler*, were a disciplinary exercise. Hitchcock stipulated that the audience arrive on time and not be permitted entry on late arrival. His practice, she argues, was a forerunner to a general disciplining of the film viewing experience with 'set show times, closely spaced screenings, elimination of cartoons and short subjects and patient waits in lines that are now standard procedure'.[8] That is, the cinematic experience is one that works within the bounds of controls. However, I contend that it is not the controls that are important, or the level of interactivity that can be achieved through such controls, but the experience itself: the scream itself; that is, the way in which the experience of cinema engages the spectator in a sensorial response. The corporealised experience of cinema promotes an 'exposure' of sensations. This 'exposure' produces an aesthetic, even *aisthetic*, effect; that is, the sensorial apparatus is revealed or 'exposed' by the operation of the cinematic apparatus.

Further, Williams argues that Hitchcock's insistence that audience members arrive on time to screenings of *Psycho* led not only to a disciplining of the film-viewing experience but also to a bargain that was struck between artist and audience – 'if you want me to make you scream in a new way and about these previously taboo sexual secrets, then line up patiently to receive the thrill'.[9] Such disciplinary pacts also generated a kind of camaraderie among filmgoers.[10] Thus, a combination of discipline and camaraderie sums up the effect of the gimmicks in Castle's films that, once installed, would determine in some way the film-viewing experience but also bonded audience members in acts such as the throwing of popcorn at the 'Emergo' skeleton.[11]

And yet such disciplining of the film spectator also demonstrates a kind of prescription on the body that, as Lyotard writes about Kafka's execution apparatus, is 'translated aesthetically in the regulating trace' of the machine in its execution.[12] The 'regulating trace' of *The Tingler* was produced by the 'Percepto' devices that were wired to the cinema seats and 'translated aesthetically' as the spine-tingling of the spectator. The film also prescribes that the spectator scream, suggesting that it was by this means the 'tingling' would stop. In a similar fashion to the way the law directs the execution of its lines on the body, the cinematic apparatus is made comprehensible by what the spectator learns on the body.

The Execution: *The Tingler* (1959)

In *The Tingler*, a convicted murderer is dragged screaming to the electric chair. Already the stage is set for the spectator to be read as the executed, the condemned. And thus also begins the recursive function of the film that will see the spectator of the film treated like the characters in the film and the spectators of the film within the film. After execution the body of the convicted murderer is delivered to Dr Warren Chapin (Vincent Price) for autopsy. During the autopsy Warren is interrupted by Oliver 'Ollie' Higgins, the brother-in-law of the executed man, and is initially surprised by the relative's attendance at the autopsy. The doctor intimates that the executed man's cracked vertebrae is a condition often seen in subjects who are frightened prior to death, and explains that he is conducting experimental research into the pathology of human fear. It is worth noting that the film *The Tingler* also appears to conduct experimental research on its spectators in attempts to induce fear.

When Warren gives Ollie a ride home he is introduced to Ollie's wife Martha Ryerson Higgins (Judith Evelyn) and is shown the cinema theatre that screens silent films that Ollie and Martha run. Martha, a deaf-mute, is nervous about the safe where they keep their cinema takings and the germs that she might contract from others. After cutting himself on a broken tea saucer, Warren witnesses Martha go into a 'psychosomatic faint' at the sight of blood, which he later deduces is because she is unable to release her fear via a scream. Such inability will be demonstrative of the film's lesson in screaming, when the film asks the spectator to scream not only to disable an extracted 'Tingler' organism but to dissipate the spectator's own spine-tingling 'Tingler'. Warren ponders the force of fear and, in the presence of his lab assistant David Morris (Darryl Hickman) and his sister-in-law Lucy Stevens (Pamela Lincoln), reaches the conclusion that what causes the vertebrae to crack when someone dies of fright must be something solid that accumulates along the spinal column:

> Anything that can exert such tremendous pressure on the spinal column *must* be something you can see, touch, hold in your hand. It may exist for only a fraction of a second, but during that fraction there's something inside every frightened person that's as solid as steel – probably stronger. Oh, by the way, I think I've found a name for it: 'the Tingler'. You like it?

Warren goes on to conduct experiments to confirm the existence of the Tingler. Often these experiments are carried out unethically, just as installing electric devices under cinema seats in 1959 could be said to be unethical. In the first of many experiments, Warren pulls an unloaded gun on his unfaithful wife Isabel Stevens Chapin (Patricia Cutts) so that her spine can be X-rayed at the moment of fright. Later Warren and David examine the X-rays that reveal the ghostly form of the Tingler against her vertebrae. Another attempt to confirm the existence of the Tingler is made by Warren when he injects himself with LSD. He screams before he manages to experience the full force of his own Tingler. Realising that they may be able to isolate the Tingler if someone were to die of fright without screaming (a scream dissipates, or in full body form, paralyses the Tingler), Warren, out of concern for her, goes to check on Martha. Ollie informs him that since her psychosomatic faint she has been unable to eat or sleep. Warren gives her a shot ('to relax her') and Ollie a prescription for barbiturates to administer to her.

Later Martha awakens in the apartment to the windows and doors slamming closed; a rocking chair rocks independent of an occupant. As she lifts the covers from a nearby bed that appears inhabited, a masked ghoul wielding a machete rises and pursues her. A hairy hand holding an axe appears through another door, and the axe is flung across the room. Taking refuge in the bathroom, Martha finds blood pouring from the basin faucet; a hand rises from a nearby bathtub filled with blood. When Martha turns to run from the room, the bathroom cabinet swings open to reveal a death certificate with her name on it, which reads: 'Cause of Death: FRIGHT'.

Discovering Martha dead on the bathroom floor, Ollie takes her to Warren's house, where the doctor places Martha on an examination table. He erects a screen between her and Ollie in preparation for autopsy. This screen is just another step in the recursive function of the film: the spectator is distanced by the screen within the screen. After determining the reason for her death – fright – we see Warren, in silhouette, prying the Tingler from Martha's spine. Martha, having been unable to scream, has cultured a full-bodied Tingler. The organism (lobster-like in appearance) that is extracted attaches itself to Warren's arm. He screams, and the organism falls to the floor, paralysed. The Tingler is placed in a locked case. Ollie leaves to take his wife's body to the funeral parlour, while the now suspiciously sweet Isabel (who has witnessed the Tingler's attack) and Warren toast the latter's research success. Having drugged Warren's drink, Isabel lets the Tingler out of the case and leaves it to find Warren's neck as he sleeps. When Isabel's sister Lucy enters to see the Tingler choking Warren, she screams and the Tingler is paralysed again.

Realising that he has 'violated the laws of nature' by removing the Tingler from Martha's body, Warren asks David to phone Ollie so that they can put the Tingler back inside her body. When Ollie doesn't answer, David phones the police and discovers that Ollie has not reported Martha's death. Warren, taking the re-caged Tingler with him, drives to Ollie's apartment. Warren confronts Ollie over his wife's death, producing the suitcase he has found in the apartment containing the gimmicks – the ghoul's mask and the hairy monster glove – that Ollie has used to frighten her to death. Martha's fear, and her inability to scream, Warren conjectures, caused the Tingler to solidify and crack the vertebrae: Martha's fear of blood provided the climax for her murder. During this conversation, the Tingler worms its way from the cage and escapes via a loose floorboard into the cinema theatre below. Warren and Ollie hurry down to the theatre, and while Henry King's *Tol'able David* (1921) is screening, they make their way along the aisles, searching for the Tingler under the cinema seats. The Tingler attaches itself to the leg of a cinema patron. As she screams, the Tingler falls to the floor and crawls away. When the film stops running and the theatre goes dark, Warren advises the audience not to panic, announcing that a girl has fainted and is being attended to. An attempt to restart the film sees the Tingler on the cinema screen crawling across the projected light source. The silhouette of the Tingler is coupled with the sound of its heartbeat, which can be heard throughout the theatre. The projector again whirs to a halt and the theatre once again goes dark. This time Warren instructs the spectators of *Tol'able David* (and, by extension, the spectators of *The Tingler*): 'Ladies and gentlemen, please do not panic! But scream! Scream for your lives! The Tingler is loose in this theatre! And if you don't scream, it may kill you! Scream! Scream! Keep screaming! Scream for your lives!'

Warren and Ollie run to the projection booth to find the Tingler around the projectionist's throat. The projectionist screams, the Tingler releases him and is paralysed. Having captured the Tingler and placed it in a film canister, Warren and Ollie return to Ollie's apartment. While they discuss Ollie's fate, given the murder of his wife, Warren puts the Tingler back into the body of Martha, and despite Ollie's remorse, goes to the police. At this moment, doors and windows in the apartment slam shut and Martha's body sits upright, her eyes fixed on Ollie. Ollie screams, and Warren intones: 'Ladies and gentlemen, just a word of warning: if any of you are not convinced that you have a Tingler of your own, the next time you're frightened in the dark, don't scream.'

Aisthesis and Prescribed Lines

Aisthesis relates to what was 'before'. Indeed, Lyotard speaks of *aisthesis* as a 'birth and infancy'.[13] Lyotard writes in his essay 'Prescription' of the kind of aesthetics that *aisthesis* entails:

> To be, aesthetically (in the sense of Kant's *First Critique*), is to be-there, here and now, exposed in space–time, and to the space–time of something that touches before any concept or even any representation. This *before* is not known, obviously,

because it is there before we are. It is something like birth and infancy (Latin, *infans*)—there before we are. The *there* in question is called the body. It is not "I" who am born, who is given birth to. "I" will be born afterwards, with language, precisely upon leaving infancy. My affairs will have been handled and decided before I can answer for them—and once and for all: this infancy, this body, this unconscious remaining there my entire life. When the law comes to me, with the ego and language, it is too late. Things will have already taken a turn. And the turn of the law will not manage to efface the first turn, this first *touch*. Aesthetics has to do with this first touch: the one that touched me when I was not there.[14]

Aisthesis, in Lyotard's sense, is that which was 'before' the law, and is already inscribed on every new birth. *Aisthesis*, for Lyotard, is also that which defies the law: 'And the application of the law always entails the same extinctive prescription: twelve hours of agony in payment for an indubitable offense, that of not having been born *first* to the law but, rather, to and through the *aisthesis*.'[15] However, Lyotard also writes in his essay 'Prescription' that 'the law needs the body, its own dwelling upon the body, as well as the body's resistance to it, in order to inscribe itself, that is, to execute itself'.[16] The relationship between the body and the inscription of the law reveals something about the relationship between *aisthesis* and aesthetics, which is that *aisthesis* requires aesthetics for it to be 'exposed'. It is aesthetics in its most primitive state that Lyotard defines, and thus the archaic form of *aisthesis* that his work explores. However, the 'theater of cruelty' produced by the law supplements the primitive aesthetics of *aisthesis* with a deployment of *aisthesis* for its own ends. Thus, the key argument that Lyotard makes in his essay 'Prescription', as far as this chapter is concerned, is how aesthetics is changed between *aisthesis* and the enactment of the 'theater of cruelty'. *Aisthesis* is a primitive aesthetics. Aesthetics, on the other hand, is made manifest in the execution of the law that inscribes the law's sentence on the body: that which brings to death in 'writing'; aesthetically, the blood that is spilled.[17] In this way, the aesthetic blood that is spilled by the 'theater of cruelty' is what will 'expose' the originary sensation of *aisthesis*.

In his short story 'In the Penal Colony', Kafka describes the workings of an apparatus used in the penal colony. The apparatus was invented by the former Commandant, is operated by the officer, and is observed by the explorer. It is an execution apparatus that inscribes with needles – upon the bodies of those condemned – the commandment that has been disobeyed. The execution apparatus takes twelve hours to complete its inscription, after which time the prisoner, the officer explains, will have understood the sentence handed to him. The prisoner attains a certain enlightenment from the judgement handed down to him through his wounds, and, upon reaching enlightenment, expires and is pushed into the pit that lies beneath the Bed of the apparatus.[18]

'In the Penal Colony' reveals how the condemned are sentenced by the law. The punishment meted out by the law is performed by an apparatus that consists of three parts – the Bed, the Designer and the Harrow. The Bed is covered in a layer of cotton wool on which the condemned lies. The Designer holds the sketches drawn by the former Commandant and controls the movement of the Harrow. The Harrow corresponds to the human form and has needles that pierce the skin, and thus, inscribe on the body of the condemned the sentence that the law has prescribed. The Harrow is made of glass and each needle fixed into the glass is accompanied by a shorter needle, which sprays a jet of water onto the skin to wash the inscription clear of blood.[19] The officer explains the punishment to the explorer: "'Our sentence does not sound severe. Whatever commandment the prisoner has disobeyed is written upon his body by the Harrow. This prisoner, for instance" – the officer indicated the man – "will have written on his body: HONOR THY SUPERIORS!"'[20] The explorer is appointed to watch the completion of the sentence prescribed by the law, a sentence that involves the sketching out of the former Commandant's designs upon the body of the condemned.

Lyotard's interest in Kafka's story lies in the ways the apparatus demonstrates *praescribere* and its variations. The sketches, like *praescriptio*, designate limitations under conditions determined by the law that are set out over a period of time. And like *praescripta*, the designs of the former Commandant traced upon the body direct the 'execution' of something; in this case, the movement of the Harrow that etches lines upon the body of the condemned. The designs that the condemned will learn in wounds on his body, however, direct the 'execution' of something else, and that is the literal execution of the condemned. Thus, a further addition is the meaning of execution in this context. Lyotard distinguishes between the execution (*praescripta*) of lines that draw a spatial and aesthetic design, and the execution (*perimere*) of the lines of the law, where *perimere* means "'to cause to perish'' only because it means first of all', he writes, "'to acquire", "to take", or "to buy". . . completely'.[21] In Kafka's story the execution of lines upon the body causes the condemned to perish. The lines of the law also take away life completely, executing in both senses. This is an aesthetic death rather than an ethical one, insofar as the aesthetic concerns the particular and the ethical the universal. The particularity of aesthetics is that of sense-experience whereas the universality of ethics is language or exchange. It is also aesthetic rather than ethical insofar as execution is completed by spatial and aesthetic design. To this end,

Lyotard writes: 'As an order deriving from the former law, the prescription is translated aesthetically in the regulating trace, the *praescriptum*, which the machine will follow in order to execute the final *inscriptio*.'[22]

As much as this aesthetic death might be represented in the *praescripta* or designs themselves, the lines of the law are indecipherable by the eye. 'He'll learn it on his body', the officer tells the explorer.[23] When the officer retrieves the designs drawn by the former Commandant from a leather wallet, the designs that the apparatus etches on the body appear to the explorer as no more than an illegible cross-hatching of lines:

> "Read it," said the officer. "I can't," said the explorer. "Yet it's clear enough," said the officer. "It's very ingenious," said the explorer evasively, "but I can't make it out." "Yes," said the officer with a laugh, putting the paper away again, "it's no calligraphy for school children. It needs to be studied closely. I'm quite sure that in the end you would understand it too. Of course the script can't be a simple one; it's not supposed to kill a man straight off, but only after an interval of, on an average, twelve hours; the turning point is reckoned to come at the sixth hour. So there have to be lots and lots of flourishes around the actual script; the script itself runs round the body only in a narrow girdle; the rest of the body is reserved for the embellishments. Can you appreciate now the work accomplished by the Harrow and the whole apparatus?—Just watch it!"[24]

The purpose of Lyotard's argument is to demonstrate an aesthetics that relates to the body and to the law. It is important to note, however, that aesthetics may not be simply found in the indecipherable lines of the regulating traces (*praescripta*), but also in their execution, in the action of the law upon the body. That is, aesthetics is also in blood spilled. As Lyotard writes: 'The condemned pays with his blood, in full, to the point of its complete drainage. The authority of the forgotten, violated prescription costs him his life.'[25] The law executed on the body and the body executing itself in its reception to the law – paying with blood, buying the law – is an aesthetic death. Thus, the aesthetics to which Lyotard refers is an aesthetics first of the inscription of this 'writing' – the inscription of the law – on the body, and second, of the blood that is spilled. This second aesthetics is one of 'executing' the lines of this inscription, which constitutes the 'theater of cruelty'.

It is under these terms of execution that Lyotard demonstrates that aesthetics – in fact, *aisthesis* – is changed by the 'theater of cruelty'. And this change is one that is understood in terms of blood. Between the blood that circulates freely (*sanguis*) and the 'blood that is spilled' (*cruor*),[26] there is not only a change in the state of the body – which could be called material and energetic – there is also a change in the nature of aesthetics, which gives precedence to *aisthesis* as inspiring all aesthetics. Circulating blood is the literal impression of *aithesis* and, in this sense, of the pulse.

Lyotard's essay 'Prescription' brings into focus the question of aesthetics as it relates to sensibility, and he does so by suggesting that it is via the action of the law upon the body that *aisthesis* is 'exposed'.[27] If *aisthesis* must be 'exposed' for the purposes of the law, the law must act on the body. For Lyotard, *aisthesis* comes to be understood through the 'theater of cruelty'. The body here is heteronomous insofar as it is 'intractable'.[28] The intractable here is 'that which resists all law'.[29] The pulse equally could be said to resist all universal statements in language and exchange. The intractable also, Lyotard writes, is an 'absolute condition of morals'.[30] What the body is unable to resist, however – what the body is not intractable to – is the violence of the 'theater of cruelty'. This is because the violence of the 'theater of cruelty' places the body at the centre of its operations. Thus, Lyotard writes, to retain its function – to sidestep the 'absolute conditions of morals', if you like – the law relates to the body via the violence of the 'theater of cruelty'. That is, the law relates to the body through the sensible. But the 'insensible touch' is equivalent to 'the first turn, this first *touch*' – the touch of 'birth and infancy'. Like it, *aisthesis* is imperceptible, 'insensible'; it is brute sensibility prior to the sensible event of the 'theater of cruelty'.[31]

Prescription and the Aesthetics of Blood Spilled

To understand precisely what is at stake in Lyotard's essay it is necessary to recount Lyotard on aesthetics, and the ways prescription, and specifically the prescriptive work of the apparatus in Kafka's story, is considered aesthetic. Lyotard's definition of aesthetics as an originary 'touch', 'before any concept or even any representation',[32] has ramifications for thinking about the relationship between the body and the law, *aisthesis* and the 'theater of cruelty', and sensation and the sensational (which is also discipline in Castle's films).

Lyotard writes that prescription is aesthetic for two reasons. First, prescription is aesthetic by virtue of the distinction between the letter and the design. We have already seen that the *praescripta* etched upon the body of the condemned are less letters than they are designs. Lyotard writes that while letters would show the 'noble', or ascetic, qualities of writing wherein *ascesis* designates 'an inner emptying, an elimination of every idiosyncratic passion or intention',[33] the marks mechanically inscribed in flesh are designs (and designed) to execute. The 'noble' or ascetic qualities of writing would suggest an atonement of the scribe through mortification, but Lyotard writes that this is not the kind of aesthetics that we find in Kafka's story, which is instead 'the preoccupying influx of the sensible' produced when the apparatus inscribes the designs directly on the flesh of the condemned to spill blood.[34] Indeed, it could be argued that these designs inscribed by the law maximise the sensible influx of the body as a fact of the body in pain in a way that legible letters are unable to. As Elaine Scarry writes in her book *The Body in Pain: The Making and Unmaking of the World*: 'Physical pain does not simply resist language but actively destroys it, bringing about an immediate reversion to a state anterior to language, to the sounds and cries a human being makes before language is learned.'[35] Language is already there in the 'theater of cruelty', inscribing itself on the body. However, the 'writing' inscribed on the body by the Harrow is not a 'read' language, but one that the body learns through its wounds: *aisthesis* is 'exposed'.

The second reason Lyotard gives for calling prescription aesthetic concerns the way the law passes into a 'corporeal impression'.[36] Drawing on Freud's work on hysteria, Lyotard writes: 'The body effects the law, immediately, *in actu*, upon itself – like the hysteric whose wrist is locked, whose nasolabial ridge contracts, or whose stigmata in the hollow of the palms begins to bleed.'[37] In Lyotard's description, the body 'acts out' the law. The body takes the obligation of the law upon itself, allowing the law to be inscribed upon it. Lyotard writes: 'The body (but what are we saying, exactly, with the words, *the body*?) is exposed not only to the obligation of expressing the fault, that is, the unbearable fulfilment of desire, but also to paying for it through suffering.'[38] The second reason for calling prescription aesthetic Lyotard writes, is stronger and concurrent with the function of Kafka's apparatus because the law, as it passes into a 'corporeal impression', makes the body pay through suffering. The law subjects the body to aesthetic determination when the body forsakes the freedom of its originary state and becomes a canvas on which the law etches its bloody designs. The body's open receptivity to the law results in an aesthetics, but one that differs in kind from the freedom of *aisthesis*:

> The machine of *In the Penal Colony* is the theater of cruelty—the aesthetics of spilled blood demanded by the ethical law when it is enacted. Between the first touch and the second, (which is the last), the touch of the incisive Harrow, the touch of the law, aesthetics changes meaning.[39]

What is important for my argument is the way in which the second touch suggests an impression that is made on the body that changes the originary meaning of aesthetics. The material and energetic body, if you like, is the site where aesthetics is changed. The freedom of the body to 'feel' is changed to the law's ability to make the body 'feel' via cruelty in a prescription that claims that the body's prior sensibility was 'savage'.

The aesthetic of the law 'exposes' the *aisthesis* of the body by exposing the body's capacity for sensibility through pain. As Lyotard writes: 'If the law is to execute itself, it must, like a touch, inscribe itself on the body.'[40] And this 'touch', Lyotard tells us, is a touch that inscribes the body and 'exposes' it as 'savage'. This is a touch that seeks to direct and suppress the primordial sensibility of the *aisthetic* body:

> Following the requirement of its own cruel aesthetics, the body will have to be *touched*. It will have to be cut into—that is, initially incised. The root of the very late Latin *intaminare* remains *tangere*: "to touch . . . toward and inside."[41]

The law commandeers the outlawed savagery of the body in an aesthetics that the body understands, while commanding atonement for that savagery.

This 'atoning for' savagery, Lyotard tells us, is the meaning of the 'blood debt':

> *Sanguis*: the blood of life in the arteries and veins; and *cruor*: the blood that is spilled. The first nourishes the flesh. It gives it its hue of blueness, its pinkness, its pallor, its sallowness, its early-morning freshness, the infinite juxtaposition of nuances that drive the painter and the philosopher crazy; an immaterial matter. As for the law, this innocence of the flesh is criminal. It must expiate this fleshly innocence. The blood that flows is called *cruor*. Expiation requires cruelty, *crudelitas* versus *fidelitas*.[42]

Blood here relates to two forms: the blood that circulates (*sanguis*) and 'the blood that is spilled' (*cruor*), and by extension, to two touches (the 'there before we are'[43] of *aisthesis* and the touch of the 'theater of cruelty'[44] that is aesthetic). Where once there was the freedom of the blood to circulate in the body, the law changes aesthetics to something that is no longer tied to a primordial and originary sensibility, but is found in the 'aesthetics of spilled blood'.[45] The 'aesthetics of spilled blood' is demanded, but is also what must be achieved by the law.

For Lyotard, the blood that circulates is depictive of *aisthesis* and the blood that is spilled is depictive of aesthetics.[46] Lyotard writes: 'We find aesthetics now, placed in the service of the former law, upon and in the tortured body of the condemned man.'[47] The law *passes* into a 'corporeal impression', but the 'body effects the law . . . upon itself'.[48] *Aisthesis*, formerly of the body, is taken up by the 'theater of cruelty' and blood is spilled, since this is what the body will understand. Lyotard writes:

> The executor of the law knows that the infant body is ignorant of the law and can know nothing of it (in the sense of an explicit knowledge), unless the law is incised into it to the point where it draws blood. What it *can* know of the law, it can know only in the sense in which *sapere* means to *savor*, to be aesthetically passible, to be touched.[49]

The law directs the body in the execution of its lines, literally sketching its design on the body. Thus, aesthetics changes meaning between the touch of the body and the re-touch of the law – a change that comes about between the aesthetics of the blood that circulates (the bodily mode of *aisthesis*) and the aesthetics of the blood that is spilled (the 'theater of cruelty').

Aesthetics changes meaning in another way and that is from the pulsatile to the rhythmic. This change comes about by the economy of the apparatus that inscribes itself in a temporal and repetitive way on the body. The economy of the body is one in which the blood circulates freely. The executing action of the law will spill the blood irredeemably and completely over a period of twelve hours. And what is more, the action to spill blood must be repeated as a demonstration for other bodies, as Lyotard tells us: 'Without deliberation or warranted judgement the sacrificial execution must be repeated automatically each time a criminal birth occurs. The cruelty will be machine-like.'[50] By 'machine-like' I take Lyotard to mean rhythmic rather than pulsatile; sequential rather than organic. The rhythmic action of the apparatus and the repetitive act of demonstration of the 'theater of cruelty' changes aesthetics. This is the difference between an aesthetics of the body associated with the pulse (*aisthesis*) and an aesthetics of inscription associated with the rhythmic action of the apparatus ('theater of cruelty').

By defining *aisthesis* what is delineated is *aisthetic* cinema's difference from aesthetic cinema. Just like the inscriptions made upon the body by the mechanical cinematic apparatus – in *The Tingler* the electric device that tingles the spine – the images of blood spilled in horror cinema constitute an aesthetic cinema, but seek to 'expose' the sensations of originary *aisthesis*. That is, blood spilled 'exposes' the pulse.

The Pulse 'Exposed'

The significance of originary aesthetics for a conception of the pulse is that it provides for an *aisthetic* understanding of cinema concerned primarily with sensation. The pulse is the minimal condition of sensation and *aisthesis* is a primitive kind of aesthetics – what is 'exposed' by aesthetics – as that which was 'before'.[51] *Aisthesis*, in other words, is the sensation that is not ready, never ready. Neal Curtis writes: 'Aesthesis [sic], then, is an exposure, an openness, a candour; the susceptibility of a bodily mode not prepared.'[52] This is how I conceptualise the pulse aesthetically as *aisthesis*. The pulse is the Open and is Open upon the world that is Open. The pulse is the force of intensity that 'opens out' the body to the world. But the pulse is also 'exposed' or opened by the world. This 'exposure' or 'openness' of the pulse to the world is revealed by 'the susceptibility of a bodily mode not prepared' when, for instance, the pulse is jolted or shocked to a faster pace when one runs up a hill, or even, when one watches a scary film.

In cinema, *aisthesis* is the sensation that inspires a kind of seeing anew, an estranged seeing. Sensation is not a recognition of the object in the world (as representation) but an encounter with the energetic and material qualities of the world. Thus, in this book *aisthesis* is used to describe a different kind of spectatorship: it is not a cognitive but a bodily way of conceiving of film spectatorship. The pulse in cinema can be characterised by this *aisthetic* 'sensing' because the pulse engages the body at this energetic and material level. The pulse's sensorial encounter with the world is 'exposed' by the 'theater of cruelty' when the blood is spilled.

What is 'exposed' by blood spilled is the freedom of the circulating blood that was 'there before'.[53] That is, what is 'exposed' by blood spilled is the pulse. The economy of the body as the blood that circulates is an economy of the pulse; the economy of the action of the apparatus upon the body and of blood spilled is the economy of mechanical rhythm. *Aisthesis*, in this way, is paired with originary sensation as a minimal condition of the pulse; aesthetics is paired with the action and inscription of rhythm. The inscriptive and rhythmic action of the apparatus upon the body that spills blood gives us a way of understanding the 'exposure' of the pulse by the rhythms of the apparatus.

Dispositif: Lines of Fright

In *The Tingler* cruelty is as 'machine-like' as the 'theater of cruelty' found in 'In the Penal Colony'[54]: Castle cannot have his audience thinking anything else. The cinematic apparatus prescribes the 'execution' of its spectators, and the film prescribes that the audience scream. At the heart of this prescription is a *differend*: a conflict that cannot be resolved.[55] In the case of *The Tingler* the *differend* is between what is prescribed by the film for its spectators and the action of the cinematic apparatus on the body. That is, the film, by prescribing that the viewer scream, asks the body to express its 'savagery'[56] as an affective response, while the cinematic apparatus that demands the disciplining of its viewers seeks to suppress this savagery and 'execute' the body for this fault. The conflict of the *differend* is between the savagery of an affective response and the intention to discipline. At the moment that the spectators of *Tol'able David* – the film within the film – and the spectators of *The Tingler* are plunged into darkness amid the sound of the heartbeat of the Tingler organism and asked to scream, the cinema seats, rigged with electric devices would 'tingle' the spectator of *The Tingler*. That 'the cruelty will be machine-like',[57] is a proposition that is at the crux of my investigation of the *dispositif*. Such a proposition is found in the ways in which the 'machine-like' prescription breaks into the energetic work of the *dispositif* of cinema at the site of the spectator, and more broadly, where the *dispositif* of cinema stands as a social apparatus in what is, in this case, a disciplinary act. By this thinking it is possible to move from a reductive idea of the machine to an expansive idea of the *dispositif*. And yet, with such a focus on the mechanical cinematic apparatus in this analysis, even this may be too mechanistic a way of describing the *dispositif*. It is imperative here to ensure a *dispositif* that takes account of the energetic disposition and cathexis of cinema.

To consider the 'cruelty' of the machine is to consider its 'execution'. Execution in *The Tingler* is propounded across two senses of the term: in the film's exhibition, execution prescribes the lines of experience for the body, and, as it 'executes' these lines of experience, the body is changed aesthetically; that is, *aisthesis* is 'exposed'.[58] Second, execution suggests that all spectators are criminal or 'savage' in some way, and it is the film that will discipline this 'savagery' of the body. A film poster that accompanied *The Tingler*'s theatrical release asked the spectator: 'Do you have the GUTS to sit in this chair?' The film, then, asks: 'Do you have a body to execute?' *The Tingler* dares the spectator to reveal the 'savagery' of their body so that they can be committed to the 'electric chair' to be prescribed by the law. This dare also challenges the spectator's tolerability to withstand the accumulation of fear in his/her own body. At the site of the body there is always potential for savagery and thus for punishment for this savagery. As Lyotard writes: 'this savagery or this sinful peregrination, it is always there as a potentiality of the body'.[59] It is evident from the opening sequence of *The Tingler*, in which Ollie's brother-in-law is executed, up until a number of spectators are asked to scream and are 'executed' in their chairs in the cinema, that the apparatus intends to discipline the body.

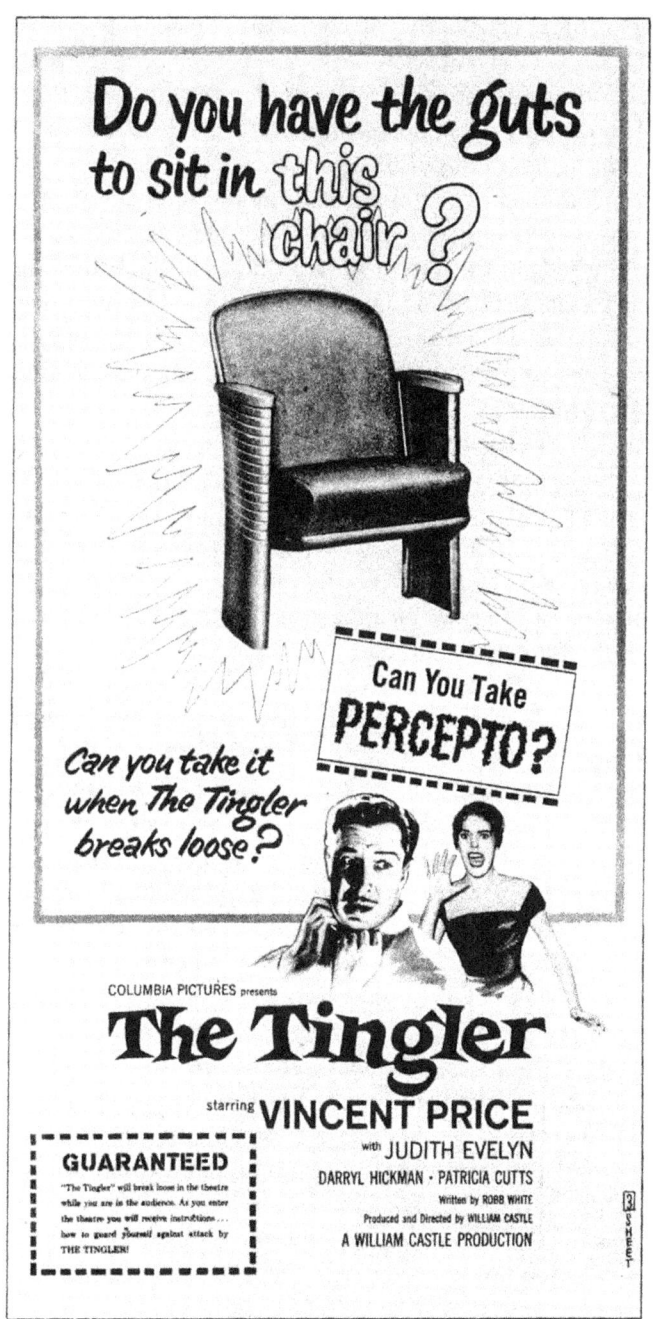

Figure 3.1 'Do you have the guts to sit in this chair?' A theatrical film poster from *The Tingler* (William Castle, 1959) © 1959, renewed 1987 Columbia Pictures Industries, Inc. All Rights Reserved. Courtesy of Columbia Pictures. Photo credit: *Fangoria*

In horror film particularly, the apparatus of cinema prescribes an aesthetics of the spectator as it relates to *sanguis* (the blood as it circulates), and an aesthetics of the image as it relates to *cruor* (the 'blood that is spilled').[60] The spilled blood we see in horror film images may be read as aesthetic in that the *aisthetic* sensations of the spectator are 'exposed'. *The Tingler* also puts into operation two economies: an economy of circulation (freedom or *aisthesis*) and an economy of expenditure ('cruelty' or aesthetics). Cinema resides in the body of the former in an economy of the latter. That is, horror cinema resides in the sensations that are inspired by the cruelties of the cinematic apparatus. The apparatus repeats the 'seizure' (appropriation) of the body, just as the body is 'constituted by its non-belonging to itself, its primary disseizure'.[61]

In *The Tingler* it is *aisthesis* and the economy of the body that determine the kind of pulse of which I will speak. In a reversal of the 'theater of cruelty', the body flaunts its savagery by investing the machine-like inscriptions with a libidinal economy, even as the mechanical apparatus seeks to discipline its audience. The investiture by the libidinal economy is the meaning of the *dispositif*: an apparatus (which is also a social apparatus) charged with libidinal investment.

What do we mean by these 'machine-like' prescriptions in the context of cinema? It is worth defining the *dispositif* in this regard since it can be understood to actively destroy the authority (autonomy) of any single machine, subject, object, meaning in exchange for a configuration of heterogeneous elements. That is, it is the authority of the cinema machine that makes reductive the work of the *dispositif* and the ways by which the spectator is constituted for cinema. Despite the law's efforts to inscribe its sentence on the body, in the 'theater of cruelty' language will not be found, as such. Rather, an energetics will be found in the arrangement of machines and their operations and relations. However, there is a tendency to refer to a 'cinema machine' rather than a system of relations that connect heterogeneous elements, including social, cultural, and institutional elements in the *dispositif*. This latter way of describing the cinematic apparatus as a system of relations has the potential to demonstrate the complexities that are inherent in the *dispositif*.

In his essay 'The Confession of the Flesh', Foucault proposes three ways of understanding the *dispositif*. First, it is a 'thoroughly heterogeneous ensemble consisting of discourses, institutions, architectural forms, regulatory decisions, laws, administrative measures, scientific statements, philosophical, moral and philanthropic propositions – in short, the said as much as the unsaid'.[62] He continues:

> Secondly, what I am trying to identify in this apparatus is precisely the nature of the connection that can exist between these heterogeneous elements ... In short, between these elements, whether discursive or non-discursive, there is a sort of interplay of shifts of position and modifications of function which can also vary very widely. Thirdly, I understand by the term 'apparatus' a sort of—shall we say—formation which has as its major function at a given historical moment of responding to an *urgent need*. The apparatus thus has a dominant strategic function.[63]

The apparatus (*dispositif*), by Foucault's definition, is a system of connections between heterogeneous elements that are discursive and non-discursive.[64]

However, in defining a system of connections between heterogeneous elements as both discursive and non-discursive, it becomes apparent that what Foucault cannot come to terms with is the way the apparatus (*dispositif*) 'is a much more general case of the *episteme*'.[65] That is, although Foucault describes the way the apparatus is discursive, he is unable to describe how it is non-discursive: 'the *episteme* is a specifically *discursive* apparatus, whereas the apparatus in its general form is both discursive and non-discursive, its elements being much more heterogeneous'.[66] The discursive is apparent because Foucault is concerned with *episteme* as it is derived from the power produced by knowledge and the institutions that hold that knowledge:

> The apparatus is thus always inscribed in a play of power, but it is also always linked to certain coordinates of knowledge which issue from it but, to an equal degree, condition it. This is what the apparatus consists in: strategies of relations of forces supporting, and supported by, types of knowledge.[67]

In fact, we could say that what is non-discursive comes about in the relations or connections that the discursive makes in the apparatus. Such a relation between the discursive and non-discursive in the apparatus is important to my argument in defining the prescription of the spectator to scream. The question to ask is whether the scream for the film *The Tingler* should be defined as discursive and inscriptive (prescriptive and aesthetic) or non-discursive and savage (connective and *aisthetic*).

Deleuze's essay 'What is a *Dispositif*?' is not concerned with 'concrete social apparatuses (*dispositifs*)',[68] as such: of *episteme* derived from institutions (subjects or objects). Rather, he describes 'lines' or 'regimes of enunciation'.[69] Regimes of enunciation 'are neither subjects nor objects, but regimes which must be defined from the point of view of the visible and from the point of view of that which can be enunciated'.[70] Such 'lines' are 'broken' and 'subject to *changes in direction*', while also 'break[ing] through thresholds'. As Deleuze continues: 'And in every apparatus (*dispositif*) the lines break through thresholds, according to which they might have been seen as aesthetic, scientific, political, and so on.'[71] Thus, defining the *dispositif* Deleuze writes of

> a tangle, a multilinear ensemble. It is composed of lines, each having a different nature. And the lines in the apparatus do not outline or surround systems which are each homogeneous in their own right, object, subject, language, and so on, but follow directions, trace balances which are always off balance, now drawing together and then distancing themselves from one another. Each line is broken and subject to *changes in direction*, bifurcating and forked, and subject to *drifting*. Visible objects, affirmations which can be formulated, forces exercised and subjects in position are like vectors and tensors.[72]

The lines that Deleuze refers to are 'lines of visibility' and 'lines of enunciation', 'lines of force', 'lines of subjectification' and 'lines of splitting, breakage, fracture'.[73] It is 'lines of subjectification' on which I will focus because what I am concerned with is the relationship of the social apparatus (*dispositif*) and thus theatre, to the spectator. Writing about the 'Self' as a 'production of subjectivity in a social apparatus (*dispositif*)', Deleuze declares:

> This dimension of the Self is by no means a pre-existing determination which one finds ready-made. Here again, a line of subjectification is a process, a production of subjectivity in a social apparatus (*dispositif*): it has to be made, inasmuch as the apparatus allows it to come into being or makes it possible. It is a line of escape. It escapes preceding lines and escapes *from* itself. The Self is neither knowledge nor power. It is a process of individuation which bears on groups and on people, and is subtracted from the power relations which are established as constituting forms of knowledge (*savoirs*): a sort of surplus-value. It is not certain that all social apparatuses (*dispositifs*) comprise these.[74]

Deleuze thus gives us a particular way of understanding the 'Self' – and for me, understanding the spectator of cinema – as a 'process' in the production of subjectivity. If the 'Self' is a 'line of subjectification' it is also a 'line of escape'. In this way Deleuze describes the 'Self' as a 'surplus-value' that is 'neither knowledge nor power'[75]: it is, in fact, what we might call a point of excess. And to consider this 'line of escape' is to consider the ways in which the spectator of cinema *aisthetically* 'escapes' from the prescribed lines of the apparatus (*dispositif*). Of thresholds and the prescribed lines of subjectivity from which one might think of a 'line of escape', Deleuze writes: 'And in every apparatus (*dispositif*) the lines break through thresholds.'[76] This 'process' of subjectification is also for Deleuze a 'becoming-other':

> We belong to social apparatuses (*dispositifs*) and act within them. The newness of an apparatus in relation to those which have gone before is what we call its actuality, our actuality. The new is the current. The current is not what we are but rather what we are in the process of becoming – that is the Other, our becoming-other.[77]

Thus this 'becoming-other' demonstrates the 'process' that is at the heart of Deleuze's 'Self' as it belongs to and acts within the (social) apparatus (*dispositif*). In describing a 'line of flight' or 'escape' for the 'Self', 'becoming-other' works to a production of the new just as it is swept along in the current of the now: of actuality. It is this 'line of flight' or 'escape' that must be considered for the spectator of *The Tingler* in relation to that which could be said to escape from the prescriptive mechanism of the apparatus. What escapes, as such, is what I call *aisthesis* or what is the potentiality of the body. That is, what escapes is *aisthesis* as an encounter with sensation. The scream might also be said to 'escape' from the body as a product of this encounter with sensation: the scream as a 'surplus-value' in the 'lines of enunciation'. And yet, for *The Tingler*, the encounter with sensation is also an encounter with prescription, since it is prescribed that the spectator screams when they feel a tingling in the spine. The excess or 'surplus-value' of sensation and the scream is the investment of energetics in the *dispositif* of *The Tingler*.

As I have noted previously, Lyotard writes in *Libidinal Economy* that the *dispositif* is a structure that involves both a libidinal formation and a discursive formation, and that 'there is no notable difference between a libidinal formation and a discursive formation, insofar as they are both formations, *Gestaltungen*'.[78] While a discursive formation is important for unravelling Foucault on the discursive and non-discursive as it relates to the *dispositif*, it is the libidinal formation that will suggest a way of understanding *aisthesis* in the *dispositif*, even as, to reiterate this imbricating relation, Lyotard writes that 'there is no notable difference between a libidinal formation and a discursive formation'.[79]

As noted in Chapter 2, what Lyotard describes as the 'bar of disjunction' is a segment of the libidinal band/skin slowed, 'disintensified', and exteriorised to conceptual exclusion. This slowing of the 'bar of disjunction' as a segment of the libidinal band/skin means that the intensive passages of the libidinal band/skin are, as Lyotard writes, 'abandon[ed] ... to the significative sign'.[80] The attribution of the sign is the work of recuperation and nostalgia.[81] As Lyotard writes:

> the theatre comes with the concept. The bar stops turning; on the contrary, it circumscribes. The intense sign which engenders the libidinal body abandons this vast Moebian skin to the significative sign, the singularity of a passage or a voyage of affects is herded, closed up into a communicable trace.[82]

I have spoken previously about the way that passages of intensity can be characterised by the Open of the pulse. We now see that this 'clos[ing] up into a communicable trace' amounts to the inscription of the rhythm of the pulse.[83] Lyotard defines the *dispositif*, and specifically the libidinal *dispositif*, in relation to structure, writing: 'every energetic configuration ... is a structure'.[84] This is because, as Lyotard writes, 'intensities stabilize themselves into configurations ... into *voluminous bodies*, into *simulacra*, and equally, therefore, into fixed organizations of elements of the "formerly" libidinal skin become organism, psychic apparatus, or whatever you like of this kind of thing'.[85] Thus, the *dispositif* is a structure, or formation, as of an energetic formation. As Grant writes, 'the "dispositif" [is] a disposition to invest, a cathexis'.[86] Defining the libidinal formation or *dispositif* in this energetic way Lyotard writes:

> A libidinal *dispositif*, considered, precisely, as a stabilization and even a stasis or group of energetic stases, is, examined formally, a structure. Conversely, what is essential to a structure, when it is approached in economic terms, is that its fixity or consistency, which allows spatio-temporal maintenance of identical denominations between a this and a not-this, work on pulsional movement as would dams, sluices and channels.[87]

Thus, as a 'stasis or group of energetic stases' – an economy that has structure – the libidinal *dispositif* describes the way that the formation's 'fixity or consistency ... work on pulsional movement', where 'pulsional movement' or 'pulsion' is translated by James Strachey as instinct (*Trieb*).[88] That is, the 'dams, sluices and channels' act like passages of intensity as intensities are corralled by structure.[89] Thus, Lyotard develops the concept of the *dispositif* to mean a disposition for the investment of energy or a cathexis suggesting operation and connection, where the investment of energy is Open and heterogeneous but also meets resistance.

The *dispositif* is not a mechanical apparatus, rather, the libidinal economy of the *dispositif* is a 'disorder of machines', or even, the libidinal economy invests machines which act to libidinally prescribe and inscribe. As Lyotard writes:

> Libidinal economy is a disorder of machines, if you will; but what *for ever* prevents the hope of producing the systemization and functionally complete description of it, is that, as opposed to dynamics, which is the theory of systems of energy, the thought – but this is still to say too little – the *idea* of libidinal economy is all the time rendered virtually impossible by the indiscernability of the two instances. This 'duality' is not at all that of the dialogue, it sets no dialectic in motion, it does not accept a dualism, since the two instances are indiscernible *a priori*, and it is only by examining a particular effect with patient, almost infinite care (as Proust

does with a gait, a smile, a taste, contact with a field, the lamplight on a staircase, each event inexchangeable, and therefore lost for the memory), that it will be possible, bit by bit, to attribute a particular *Gestaltung* to life and the conservation of a particular organized whole, a particular unbinding and disruption rather to death through excess or lack.[90]

The *dispositif* in this sense is one that pertains to a certain kind of subject, even 'partial' subject, of *aisthesis*.[91] The encounter with effects is the investment of energy – a cathexis – that has the force of a libidinal economy. As Lyotard writes, the libidinal economy 'escapes' the 'mechanical analogy',[92] because the libidinal economy is not 'thought' even as it exists as an analogue – a band/skin – for libidinal investment. Second, Lyotard writes that this libidinal economy has energetic force (*puissance*), which is different to the 'cruelty' or violence of the power (*pouvoir*) of the disciplinary apparatus.[93] This is the difference in the force of sensation that arises in *aisthesis* and the 'theater of cruelty', which could be said to have disciplinary power. And yet, even the 'theater of cruelty' must 'expose' the forces of sensation that constitute *aisthesis* by which to enact itself.

The apparatus in Castle's films mortify (in all senses of the term), and thus cause, a particular economy to arise in the relationship between apparatus and body, or more to the point, in the economy of the apparatus that inscribes the body. The opening of the libidinal band/skin is an analogue for the connective 'being in relation to' by which the libido invests and thus invests the *dispositif*. This mortification is both an investment in the death drive and an opening of the body to the discomforts of the apparatus's prescription. The 'being in relation to' of the apparatus and body is not a matter of ethics, but of aesthetics, because the apparatus makes a 'corporeal impression'. Such an aesthetics is one that relates to what Lyotard situates in 'the first turn, this first *touch*': an *aisthesis* 'exposed' as a sensorial openness of the body.[94]

Aisthesis, as Lyotard defines it, is an aesthetics that relates to the openness of the body, rather than an aesthetics that is caught up in the execution of a line, found in the letter of the law – a *praescripta* or 'graphy'. In other words, *aisthesis* is an openness of the body, which, when prescribed by the 'theater of cruelty' becomes nothing short of a particular kind of *dispositif*. This *dispositif* is a theatre of analogues of the body: the heart that throbs, the spine that tingles, the mouth that screams. Like the analogue of the libidinal band/skin, these analogues are ways of conceptualising intensity. Just as the pulse is inscribed by its rhythm, *aisthesis* is prescribed in analogues. Analogues are the ways by which inscription gets in on the act of *aisthesis* but only inasmuch as it is mortifying.

What my argument has tracked is, in Foucault's words, the discursive and non-discursive, or in Lyotard's words, the discursive and the libidinal. It is between the discursive and the non-discursive (libidinal) that there is particular relation. The scream can, because of the film's prescription of it, be described as having a signifying or discursive function. That is, prescribed by the film, the scream takes on a signifying or discursive function within the *dispositif* as opposed to a non-discursive articulation, or what Scarry calls a 'state anterior to language'.[95] This prescription could be considered the work of the social apparatus (*dispositif*) as a disciplinary function. Just as Williams's essay is titled 'Learning to Scream', *The Tingler* determines what is learned on the body; prescribed by its disciplinary function.[96] Laughter, rather than the scream, is the non-discursive articulation for the spectator of *The Tingler*, as the failure of prescription gives way to the *aisthetic* trace.

It is evident that a frustration of representation occurs in many ways in Kafka's 'In the Penal Colony'. The libidinal nature of the apparatus – the forces and relations within it – make of the apparatus, what could be called, an energetic set-up or *dispositif*. The excessive and heterogeneous body frustrates or scandalises the inscription of the law: in Kafka's story, the needles that make the inscription on the body are accompanied by a jet of water washing away the blood to ensure that the body, even in this moment, does not obscure the inscription of the law. *Aisthesis* frustrates the 'touch' of the law and its inscription. The 'first turn, this first *touch*' on the body that is already 'there', like 'birth and infancy (Latin, *in-fans*) – there before we are',[97] implicates the inscription of the law upon the body, which can only prove to be the bloody etchings of a re-touch: a touch '*after the event*'.[98] As Lyotard writes: 'If the law is to execute itself, it must, like a touch, inscribe itself on the body.'[99] Or as the officer tells the explorer: 'There would be no point in telling him. He'll learn it on his body.'[100]

The re-touch of the law is frustrated by the body just as the body frustrates representation: such de/formation is scandalous. The libidinal body of incompossible zones and positions frustrates or scandalises the 'theater of cruelty' because there is no conceptual opposition for that which has no discourse: the libidinal band/skin is fundamentally unrepresentative. It is in the incompossible multiplicity of libidinal investitures in the *dispositif* that we see the libidinal as an economy: a theatre only as much as it is 'one *dispositif* among others'.[101] While the law inscribes the body in a certain way, the body has the potential of excess to disturb the law, or invest it with libidinal excess. As Curtis writes: 'This body has no limits because various things such as books, food, images, as well as words, machines and even sounds can be charged with libidinal investment and therefore become areas of the body.'[102]

The apparatus in Kafka's 'In the Penal Colony' is charged with libidinal investment. The apparatus becomes a theatre of metonymy upon which the excess of the body expends itself. As Lyotard writes in *Libidinal Economy*: 'The symptom, or at least the syndrome, will be able to be *read*, analysed and reconstituted as a structure . . . from a metonymy without end.'[103] By metonymy I mean the substitution for that which is unrepresentable and made visible by equivalents in analogical figures, which, when placed next to each other have contiguity. This is why the inscriptive beat of rhythm (the part) is a metonym, or analogue, for the pulse (the whole), because rhythm is the visible inscription of the movement of the pulse.

Figural Analogues or 'a Metonymy Without End': The Heart that Throbs, the Spine that Tingles, the Mouth that Screams. Do you have the Guts?

The Tingler is notable, particularly during its final sequences, for the way in which it establishes multiple and simultaneous positions for the spectator. The spectator in the screening of *The Tingler* responds interchangeably with the spectator of the film within the film, *Tol'able David*. The spectator of *The Tingler* is in fact interpellated into the cinema space just when the projection of *Tol'able David* is interrupted and the cinema goes dark. Warren's instruction to scream reiterates Castle's direct address to the spectator of *The Tingler* at the beginning of the film and pitches the substituting force of the scream – the screams of the spectators of *Tol'able David* would have merged with the screams emanating from within *The Tingler* theatre. Allegedly, at the moment the diegetic cinema patron screams, faints, and is attended to in the film, a correlating scene took place within selected cinema screenings in *The Tingler*'s original theatrical release in which an ersatz screamer and fainter was carried from the cinema to be attended to by the nurses stationed in the foyer.

The throbbing heart of (we can assume) the Tingler organism that pervades this sequence beats towards dissolution as it finds its answer in the throb of the spectator's heartbeat. The collapse of the cinema into darkness pads out the driving return of the pulse to the body. Without a visual image, the throb of the Tingler's heartbeat pervades the darkness of the cinema theatre, dissolving the distinction between theatre space and spectator: the heartbeat seizes the spectator by closing in around him or her. Here, what becomes evident is the confusion at the site of zones, pleasures and places in the 'dissolution into workings' by which rhythms 'solicit an answering rhythm in the body of the viewer'.[104]

Figure 3.2 Audience participation: the collapse of the theatrical space into the cinema space in *The Tingler* (William Castle, 1959) © 1959, renewed 1987 Columbia Pictures Industries, Inc. All Rights Reserved. Courtesy of Columbia Pictures.

Warren's encouragement to 'Scream for your lives!' is accompanied by the electrifying 'tingling' of the cinema seat. Sensation is directed internally as a force that wells up from within, rather than as the effect of an image that frightens the spectator externally, and can be found in the reverberating beat of the heart, the tingling spine and the scream. The darkness of the interrupted *Tol'able David* film, the throbbing heart and the spine-tingling sensation released as a scream, is a cinematic experience of the spectator opening and discharging their tensions on the cinema space, rather than an eye that takes in external stimuli from its surroundings. Instead of an exterior visual image producing interior sensations, interior and intensive sensations produce exterior and extensive sounds, causing the spectator to become aware of surrounding spectators. Without a visual image, the spectator becomes aware of their own sensations as they are released, via the scream, for the audibility of their surrounding spectators.

My point is that the heart that throbs, the spine that tingles, and the mouth that screams are figural analogues for signifying *aisthesis*. By figural analogue I mean that which 'will be able to be *read* . . . from a metonymy without end'.[105] Signified by the spectacle – that which is prescribed – the heart that throbs, the spine that tingles and the mouth that screams are intensities that are in themselves unrepresentable, and form analogic chains for the sensations that the film attempts to elicit from its spectators. Like Lyotard's 'intense passages', these analogues that signify intensities 'take on value, as elements, from their continuation, from their opposition, from a metonymy without end'.[106] Such figural analogues are 'figural' because they are moving and sensorial, and 'analogic' because they are not the thing itself but a signifying metaphor in a line of contiguous metonyms that are linked by association. Figural analogues are a way of understanding the prescriptive mechanism of that which is already *aisthetic*. Figural analogues represent prescription trying to get in on the act of *aisthesis*. The effect which is, of course, generated, is not *aisthetic* but rather metonymic: a structure, value, sign that is a closing to signification in the opening to something else/the world.

What is also constructed by the figural analogue is a failure/comedy of that which would be *aisthesis*. This is because the analogue cannot capture all that can be found in *aisthesis* and in its transparent attempt makes a joke unto itself. While *The Tingler* would like to think that fear is cultivated by the film, instead it must prescribe the body to be 'inscribed' by the electric device. In other words, the fear that is cultivated by the film is a failure/comedy. However, this can only be supposed if we go on to suppose that corporealisation for this film also fails. Only by a certain reading does corporealisation fail for *The Tingler*, because if the spectator does not scream they certainly do laugh.

Thus, the resistance this argument meets is that the 'tingling' of the spectator in *The Tingler* is not designed to hurt or to spill blood, even if its embodiment in the film narrative is electrocution by chair. It is a gimmick designed for the purposes of the spectacle and to thrill audience members: to have them scream with delight. *The Tingler* is theatre but it is not a 'theater of cruelty'. What happens then when 'cruelty' is turned into a gimmick? James Williams writes on the exploitation of desire on the libidinal band/skin:

> The dispositions control feelings and desires, for example they give accounts of the 'proper' use of a feeling or of the 'proper' way to exploit and satisfy desires. But the feelings also have a hold over the dispositions, that is, the occurrence of feelings and desires can challenge any given disposition and thereby demand a new set-up.[107]

In cinema, the gimmick is made possible because of the way the 'occurrence of feelings and desires can challenge any given disposition'.[108] Gimmicks are a challenge, not necessarily to 'the "proper" use of a feeling' or to 'the "proper" way to exploit and satisfy desires', but in that they generate the feelings that challenge 'any given disposition'.[109] The gimmick demands a new way of generating sensation; it demands a 'new set up'.[110] For film spectatorship, the gimmick's challenge to the 'disposition' means an exploitation of the intensities by cinema with no guarantee of the effectiveness for its spectator.

The 'execution' of the body by an apparatus has been taken up by filmmakers in exploitative ways, and becomes apparent through the exploitation of desires on the libidinal band/skin. Castle is one such filmmaker, setting out to 'execute' the audience of his films using electric devices, and telling them that the torment will only halt once they have screamed. The scream always exceeds the forms and methods that attempt to elicit it. The gimmickry of *The Tingler* means that this 'execution' and prescription to scream is always a failure/comedy of the 'theater of cruelty'. Nonetheless, Lyotard's insight into the 'position of the Signifier or of the Other' can perhaps be applied to the making of *The Tingler*: 'in the concentratory *dispositif*, itself an enjoyable (*jouissive*) position . . . the "rigour of the law" gives more than one person a hard-on'.[111]

The difference then, between B-grade exploitation films and A-grade practices, is that the sensations that the mechanical cinematic apparatus incites the spectator to 'feel' in B-grade exploitation are of an unpredictable range. The spectator, in fact, expresses a 'savagery' of feeling that cannot be controlled. Waters writes of one spectator's response to Castle's *The Tingler* in its original theatrical release: 'In Philadelphia one beefy truck driver was so incensed that he ripped his entire seat from the floor and had to be subdued by five ushers.'[112] *Aisthesis* is apparently 'exposed' by the mechanical cinematic apparatus in all its savage potential even when a certain response is prescribed. Despite A-grade horror's simulation of real horror, the B-grade exploitation of *The Tingler* works with a mechanism that, by directly 'touching' the body, incites *aisthesis*.

Countering the argument of figural analogues as the result of prescription, as one in a chain of analogues found in *The Tingler* that includes the heart that throbs, the spine that tingles, the mouth that screams, the scream can be considered *aisthesis* par excellence. Williams describes it as such when he writes of the appearance of the scream on the libidinal band/skin:

> With nowhere to go they [desires and feelings] circulate in desperation, until 'with a scream', another feeling, affect or desire emerges on the surface of the libidinal band. The scream that goes with a sudden crack-up marks the shift from one disposition to another. A crisis has occurred in one system through the emergence of an intensity that it cannot handle. A new system will have to be built to contain it.[113]

Williams demonstrates here the build up of intensities on the libidinal band/skin and the dispositions that structure them. The scream by this reading is the height of affective change 'from one disposition to another'. That is, the scream, as the response to an effect on the body, tears or bursts out of the body as affect. Castle's *The Tingler* simply implicates the spectator in an enforced version – a prescribed inscription – of the scream.

Aisthesis is used in this book to describe the sensibility of the pulse 'exposed' by the 'theater of cruelty'. It is in the aesthetics of spilled blood by which the 'theater of cruelty' 'exposes' *aisthesis*: aesthetics versus *aisthesis*; spilled blood versus the blood that circulates; *cruor* versus *sanguis*. And it is the apparatus – whether a machine or the law – that spills blood. In this sense, it is the rhythm of an inscriptive apparatus that 'exposes' the circulating blood of the pulse.

Significantly, *aisthesis* defines a sensible aesthetics distinct from that found in 'writing', inscription, the 'execution' of a line for meaning or limitation, and the 'execution' of and by the law. *Aisthesis* inaugurates a significant argument because it entails an aesthetics found in the opening of the spectator to the sensorial manifold. *Aisthesis* is 'felt' sensation 'exposed', and 'exposed' most spectacularly when 'exposed' by the 'theater of cruelty': blood spilled is an aesthetic that 'exposes' an affective *aisthesis* that is already 'there, here and now' for the body.[114]

In the energetic arrangement of apparatuses and spectators, these components are charged with libidinal cathexis. By these energetic arrangements, apparatuses are *dispositifs*. And yet, the apparatus – whether Kafka's apparatus in his story 'In the Penal Colony', the inscriptive prescription of Lyotard's 'theater of cruelty', or the prescriptive cinematic apparatus of Castle's *The Tingler* in its cinema release – can only hope to produce figural analogues for the affective *aisthesis* of the pulse. When talking about a prescribed and disciplinary incitation of the affective pulse – a pulse that by its nature is fundamentally unrepresentative – the prescription can only be but failure/comedy. This is precisely what can be said of the figural analogues in Castle's *The Tingler* – the prescribed responses to the image, such as the fear produced by the tingling of the spine or the demanded scream, makes dissolvent real effects because of the failure or comedy of the apparatus to produce real effects; real *aisthesis*. The body acted upon by the 'theater of cruelty' will only ever resemble the originary sensations of *aisthesis*. By presenting *aisthesis* with blood spilled and forcing from it a scream, the violence of the 'theater of cruelty' produces just a callous mimicry of the originary sensations entailed in *aisthesis*.

However, the sensations inspired by the cinematic apparatus in *The Tingler* – the heart that throbs, the spine that tingles, the mouth that screams – are still sensations that arise in the spectator to be exploited by the film, even if the full extent of these intensities can only be represented as analogues. *Aisthesis*, and by extension, the originary sensations of the pulse are 'exposed'; *dispositifs* are energised. If, as Williams writes, the scream is the way by which a 'feeling, affect or desire' emerges on the libidinal band/skin,[115] what we find is that the intensities that escape via the scream are nonetheless *aisthetic*.

Notes

1. In his direct address to the cinema spectator, William Castle introduces *The Tingler* (and the device of 'Percepto') as a hawking exhibitor. This style of directorial showmanship and the guarantee of a scare continued into Castle's other works such that Castle's silhouette, cigar in mouth, became a recurring 'brand' for the films he was touting.
2. Lyotard, 'Prescription', p. 179.
3. Lyotard, 'Prescription', p. 179.
4. Waters, 'Whatever Happened to Showmanship?', p. 57.
5. Odorama utilised scratch-and-sniff cards that were distributed to audience members. When a number (from 1 to 10) popped up on the screen, the corresponding number on the card could be scratched and sniffed. The smells correlated with the narrative, for example: the smell of air freshener when Francine Fishpaw (Divine) – who has an odour fetish – sprays it around her; the smell of human gas when Elmer Fishpaw (David Samson), Francine's husband, passes wind in bed; the smell of natural gas when Lu-Lu Fishpaw (Mary Garlington) puts her head in the oven. These smells are critiqued by Laura U. Marks as being largely 'synthetic smells – new-car smell, air freshener' (Marks, *Touch*, p. 124). Notably, they are all smells that Francine smells with her sensitive nose, and thus the film suggests a kind of spectatorship substitution for Francine and her odour fetish, rather than smell as a general atmospheric substance for the nose of anyone.
6. The teething problems of, or unexpected reactions to, Castle's gimmicks tend to be the most propagated, and Castle's coffin entrance is no exception. In his autobiography, Castle describes how he arrived at a Minneapolis screening of *Macabre* in a coffin and black hearse. Castle felt the coffin lifted to the sidewalk and, ready to pop out of it, reached up to open the lid. The coffin lid became stuck and Castle was left pounding on it as the audience filed in to watch the film (Castle, *Step Right Up!*, p. 144).
7. Skal, *The Monster Show*, p. 259.
8. Williams, 'Learning to Scream', p. 15.
9. Williams, 'Learning to Scream', p. 16.
10. Williams writes in her essay 'Learning to Scream' about the release of Hitchcock's *Psycho*: 'This audience, despite its mix of class (mink and hamburgers)

and gender, has acquired a new sense of itself as bonded around certain terrifying sexual secrets. The shock of learning these secrets produces both a discipline and, around that discipline, a camaraderie, a pleasure of the group that was both new to motion pictures and destabilising to the conventional gender roles of audiences' (Williams, 'Learning to Scream', p. 16).
11. Waters, 'Whatever Happened to Showmanship?', p. 56.
12. Lyotard, 'Prescription', p. 177.
13. Lyotard, 'Prescription', p. 179.
14. Lyotard, 'Prescription', p. 179.
15. Lyotard, 'Prescription', p. 184.
16. Lyotard, 'Prescription', p. 185.
17. Lyotard, 'Prescription', p. 180.
18. Kafka, 'In the Penal Colony', pp. 203–4.
19. Kafka, 'In the Penal Colony', pp. 193–200.
20. Kafka, 'In the Penal Colony', p. 197.
21. Lyotard, 'Prescription', p. 177.
22. Lyotard, 'Prescription', p. 177.
23. Kafka, 'In the Penal Colony', p. 197.
24. Kafka, 'In the Penal Colony', pp. 202–3.
25. Lyotard, 'Prescription', p. 177.
26. Lyotard, 'Prescription', p. 180.
27. Lyotard, 'Prescription', p. 179.
28. Lyotard writes in his essay 'Prescription': 'The heteronomy of the body understands nothing of physical time or of ethical time because the *aisthesis* that governs it is neither linked/linking (in the sense of intelligibility) nor unlinked/linking (in the sense of responsibility). The paradox of this body's time – insofar as it is constituted by its non-belonging to itself, its primary disseizure – is that it lacks the modality of any kind of linkage' (Lyotard, 'Prescription', p. 187).
29. Lyotard, 'Prescription', p. 176.
30. Lyotard, 'Prescription', p. 176.
31. Lyotard, 'Prescription', p. 179.
32. Lyotard, 'Prescription', p. 179.
33. Lyotard, 'Prescription', p. 178.
34. Lyotard, 'Prescription', p. 178.
35. Scarry, *The Body in Pain*, p. 4.
36. Lyotard, 'Prescription', p. 178.
37. Lyotard, 'Prescription', p. 178.
38. Lyotard, 'Prescription', p. 178.
39. Lyotard, 'Prescription', p. 180.
40. Lyotard, 'Prescription', p. 179.
41. Lyotard, 'Prescription', p. 179.
42. Lyotard, 'Prescription', p. 180.
43. Lyotard, 'Prescription', p. 179.

44. Lyotard, 'Prescription', p. 180.
45. Lyotard, 'Prescription', p. 180.
46. Lyotard, 'Prescription', p. 180.
47. Lyotard, 'Prescription', p. 180.
48. Lyotard, 'Prescription', p. 178.
49. Lyotard, 'Prescription', p. 180.
50. Lyotard, 'Prescription', p. 181.
51. Lyotard, 'Prescription', p. 179.
52. Curtis, 'The Body as Outlaw', p. 257.
53. Lyotard, 'Prescription', p. 179.
54. Lyotard, 'Prescription', p. 181.
55. As Lyotard writes in his essay 'Prescription': 'The differend between the body and the law cannot be converted into a litigation. Only the sacrifice of the body maintains the sanctity of the law. Without deliberation or warranted judgement the sacrificial execution must be repeated automatically each time a criminal birth occurs. The cruelty will be machine-like' (Lyotard, 'Prescription', p. 181).
56. Lyotard, 'Prescription', p. 179.
57. Lyotard, 'Prescription', p. 181.
58. Lyotard, 'Prescription', pp. 177–9.
59. Lyotard, 'Prescription', p. 179.
60. Lyotard, 'Prescription', p. 180.
61. Lyotard, 'Prescription', p. 187.
62. Foucault, 'The Confession of the Flesh', p. 194.
63. Foucault, 'The Confession of the Flesh', pp. 194–5.
64. Foucault, 'The Confession of the Flesh', p. 194.
65. Foucault, 'The Confession of the Flesh', p. 197.
66. Foucault, 'The Confession of the Flesh', p. 197.
67. Foucault, 'The Confession of the Flesh', p. 196.
68. Deleuze, 'What is a *Dispositif*?', p. 159.
69. Deleuze, 'What is a *Dispositif*?', p. 160.
70. Deleuze, 'What is a *Dispositif*?', p. 160.
71. Deleuze, 'What is a *Dispositif*?', pp. 159–60.
72. Deleuze, 'What is a *Dispositif*?', p. 159.
73. Deleuze, 'What is a *Dispositif*?', p. 162.
74. Deleuze, 'What is a *Dispositif*?', p. 161.
75. Deleuze, 'What is a *Dispositif*?', p. 161.
76. Deleuze, 'What is a *Dispositif*?', p. 160.
77. Deleuze, 'What is a *Dispositif*?', p. 164.
78. Lyotard, *Libidinal Economy*, p. 25.
79. Lyotard, *Libidinal Economy*, p. 25.
80. Lyotard, *Libidinal Economy*, p. 25.
81. Lyotard, *Libidinal Economy*, p. 25.
82. Lyotard, *Libidinal Economy*, p. 25.

83. Lyotard, *Libidinal Economy*, p. 25.
84. Lyotard, *Libidinal Economy*, p. 27.
85. Lyotard, *Libidinal Economy*, p. 26.
86. Grant, 'Glossary', p. x.
87. Lyotard, *Libidinal Economy*, pp. 25–6.
88. Grant, 'Glossary', p. xi.
89. Lyotard, *Libidinal Economy*, p. 26.
90. Lyotard, *Libidinal Economy*, p. 30.
91. Trahair, 'Jean-François Lyotard', p. 223.
92. Lyotard writes: 'If he [Freud] introduced the principle which he names Nirvana, it is in order that his libidinal economy escapes the thermodynamic and, more generally, mechanical analogy, and so that this thought of the unconscious does not precisely close up into a theoretical system; so close to Nietzsche in this respect' (Lyotard, *Libidinal Economy*, p. 30).
93. Lyotard, *Libidinal Economy*, pp. 31–2.
94. Lyotard, 'Prescription', p. 179.
95. Scarry, *The Body in Pain*, p. 4.
96. Williams, 'Learning to Scream', pp. 14–17.
97. Lyotard, 'Prescription', p. 179.
98. Lyotard, *Libidinal Economy*, p. 17.
99. Lyotard, 'Prescription', p. 179.
100. Kafka, 'In the Penal Colony', p. 197.
101. Bennington, *Lyotard*, p. 27.
102. Curtis, 'The Body as Outlaw', p. 260.
103. Lyotard, *Libidinal Economy*, p. 27.
104. Lyotard, 'Several Silences', p. 101; Bennington, *Lyotard*, p. 57.
105. Lyotard, *Libidinal Economy*, p. 27.
106. Lyotard, *Libidinal Economy*, p. 27.
107. Williams, *Lyotard*, p. 48.
108. Williams, *Lyotard*, p. 48.
109. Williams, *Lyotard*, p. 48.
110. Williams, *Lyotard*, p. 48.
111. Lyotard, *Libidinal Economy*, p. 5.
112. Waters, 'Whatever Happened to Showmanship?', p. 57.
113. Williams, *Lyotard*, p. 46.
114. Lyotard, 'Prescription', p. 179.
115. Williams, *Lyotard*, p. 46.

CHAPTER 4

Automutilation and Metonymy: The Economy of the Pulse

In his essay 'Acinema', Lyotard writes that the 'misspending' or expenditure of energy causes 'uncompensated losses' for the spectator.[1] Lyotard extends such 'uncompensated losses' of energy to the cinematic image in what he calls 'acinema'.[2] This chapter will propose that the site in which Lyotard's conception of these kinds of 'uncompensated losses' of energy can be identified is horror or 'splatter' cinema. This chapter will also analyse Lyotard's essay 'The Idea of a Sovereign Film', in which Lyotard uses Bataille's notion of sovereign operations that I argue characterises the films that align with a cinema of the pulse. By calling on the operation of the pulse to theorise both the affective 'splatter' shots that generate intensities and the 'opening' of the spectator to communication/communion, this chapter will conceptualise a sovereign spectatorship. Sovereignty is what Derrida in his essay on Bataille calls a 'putting at stake' of mastery or identity.[3] The 'putting at stake' of mastery or identity is a risking or an 'opening' of oneself to intensities. To consider 'Acinema' in terms of such 'putting at stake' is an attendance to the kinds of movement that do not give signifying value or return, but rather result in 'intense enjoyment and sexual pleasure (*la jouissance*)' for the spectator.[4] In outlining a spectatorship of the pulse in terms of sovereignty, this chapter takes the energetic exchanges and expenditures of cinema outside the terms of subjectivity and identity to interpret spectatorship in its operations.

In this chapter I implement sovereignty's 'putting at stake' in an analysis of the spectatorship of two films: George A. Romero's *Dawn of the Dead* (1978) and Lucio Fulci's *L'aldilà / The Beyond* (1981). While the two films I have chosen are films integral to the zombie canon, it is only inasmuch as they reverberate facets of what can be called a general economy of expenditure for a film spectator that I take them up here. I do not set out to define the zombie as a genre figure or the zombie film as a genre film.

Dawn of the Dead is the second entry in the series of six *Dead* films directed by Romero. The six include *Night of the Living Dead* (1968), *Dawn of the Dead* (1978), *Day of the Dead* (1985), *Land of the Dead* (2005), *Diary of the Dead* (2007), and *Survival of the Dead* (2009). While the first, Romero's *Night of the Living Dead*, is an influential film and is often considered the blueprint film in terms of the development of the zombie sub-genre as a whole, the figure of the zombie had an established and thematically diverse filmic history prior to 1968 in films such as Victor Halperin's *White Zombie* (1932), Jacques Tourneur's *I Walked with a Zombie* (1943), Roger Corman's *The Undead* (1957), Ubaldo Ragona's *The Last Man on Earth* (1964), and John Gilling's *The Plague of the Zombies* (1966).

Set and filmed on location in Louisiana, *L'aldilà* is an Italian produced film directed by Lucio Fulci. The film was released internationally in different cut versions under different titles and blacklisted in Britain in 1984 as a 'video nasty'. *L'aldilà* is the second film in the trilogy, and is bracketed by *Paura nella città dei morti viventi/ City of the Living Dead* (released in the United States as *The Gates of Hell*) (1980) and *Quella villa accanto al cimitero/ The House by the Cemetery* (1981). Each film in the trilogy deals with one of the seven gates of hell, which, once opened, emit the 'living dead'. Prior to these three films Fulci had directed *Zombie Flesh Eaters*, which was released in 1979. Critics were vehement that *Zombie Flesh Eaters* mimicked Romero's *Dawn of the Dead*, a notion that was perpetuated by the fact that it was released by distributors under the title *Zombi 2* in most of Europe and *Zombie* in the United States.[5] Distributers had used this as a selling point, feeding on the popularity of *Dawn of the Dead*, which had been released as *Zombi* in Europe.

These films belong to identifiable modes of production at a particular politico-economic moment that produces a correspondingly unique economy of spectatorship. Both *Dawn of the Dead* and *L'aldilà* are considered exploitation films. Made in the late 1970s to early 1980s, both demonstrate continuity editing systems interspersed with affective 'splatter' shots. *Dawn of the Dead*'s modern capitalist allegory is integrated with the kind of 'splatter' effects of which Romero's zombie films were progenitor.[6] The 'splatter' effects in *L'aldilà*, many of which illustrate eye-gouging gore, reinforce the position of the spectator. It is 'splatter' that generates the investment and exploitation of intensities: an 'opening out' of intensities that 'opens out' the viewer in it.

Bataille gives us two great examples of sovereign operations in aesthetic procedures: automutilation and metonymy. Automutilation and metonymy are both continuous processes that have surplus as their operative function and result in communication/communion. Automutilation puts subjectivity 'at stake' and metonymy puts identity 'at stake'. Automutilation entails an 'opening out' or investment of energies. Metonymy is understood here as 'contagion' or the displacement of energies. Automutilation gives the meaning 'auto', referring to 'self', in the sense of 'one's own' but also 'automatic' (instinct, *Trieb*, *pulsion*): thus, one's own/automatic mutilation. I argue here for an 'opening out' in automutilation as a way of getting closer to a kind of bodily spectatorship of horror cinema. Metonymy describes an 'opening out' of identity to the quasi-physical via 'contagion'.

Zombies are automutilative and metonymic figures. Zombies work by instinct, eating living flesh; that is, they automatically (self-)mutilate. Zombies are contagious – once bitten, a living person will become one of the 'living dead' – which gives zombies something in common with my conception of metonymy as 'contagion'. However, these terms are applicable to more than the zombies in such films. I am interested in the internal operational functions of automutilation and metonymy, rather than what they represent of what is external to the films. I find the 'opening out' of automutilation and the metonymic 'contagion' generative of a 'putting at stake' of subjectivity and identity in the films' spectators. My focus is on a cinematic experience that involves the Open or continuum: a sensory manifold by which flesh is 'opened out' in the action of automutilation and by which metonymy operates to 'sustain' sensation by 'contagion'. It is nevertheless worthwhile to consider why the terms 'automutilation' and 'metonymy' themselves can be considered elements that pervade the zombie film landscape.

Automutilation and metonymy retain economies that are counter to the production and circulation of subjectivity and identity. A different kind of communication arises through risk or sacrifice – a 'putting at stake'[7] – that is made at the site of horror. Neither automutilation nor metonymy are representations. Rather, they are movements or actions; moreover, they are sovereign operations. The sovereign operation is an experience of the 'loss' by expenditure that is 'constant' or continuous.[8] Automutilation and metonymy are ways of thinking about a particular kind of operation or economy of spectatorship that seizes the body from within while giving way to communication with the image/world in 'sustained' sensation.[9] Automutilation and metonymy are continuous processes that have expenditure as their operative function and result in communication/communion. Automutilation and metonymy then – separated by (and 'sustained' in) horror – share this communication/communion by which 'I' am 'put at stake'.

General Economy as Energetic Expenditure

Lyotard's understanding of what constitutes 'acinema', but also sovereign cinema is cinema that makes provision for spectatorship in terms of expenditure or 'uncompensated losses'.[10] The spectator's investment of libidinal energies in the image is imbricated with the exploitation of libidinal energies in cinema. It is the investment and exploitation of energies that make up the arrangement or *dispositif* of cinema. Beyond this exchange of energies, there are also 'uncompensated losses' of energy in the *dispositif*. That is, the investment of energies must also give way to 'uncompensated losses' that cannot be exploited, circulated and returned to give signifying value for cinema. 'Acinema' is described by Lyotard as having 'two poles': 'immobility and excessive movement'.[11] Sovereign cinema is described by Lyotard as having 'intense instants, temporal spasms'.[12] While the 'immobility' of the image produces the 'excessive movement' of the spectator in Lyotard's 'acinema', the 'intense instants, temporal spasms' of Lyotard's sovereign cinema are both in the image, even as they generate a particular kind of communication between the image and the spectator. Both 'acinema' and sovereign cinema are concerned with intensities.

It is the force of intensities that constitutes the pulse, and which is communicative in the *dispositif*. 'Acinema' and sovereign cinema produce a different kind of communication that does away with signification, unified subject spectators and identifying structures of spectatorship. The energetic exchange in which the pulse functions is an Open relationship between the spectator and the image/world, rather than one based in subjectivity/identity and identificatory spectatorship. The pulse thus has broader meaning that extends beyond the physiological response of the spectator to the image.

With regard to the cinematic experience as an Open and energetic relation, this chapter argues that there is a problem of mastery in the spectatorship of horror cinema, and thus there is a necessity to consider spectatorship as a sovereign operation. The problem of mastery rests on a Hegelian reading of cinema that puts the identity of a unified subject in terms of the master–slave dialectic and knowledge (in this case, of film) in terms of the exchange of meaning. Bataille reworks Georg Hegel's concept of experience (*Erfahrung*). For Hegel, experience is the 'becoming' of absolute Spirit.[13] It is a dialectical process of self-revelation whereby knowing transforms the object known. 'Becoming' is constituted as sublated 'moments' such as 'being' and 'nothing'. In Bataille, experience is 'sustained' and unknown.[14] As Bataille writes in *Inner Experience*: 'experience attains the fusion of the object and the subject, being as subject non-knowledge, as object the unknown'.[15]

The experience of the pulse is not found in our knowledge of it, but is 'felt'. The pulse is rarely experienced at the level of cognition and, therefore, just as there is un-knowing at the site of death, terror and ecstasy, sacrifice, laughter, the erotic, the poetic and the sacred, the pulse is unknown. Such un-knowing is important for the pulse precisely for the 'fusion' of the object and subject that it entails in the opening of the self to the world. This means that in the energetics of the pulse there is no mastery of subjectivity or identity, as such. Rather, sovereignty highlights the potential of the pulse for energetics beyond subjectivity and identity. Sovereignty, that is, highlights the energetics of a general economy: an economy that incorporates the expenditure of subject and object in energetic operation, sacrifice, and wasteful disbursement.

The concept of sovereignty reveals the problem of mastery. Sovereignty, as Bataille describes it, is the 'putting at stake' of subjectivity/identity that risks the master's recognition of himself in relation to the slave.[16] Such a 'putting at stake' can be constituted as energetic expenditure. Bataille, that is, uses sovereignty to explicate a relation to sacrifice, or the exposing and 'risking' of one's life to expenditure or 'loss'. 'Risking' or 'putting at stake' is what Bataille calls sovereignty because it risks the 'absolute loss of meaning'.[17] Sovereignty, in Bataille's terms, is then not about unified subject positions, monarchy, or subjectivity, but is the freedom outside signifying exchange and return. Sovereignty is the 'loss' of signifying exchange and return, with regard to being, by the fact of 'putting at stake' of oneself. It is this economy of expenditure and 'loss' that describes sovereignty. Defining general economy and its relation to sovereignty in his text *Inner Experience*, Bataille writes:

> *General economy* makes evident in the first place that a surplus of energy is produced that, by definition, cannot be used. Excessive energy can only be lost without the slightest goal, consequently without any meaning. It is this useless, senseless loss that *is* sovereignty. (In that the *sovereign*, like the *solid*, is an inevitable and constant experience).[18]

Sovereignty is important for spectatorship because it suggests that the spectatorship of horror film can be constituted at the site of a 'putting at stake' of oneself in an operation of energetic expenditure: an expenditure that gives way to a kind of communication and communion. Such an experience of energetic expenditure is 'inevitable', in the sense that it is un-thought (un-known) and happens in the instant; and is 'constant' in the sense that it is not developmental as the dialectic is, but is in surplus and constitutes a continuous energetics of communication that is communion.[19]

Sovereign operations bear on an understanding of film in relation to affect. We might see affect as impinging upon subjectivity, though sovereignty does not refer to subjectivity at all. There is no unified subject by which sovereignty defines itself. Rather, sovereignty refers to a sacrifice of the self and expenditure without reserve or return of meaning, giving up all positions of mastery and the dialectical 'other'.[20] I describe the pulse as being defined by intensities that, as affects or feelings, have their expression in events that take place in the world but that are 'structured' (channelled and exploited) by *dispositifs*. Sovereign affect then, refers to the way in which intensities are exploited, even as there are 'uncompensated losses' of energy in the arrangement. Affects consume and 'carry us away from ourselves'.[21] Affect, in this way, is understood as both 'asignifying' and 'asubjective'.[22] Ultimately the affect of intensities provides a means of understanding sovereign operations: the condition of viewing cinema as communication/communion rather than via identificatory structures. The difference is that in the communication/communion of general economy, there is no signifying exchange value and hence, unified subjects or identities involved in the exchange of meaning. Rather, communication/communion in terms of general economy is situated according to 'loss' or the 'putting at stake' of self – that which Bataille also describes in the excretory – and is an 'expulsion', 'projection', or even a way of 'liberating impulses'.[23] The sovereign operation functions in accordance with the conditions of general economy.

Sovereignty is a germane way of explaining the kind of subject, rather, 'loss' of subjectivity that is extant for horror. Sovereignty is characterised by Bataille in the experience of 'death, tragic terror, and sacred ecstasy'.[24] As an operation of exposing oneself to 'risk' – a sacrifice or putting 'at stake' of oneself – sovereignty demonstrates that it is in the 'instant' that 'splatter' 'bursts out', just as for Bataille, laughter does.[25] The sovereign operation has been theorised in relation to comedy,[26] but is, in this chapter, theorised in relation to the blood splattering effects of horror; in the force of the ecstasy or *jouissance* of intensities in the 'splatter' image, and the excessive intensities or affects that make up horror spectatorship.

Two General Economies of Communication and Communion

Automutilation: Effects on the Flesh

Automutilation is described by the art theorist Krauss in her reading of Bataille. This is significant in that Krauss, through her work, tracks a corporeal spectatorship, but one in which desire decomposes vision and excess dismembers subjectivity. In her essay 'The Im/Pulse to See', the stimulation and enervation of the pulse as the beat of desire decompose and dissolve 'the very coherence of form on which visuality may be thought to depend',[27] and in her earlier essay, 'Antivision' – the essay that directly refers to Bataille's concept of automutilation – Krauss expresses the 'scandalous relation of art to vision' that defiles, autodefaces and even automutilates the self.[28]

The automutilation to which I refer is an automutilation of the unified spectator subject – that is, the unified subject is 'opened out' and in this 'operation', automutilated. The prefix 'auto' in its combining form relates to 'chemical, biological, or organic processes, with the sense "originating within or acting on the body or organism in question; self-produced; self-induced"'.[29] This means that automutilation is a mutilation of the 'self', but it is the process that will be important here. Automutilation is a heterogeneous and continuous expenditure, and very different to the mimesis that Shaviro names as an aspect of the zombie film.[30] Krauss pairs mimesis with automutilation, writing:

> There [in automutilation] we find the body inscribed in a mimetic response to external forces; the body bursting its bounds as it is assaulted from without; the body assuming both the signs of castration and the forms of the fetish.[31]

Automutilation goes one step further than mimesis, however, because the automutilative is characterised by sovereign operations and, by such operations, continually dismembers subjectivity.

In essays written between 1929 and 1930, such as 'Rotten Sun', 'Sacrificial Mutilation and the Severed Ear of Vincent Van Gogh', 'Eye' subtitled 'Cannibal Delicacy', and the essay 'Van Gogh as Prometheus' written in 1937, Bataille demonstrates his interest in automutilation. In 'Sacrificial Mutilation and the Severed Ear of Vincent Van Gogh', van Gogh's obsession with the sun is paired with automutilation. The practice of staring into the sun, according to Bataille, foresaw van Gogh's automutilative act of cutting off his own ear. In Bataille's essay, the surplus of the sun and the general economy of expenditure is delayed in, and even relocated to, the body as the site for automutilation: an investment of intensities. This relocation of intensities is not mimetic – in the sense that the body imitates the sun while retaining its integrity – but is a heterogeneous continuation of the intensities of the sun. The sun produces excesses of energy that are expended without reserve on the body. The body 'returns' such expenditure by 'opening out' the surface on which the sun expends itself, by which the body is 'lost' to the excessive and automutilative act. Such an automutilative act can be paired with the visceral 'opening out' of flesh that we view in horror films and that conveys the expenditures of a general economy of film spectatorship.

Figure 4.1 The surplus of the sun. *The Sower* (Vincent van Gogh, November 1888) © Van Gogh Museum, Amsterdam (Vincent van Gogh Foundation)

Automutilation is a way of theorising Bataille's concept of a general economy of expenditure as an 'opening out' that makes the body continuous in an energetics that communicates/communes with the image/world. Bataille links general economy to the cosmic through the expenditures of the sun. For Bataille, the sun is general economy *par excellence*. The radiation of the sun '*loses itself without taking account, without compensation. The solar economy is founded on this principle*'.[32] The solar economy can be restricted (delayed and returned) but is, in the end, 'loss'. Humans are both a momentary effect (delay) and a continuation of this expenditure. As Bataille writes: 'The solar energy that we are is an energy that *loses itself*. And undoubtedly we can delay it, but not suppress the movement that demands that it lose itself.'[33] In this sense, the economy of the sun has both a restricted economy and a general economy, for what is waste is returned in growth, but beyond this return there is loss that does not enter exchange. It is general economy and the expenditures that do not enter exchange that are of interest here.

In an anthropological study in his essay 'Rotten Sun', Bataille connects the sun to madness ('the scrutinized sun can be identified with a mental ejaculation, foam on the lips, and an epileptic crisis'[34]), and various frenzied automutilative and sacrificial practices that envisage the sun as a solar god ('In mythology, the scrutinized sun is identified with a man who slays a bull (Mithra), with a vulture that eats the liver (Prometheus): in other words, with the man who looks along with the slain bull or the eaten liver'[35]). Bataille links solar expenditure to base materialism by which the solar god is brought down in all its wasted glory via the energies that course through the material. The effects of an excess of energy suggest, as Bataille writes: 'The rupture of personal homogeneity and the projection *outside the self* of a part of oneself.'[36] This 'projection' (or even excretion) is also 'loss' as in a 'loss' of energy by expenditure. Automutilation entails one expending everything, including the self, which highlights the drive to heterogeneity or 'loss' of self.

Automutilation allows for a radical conceptualisation of the cinema spectator. The spectator through automutilation is not conceptualised as a Cartesian subject finding its body, but that body dismembering subjectivity. Automutilation has been little broached in film spectatorship theory. Cinema theorists such as Shaviro, David Bordwell, Torben Grodal, Murray Smith and Anne Rutherford tend to talk about mimesis;[37] however, what is rarely mentioned in cinema theory is the term 'automutilation'. This chapter rectifies this deficiency by suggesting that the aesthetics of cinema and film spectatorship involves automutilation as much as mimesis. Automutilation gives a way of understanding the visceral 'opening out' of bodies on screen as producing a continuous and heterogeneous energetics in the sovereign spectator.

In light of the automutilation that Bataille describes, it is apt to consider Lyotard's opening, spreading, and dissection of the libidinal band/skin in his text *Libidinal Economy* and the kind of energetics that this entails. Both the 'opening' of the libidinal band/skin and the 'opening out' of the flesh in automutilation involve a subject not as a unified subject that forms subjectivity, but as a component in an energetic arrangement or *dispositif* that takes part in continuous experience. The libidinal band/skin is the 'opening out' of an 'ephemeral' but 'heterogeneous' surface.[38] Automutilation is the 'opening out' and expenditure of self, by which 'I' lose 'myself' to the experience. While automutilation is the way through which the spectator becomes operative in the general economy by the 'opening out' of the body, the 'contagion' that makes experience continuous can further be seen by which identity becomes operative. In the next section, I describe metonymic operations as the 'opening' of identity to the quasi-physical and that which elicits a continuous, because 'contagious', affective experience.

Metonymy and the 'Operation' to Undo Identity

If automutilation 'opens' the subject to the world in a visceral sense, metonymy 'opens' identity to the quasi-physical. The *Oxford Dictionary* defines metonymy as: 'A figure of speech which consists in substituting for the name of a thing the name of an attribute of it or of something closely related.'[39] Metonymy refers to the substitution of things that invokes contiguity. Metonymy allows for the transference of meaning, whereby commonly held attributes produce a continuity or relation between things. The linguistic concept of metonymy has previously been used in the analysis of horror cinema to explain ways that horror, the disgusting or the abject, is invoked in the image. It is the meaning-making potential of the metonymic image that allows for connection between images. However, it is also that attributes of the image generate an affective response which connects them to other images, and which is of import for conventional ways of understanding metonymy. Noël Carroll, for example, understands the intimate relation between the concept of metonymy and the genre of horror. In his text *The Philosophy of Horror: Or, Paradoxes of the Heart*, Carroll writes about how metonymy is used in the horror film:

> Horrific metonymy is a means of emphasizing the impure and disgusting nature of the creature—from the outside, so to speak—by associating said being with objects and entities that are already reviled: body parts, vermin, skeletons, and all manner of filth.[40]

My interest in the concept goes beyond meaning-making, however, to define metonymy as that which enters the quasi-physical. Images via the quasi-physical have a 'contagious' quality. That is, this chapter will not simply use metonymy to describe monsters 'from the outside'; it will not treat monsters like identities and spectators like identifying subjects (albeit, abjectly identifying subjects). Rather, it tracks Bataille's use of metonymy in his fictional work *Story of the Eye* and other essays to describe a kind of 'opening out' (breaching or violation) of the spectator experience. Barthes's essay, 'The Metaphor of the Eye', shows that what I characterise as an 'opening out' of experience through the 'contagious' qualities of metonymy is, in Bataille's *Story of the Eye*, also the key to its eroticism. Eroticism, for Bataille, is the way in which beings become continuous.[41] By the 'sustaining' of sensation generated by the 'contagious' and quasi-physical qualities in images, the operation of metonymy is granted access to bodily operations. Through 'contagion', metonymy generates identity 'at stake' via a different kind of communication and communion than that which simply makes meaning.

My concern here is with sovereign cinema as a kind of *dispositif*, set-up or arrangement for the investment in and displacement of intensities. That is, if the *dispositif* is at once an investment of libidinal energies by which we can define automutilation – the investment of the flesh of a heterogeneously excessive energetics – then the *dispositif* is also subject to 'economic movements and displacements'.[42] Where metonymy and cinema intersect is not in the referent (language, as Roman Jakobson and Morris Halle are concerned) of the filmic text. Metonymy in cinema is an operation found in the displacement of energetic intensities that do not exchange meaning at all, even as communication/communion is generated. Metonymy, in this sense, refers to operation (the operation of 'contagion' that breaches and displaces) and not to identity (that of objects and subjects).

In fact, as Paul de Man has argued, the identity of the metaphor is eclipsed by the contiguity of the metonym.[43] While metaphor and metonymy are both figures, metaphor is concerned with identity, whereas metonymy is a representational discourse that opens to something else. Metonymy, that is, is an opening to the quasi-physical or an opening of signification to the whole (of the world). Such an opening to the quasi-physical, as well as the continuity of experience in metonymy, entails 'contagion'.

Jakobson and Halle make clear this difference when they align metaphor with identification and similarity ('homeopathic' or 'imitative' magic) versus metonymy, which they align with contiguity ('contagious magic').[44] Metonymy refers then, to spatial proximity or contextual meaning or a contingent relation, and is concerned with new relations: it makes images 'contagious' in a quasi-physical way. Because of metonymy's bearing on new relations or operations it can be put to use to conceptualise sovereign spectatorship. I argue against films as objects and spectators as signifying and unified subjects, that is, I argue against identity and similarity. The pulse is pre-subjective and pre-cognitive. Metonymy in alignment with general economy puts identity 'at stake' via 'passage' or 'contagion'.[45]

Evoking the quasi-physical, Barthes writes that metonymy in Bataille's *Story of the Eye* is 'eroticism itself' because the interchanging of metaphors in the metaphoric series invokes obscenity and substance.[46] In this text Bataille invokes two separate metaphoric series or chains in eye, egg, testicles and sun, and corresponding liquids in tears, egg yolk, semen or urine, and the hot, turbid intensities of light and heat.[47] Such metaphors, Barthes writes in 'The Metaphor of the Eye', 'pass from *image* to *image*',[48] with no original term: 'the paradigm begins nowhere'.[49] Metaphors for the eye and for tears, as instances in the series, stand for what cannot be represented; the contiguity between metaphoric terms – their metonymic relation – stands for surplus. Bataille writes in *Story of the Eye*, for instance: 'The caress of the eye over the skin is so utterly, so extraordinary gentle, and the sensation is so bizarre that it has something of a rooster's horrible crowing.'[50] Bataille here describes the plucked-out eye of the priest, Don Aminado, and its use to erotic effect as the character, Simone, rolls the eye over and inside her body. But the eye is linked to a rooster's crowing and therefore the rising of the sun (and potentially, the rising of the cock) in this description. In an earlier scene in which the three characters, Simone, Sir Edmund, and the narrator visit an arena in Madrid to see a bullfight, Bataille describes the actions of Simone, who has been gifted with the raw balls of a dead bull, as she watches the matador, Granero, as he is gored by a bull:

> Thus, two globes of equal size and consistency had suddenly been propelled in opposite directions at once. One, the white ball of the bull, had been thrust into the "pink and dark" cunt that Simone had bared in the crowd; the other, a human eye, had spurted from Granero's head with the same force as a bundle of innards from a belly. This coincidence, tied to death and to a sort of urinary liquefaction of the sky, first brought us back to Marcelle in a moment that was so brief and almost insubstantial, yet so uneasily vivid that I stepped forward like a sleepwalker as though about to touch *her* at eye level.[51]

The bull's testicle is here associated with the eye of the matador and also with the sun in the sky (the 'urinary liquefaction of the sky'[52]). However, what is also pertinent are the actions, or operations, at play: thrusting, spurting, liquefaction. Such actions, or operations, are indicative of an action other than that of matter and that of the liquids associated with matter: the operation of language to open signification to something else in the world.

For it is not just chains of metaphors that are invoked in Bataille's work, but that these chains of metaphors are interchanged, giving way to an absurd contiguity.[53] This is the use of metonymy in Bataille's work as Barthes describes it: a freedom found in metonymy to make contiguous any of the metaphors in the chain in Bataille's series. One of the bull's testicles is bitten into, by Simone, like an egg, and the other testicle is propelled forward in the same moment as the matador's eye is propelled out of his head.[54] The sun's beam of light is like urine, which is associated with Marcelle and her urine-stained bed sheet.[55] Barthes writes about Bataille's *Story of the Eye*,

> the result is a kind of general contagion of qualities and actions: by virtue of their metaphorical dependence eye, sun, and egg are closely bound up with the genital; by virtue of their metonymic freedom they endlessly exchange meanings and usages.[56]

Thus, if we take a definition of metaphor as the substitution of one thing for another, and metonymy as the transference, or contiguity, of qualities and actions from one thing to another, in Bataille's story, through metaphor we see the variety and endurance of the eye and its qualities, while metonymy 'sustains' sensation via 'contagion'.[57] Metaphor here operates not simply for images but gives way to metonymy's contiguous sensations of experience (from laughter to ecstasy or anguish),[58] generating a 'flow of matter' but also of experience. The very continuity of images and sensations in the metaphoric series and the contiguity of the metonym, also calls for a breach, or a 'violation of a limit to the signifying space'.[59] Barthes continues: 'the metonymy is nothing but a forced syntagma, the violation of a limit to the signifying space. It makes possible, at the very level of speech, a counter-division of objects, usages, meanings, spaces, and properties that is eroticism itself.'[60] Metonymy thus attains proximity to the body (the genital) at the same time as it operates to undo identity. Like the erotic movement that makes all substance obscene, metonymy 'sustains' experience through the displacement of energies in the images. Metonymy demonstrates the cataclysmic contiguity of terms and the fractured 'opening' – rather, 'loss' – of their identity in an economy of expenditure. The excesses they denote cannot themselves have any function and are thus as vulgar as the metaphors that stand in for them. Metonymy is then a figure of language by which writing becomes unthinkable and impossibly erotic.

As above, Barthes describes Bataille's use of metonymy not only in the 'violation of a limit to the signifying space'; it is 'eroticism itself'. Eroticism is found in the continuity of communication that both 'sustains' and breaches – or violates – the 'signifying space'.[61] In the same way, it could be argued that eroticism makes a breach in identity – risks by 'putting at stake' – and is one of the ways that Bataille writes that 'I' find myself in communion with others. Thus, it is not simply the limits of the 'signifying space' but the limits of the signifying subject that are breached in Bataille's eroticism. The erotic movement is one that 'sustains' experience, breaching the limits of both signs and subjects. The metaphoric chains produce metonymy, and, in the displacement of energies, cause a sustaining of experience by the violation of the limits of the 'signifying space'.

How does metonymy function regarding 'contagion' and the body? And more particularly, how does the displacement of energy function to generate communication/communion? Metonymy has a similar action, or operation, to that of automutilation. Where automutilation 'opens out' the flesh via the investment of energies, metonymy 'opens out' identities via the displacement of energies. Metonymy is a splitting of the sign itself in an excessive 'opening out'. This relates to the kind of communication/communion that Bataille describes because it demonstrates the 'opening out', 'sustaining', or continuation of sensation that arises between terms and subjects at the same time that identity is 'put at stake'. In relation to Bataille's account of 'loss', 'there is passage, communication', but such passage or communication does not have the distance between, and distinct existence of, object and subject.[62] Instead, there is an investment and displacement of energies between the two. Just as the operations of displacement are imbricated with those of condensation, so too are the displacement of the energies of the metonym imbricated with continuous 'contagion'. What metonymy adds to an understanding of communication/communion is that communication exists as operation; and this is an operation that violates the limits of identity even as there is an energetic exchange between components. The communication/communion of the metonym is set against this self-conscious 'one-ness' – the ideal term – that is the restricted economy of the return of signification.

Automutilation and George A. Romero's *Dawn of the Dead* (1978)

There is a relationship between the breakdown of the political economy in the world of the film in *Dawn of the Dead* and the general economy in which the spectator of the film engages. This can be seen in two opposing movements: 'immobility and excessive movement'[63] or boredom and 'splatter'. That is, while in the film the breakdown of the political economic exchange system results initially in a frenzied gathering and looting of goods by Fran (Gaylen Ross), Stephen (David Emge), Peter (Ken Foree) and Roger (Scott H. Reiniger), and later, the bikers, over time the shopping mall becomes boring for the four main characters in the film. What is important about this is that boredom, or 'immobility', intersects, in this film, with 'splatter', or 'excessive movement'. Only by laying waste to the 'living dead' via violent and blood-splattering gunshot wounds to the head is boredom attained or recuperated.

Of 'immobility and excessive movement' Lyotard writes in his essay 'Acinema': 'In letting itself be drawn towards these antipodes the cinema insensibly ceases to be an ordering force; it produces true, that is, vain, simulacrums, blissful intensities, instead of productive/consumable objects.'[64] The breakdown of exchange expressed in 'immobility' (boredom) in the world of the film and the resulting 'excessive movement' ('splatter') produces intensities for the spectator that are not 'productive/consumable objects'. Intensity is the pulsing 'immobility' to 'excessive

Figure 4.2 Blood splatter on a shop front window. *Dawn of the Dead* (George A. Romero, 1978)

movement' (*jouissance*) that is outside of all exchange, and is thus expenditure without return or reserve. 'Splatter' allows for an 'opening out' of intensities. But it is also these intensities that, after *Night of the Living Dead*, cinema production comes to exploit, even as intensities are beyond control: 'splatter' cinema as the outcome. The intensities that 'splatter' produces in the image and the spectator stimulates communication/communion even as such intensities are exploited.

But there is another kind of 'opening out' to communication/communion in *Dawn of the Dead*. Such an 'opening out' has a double form in *Dawn of the Dead* in that the oral consumption that results in contagion also becomes the 'opening out' of the flesh in automutilation. *Dawn of the Dead*'s 'feast of the dead' scene is historically renowned as the greatest zombie 'chowdown'. Holed up in the shopping mall, Fran, Stephen, Peter and Roger have made themselves relatively cosy. By locking down all entrances to the mall and destroying the 'living dead' inside, they are free to move around and access goods within the mall. Bikers raiding the mall, however, allow the 'living dead', who have been growing in number outside, entry. The bikers knock over, tease, and throw cream pies at the 'living dead' who amble slowly about. They simultaneously seltzer spray the faces of the 'living dead' and destroy goods in the mall. What at first looks like harmless fun results in several of the bikers being overwhelmed by the 'living dead'. One biker who is taking his blood pressure gets a reading of zero, rapidly loses blood, and is pulled apart limb by limb by the 'living dead'. Another is disembowelled, the camera luridly skipping between his torn stomach, his screaming mouth, and the faces of the 'living dead' as they ravenously delight in the feast, their hands filled with intestinal parts.

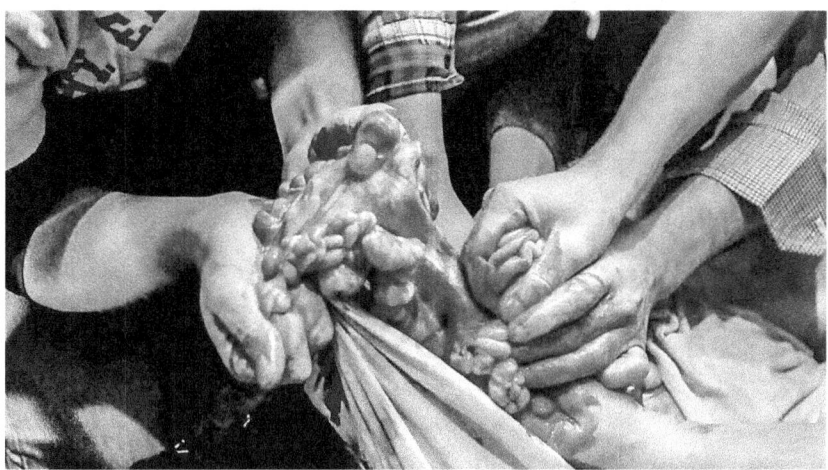

Figure 4.3 A biker disembowelled. *Dawn of the Dead* (George A. Romero, 1978)

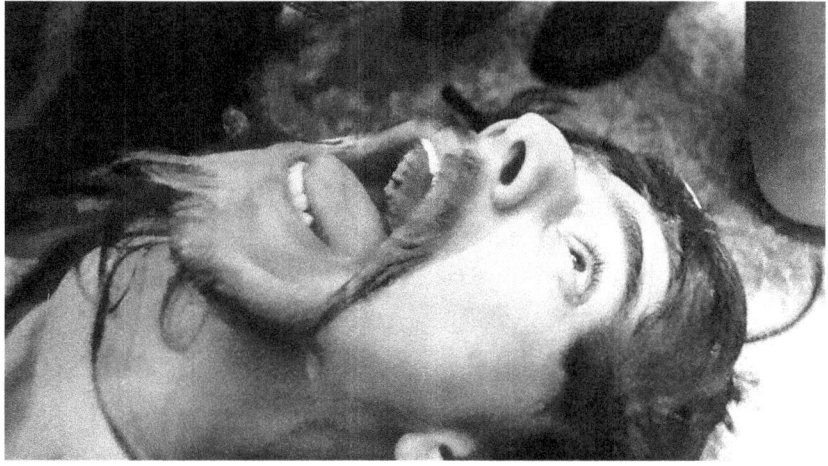

Figure 4.4 The biker screams. *Dawn of the Dead* (George A. Romero, 1978)

Figure 4.5 The 'chowdown'. *Dawn of the Dead* (George A. Romero, 1978)

Tracking the topography of gore film, Patricia MacCormack writes in her essay 'Perversion – An Introduction':

> The body is a clandestine geology. In flesh and desire we exist as plateaus over which we have no control, knowledge or, as seen in gore cinema, image. Folding flesh and desire outward through provoking images refolds and thus transforms the self. Those who resist transformation most frequently resist the encounter which brings its ecstasy (*ex-stasis*, outside of self) into being – the encounter with perverse worlds often only available in film.[65]

The clandestine geology to which MacCormack refers cannot simply be the surfaces (of inscription) of the body, but rather is an 'opening out' of the flesh that transforms the self because it is an 'encounter' with 'ecstasy (*ex-stasis*, outside of self)'.

The 'opening out' to automutilation is this 'opening out' of the 'clandestine geology' or topography and is, in fact, disruptive to the energetic system. There is surplus in this energetic system or economy because, just as MacCormack writes, we have no control, knowledge, or image of flesh and desire, we have no image of the intensities that approach ecstasy or *jouissance*, which cannot be controlled and do not enter cognition. A restricted economy engages in control/knowledge/image. Instead, we find in gore cinema the 'opening out' to automutilation of a general economy, which is also the opening of the spectator to an 'expulsion', 'projection', or even a way of 'liberating impulses'.[66] And yet, the 'living dead' find communion in this 'feast', just as the spectator finds communion in intensities that approach ecstasy or *jouissance*.

An Operation in the Morgue: Lucio Fulci's
L'aldilà/The Beyond (1981)

Although contagion is spread via contact in *L'aldilà*, it is not a simple bite from a zombie, as in Romero's films. A beaker of acid, a tide of blood, spiders and a dog are all used as 'possessed' forces for contagion. Contagion occurs through the metonymic association of quasi-physical forces and their (often inexplicably linked) action. The association of forces and their action compromises the spatial and temporal discreteness between bodies in *L'aldilà*, ultimately undoing identity. In my analysis of *L'aldilà* I will show how the metonymic relation precipitates a kind of communication/communion between images, but I argue that such communication/communion is not an exchange of meaning. Rather, the metonymic relation in *L'aldilà* gives way to expenditure and thus a 'loss' of identity and meaning that is the communication/communion of general economy.

In *L'aldilà*, a strange shell of a corpse, which we learn is that of the heretic artist Schweick (Antoine Saint-John), who was crucified and quicklime-lynched fifty-four years earlier, lies upon a slab in the morgue linked to an encephalograph (what the medics in the film modestly call a 'brain-wave machine'). His corpse, which has been removed from the basement of the hotel that Liza Merril (Catriona MacColl, credited as Katherine MacColl) has occupied, is being tested for brain activity. We cannot really be sure of the imperative of this test, and indeed Dr John McCabe (David Warbeck) says as such. The body of Joe the plumber (Giovanni De Nava), who has had his eyes gouged out by a hand reaching from beyond the gate of hell – the gate that he discovered while attempting to fix the plumbing in the hotel – lies on the slab beside Schweick's. After the last of the doctors leaves the morgue, we see in close-up the 'brain-wave machine' as it begins to beat out an electric pulse.

In long shot, Joe's daughter Jill (Maria Pia Marsala) and his wife Mary-Ann (Laura De Marchi), approach along the hospital corridor, their shoes clacking rhythmically against the hard linoleum floor. They pass two hospital orderlies. Mary-Ann directs Jill to sit in a chair, saying 'Wait here for me, Jill. I won't be long'. She enters the morgue door, which is labelled 'Do Not Entry' (an unintentional translation error). The camera pans over the plastic-covered corpses that are laid out, as Mary-Ann enters the morgue and approaches Joe's body (one of the two bodies not covered in plastic). In close-up we see the 'brain-wave machine': the electric pulse is now flat-lining. The shot pulls back to Mary-Ann leaning over Joe's body. She takes from her pocket a string of rosary beads. In continuous take, the shot zooms in to Schweick's face (in profile) and then the 'brain-wave machine' just beyond Schweick, which is still flat-lining. In mid-shot, we see Jill (in profile), still sitting on the chair in the hospital corridor. There is a mid-shot of Mary-Ann holding a white shirt, preparing to dress Joe. She tries to lift Joe's body but is unable to. She takes a pair of scissors from her pocket, and in close-up we see the scissors cutting the fabric. After a close-up of Jill's face (in profile), the camera pull focuses on an orderly wheeling a corpse on a trolley towards Jill along the hospital corridor. The wheels of the trolley squeal loudly against the linoleum floor. In close-up, we see Jill's face as the trolley goes by in the foreground. Mary-Ann arranges the rosary beads in Joe's hands. The camera pulls back from the rosary beads to a dolly pan shot of Mary-Ann standing beside Joe's now dressed corpse, with Schweick's corpse on her other side, as she grieves. In continuous take, Mary-Ann turns and sees Schweik's corpse and the 'brain-wave machine'. The camera zooms in to a close-up of Mary-Ann as she screams. We then see a close-up of Jill, who utters the word 'Mummy'. And then, also in close-up, there is a shot of a tilted beaker, acid pouring from its lip. The camera pulls out from a close-up of Jill's face (in profile) as she rises from her chair and moves toward the door. In close-up again, we see acid pouring from the beaker. There is a long shot of Jill entering the morgue with Schweik's corpse in the foreground that becomes a tracking shot (dolly with) to Joe's corpse in foreground. There is a mid-shot of Jill as she turns. The camera zooms in to a close-up of Jill's horrified face. In mid-shot we see Mary-Ann's body lying on the floor, the acid from the beaker pouring onto her face, which is slowly being burnt away, revealing blood and gore.

After what has been a series of continuous takes and sweeping dolly or zoom shots, the shots become close-ups, in a rapid series of cuts. The images that are cycled are: the close-up of the tilted beaker from which acid is pouring; the close-up of Mary-Ann's slowly disintegrating face (in profile) as acid pours onto it; a close-up of Jill's face; a close-up of Joe's face (in profile); and a close-up of Schweik's face (in profile). Then, after a close-up of Jill's face and a pan down her body to her shoes, a close-up of a pool of acidy blood from Mary-Ann's disintegrating face, which approaches Jill's shoes, also becomes part of the cycled set of images. In mid-shot we see Jill trapped by the advancing tide of blood. Jill tries to find a door through which she can exit. There is a straight-on angle shot of the tide of blood moving across floor. After a mid-shot and a reverse shot of Jill opening a cool-room door, a corpse falls towards Jill. The camera zooms in to a close-up of Jill screaming.

Later, as Jill walks from the funeral site of her father, Joe, and her mother, Mary-Ann, we glimpse her eyes, which have been transformed to a milky white. Later again, in the morgue, as John, Liza and Jill find themselves surrounded by Schweick and a multitude of possessed hospital patients, Jill turns violently upon Liza, thrusting Liza's head back with her hand and reaching with her fingers to gouge out Liza's eyes. John points his gun and shoots, and Jill's head explodes. It is interesting to note again in these shots that which is very close to what Lyotard designates as 'immobility and excessive movement'[67] in, first, the pool of blood that seeps towards Jill's shoes and her petrification before it, and then later, the splattering explosion of Jill's head.

There are many variations on the zombie body in *L'aldilà*. Objects and characters alike become conduits for and are 'possessed' by Schweick. A beaker of acid pours inexplicably via a phantom hand onto the face of Mary-Ann, creating an amorphous pool of blood that incessantly seeps towards its victim, Jill; spiders eat the face of a librarian who discovers an architectural record of the gateway to hell; a possessed dog mauls the throat of its owner, Emily (Cinzia Monreale, credited as Sarah Keller), who has come back from the 'beyond' to warn the living. Those touched by the possessed people or things become transmitters for Schweick. The slow seepage of the acidy blood across the floor of the morgue and, as the pool spreads, its proximity to the feet of Jill, not only perpetuates, but also becomes a mechanism in the operation of Schweick: an operation that allows Schweick to possess people without coming into direct contact with them. The mechanism of possession (or 'contagion') that occurs in the morgue is perpetuated through contact that invokes metonymy because of the contiguity of images: beaker of pouring acid – disintegration of Mary-Ann's face – seeping tide of acid and blood that approaches Jill's feet – Jill's hand pressed against Liza's face – the bullet that makes Jill's head explode. We pass from image to image with no original term. What is important is the operation: the acid consumes Mary-Ann's face, and Mary-Ann disintegrates into a tide of blood. The tide of blood consumes Jill's attention, and Jill's 'identity' disintegrates in that tide of blood. Jill is lost in the dissipating cries of her own scream.

Figure 4.6 Acid pouring from a beaker. *L'aldilà/The Beyond* (Lucio Fulci, 1981)

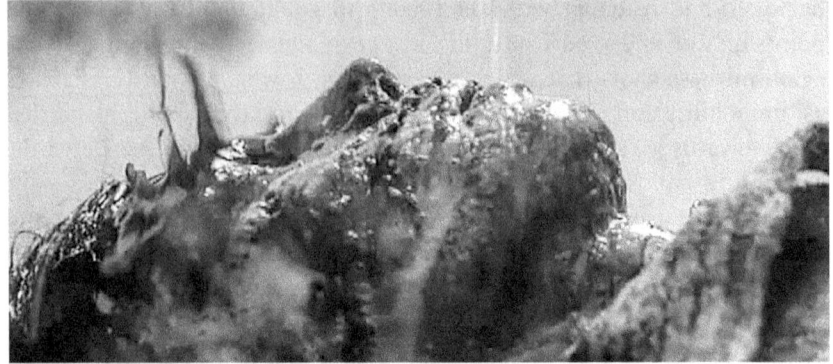

Figure 4.7 Mary-Ann's disintegrating face. *L'aldilà/The Beyond* (Lucio Fulci, 1981)

Figure 4.8 The advancing tide of blood. *L'aldilà/The Beyond* (Lucio Fulci, 1981)

Figure 4.9 Jill screams. *L'aldilà/The Beyond* (Lucio Fulci, 1981)

L'aldilà, and this scene in particular, recalls for us Bergson's ideas about a 'change of *state* or of *quality*'[68] that can be seen as a fact of metonymy in cinema. This is a change of state or a change of quality of Mary-Ann that we must also agree is a change of state or a change of quality of Jill, as well as a change of state or a change of quality of the spectator. It does not matter for the purposes of this argument that this sequence of events is not shot in continuous take (but is instead cut as a flurry of close-ups in series that indicates metonymy at work). The spreading pool of blood as it relates to a change in state has the same effect. In a sense, Bataille goes a step further than Bergson by suggesting that the change of state or of quality is not simply the opening of consciousness upon the whole but is also the opening to communication/communion. Communication/communion gives rise to a 'loss' of self as it involves the 'contagion' and 'passage' of energy that flows from one being to another.[69]

In *L'aldilà* bodies are '*declined*'[70] in ways that affect characters, causing, as Bataille says of sacrificial expenditure, him to 'throw himself suddenly *outside of himself*'.[71] In relation to Jill, the tide of blood causes her to 'throw' herself 'suddenly *outside of*' herself. Identities are lost in the 'decomposition' of bodies, and also in the expenditure of energy. The three corpses or bodies – Schweick, Joe and Mary-Ann – laid out in the morgue on this horizontal plane, threaten the upright posture of Jill. In the decompositional 'fall' of her mother and this horizontal and spreading flow of blood, Jill loses herself (loses rationality, in fact loses her head, pre-empting her literal 'decapitation'). Horrified, Jill is unable to take her eyes from the encroaching tide of blood; it almost engulfs her. As Bataille writes of experience, in this 'profound obscurity is a fierce desire to see when, before this desire, everything slips away'.[72] Jill's scream, like her mother Mary-Ann's, signals her 'fall'. This is a scream, 'spasmodic and excremental', that is an expression of the involuntary 'fall' into the heterogeneous wastefulness of the 'loss' of self.[73]

The acid that disintegrates Mary-Ann's face causes a decomposition of form – which is clearly evident – however, this decomposition is a sovereign operation; that is, a time that 'has no foundation and no head'.[74] In other words, this operation is not an abstract period of time that portends endings and would thus divide a spatial distance into present and absent moments of experience, but is as Shaviro writes, 'an absurd compulsion to repeat, to approach the threshold of disaster again and again'.[75] Time, Bataille writes, 'becomes the object of ecstasy' and 'appears as the "eternal return" in the vision of Surlei or as "catastrophe" ("Sacrifices"), or again as "time-explosion"'.[76] Bataille continues: 'Ecstatic time can only find itself in the vision of things that puerile chance causes brusquely to appear: cadavers, nudity, explosions, spilled blood, abysses, sunbursts, and thunder.'[77] Thus, the spilled blood of Mary-Ann in *L'aldilà* can be seen as complying with 'ecstatic time'.

Inasmuch as these operations function, it is the 'absolute risk' or the 'putting at stake' of self that is the mechanism in the metonymic chain. The blood, spreading from the disintegrating Mary-Ann consumes Jill, just as Jill 'falls', fascinated and horrified into the blood of the disintegrating Mary-Ann. Like standing at the edge of a dizzying void we know that this contact with blood will transform Jill. Jill abandons herself to the 'beyond' of her mother's blood just as John and Liza, fleeing from the possessed patients who walk the hospital, find themselves returning again and again to the basement of the hotel near the gate of hell and must eventually abandon themselves to what lies beyond the gate. In this crossing of the threshold their eyes are made pearly white as if obscured by the excess of the void that seems to continue infinitely in all directions.

What takes place for film is horror itself: the 'pure loss' or 'fall' into what is indescribably obscure.[78] *L'aldilà* demonstrates an economy of expenditure most prominently in Mary-Ann's disintegrating face, as it, splashed with acid, is distilled into blood. This automutilation of the form of the body, and the automutilation of the formal and temporal elements of the film (because there is no causal logic for why the beaker is tipped to the point of releasing its acid), points to a particular relationship of the spectator to economy. This economy can be described as an economy of surplus or of expenditure without return or reserve of meaning: a general economy.

The Sovereign Operation as Affective Experience

My analysis of these two films is not an allegory or social commentary in the sense that is popularly taken up in relation to *Dawn of the Dead*, nor that which is entailed in *L'aldilà*'s spiritual crisis.[79] My argument is that there is a relationship brought about in the cinema experience that directs our attention beyond the social commentary to a particular articulation of the body and the body's operation within the *dispositif* as economy. Shaviro writes that films are '*machines for generating affect*, and for capitalising upon, or extracting value from, this affect'.[80] By value, I take Shaviro to mean the value of the affect exploited as well as its pricelessness. For the concern of the 'splatter' films that I analyse is not with exchange value but with expenditure at the site of intensities. Such films are engaged in a particular investment and exploitation of the intensities of the spectator.

Thus, the apparatuses, even *dispositifs* that I identify, are not ideological ones as in the work of Jean-Louis Baudry.[81]

While affect gives the spectator 'sensuous' proximity to the image that entails an 'opening out' of the image, ideology gives the spectator distance via the cognitive 'exchange of signs'.[82] Thus, I argue that these films generate subjectivity, even while their affectivity means that they are in the more immediate realm of an asubjective or pre-subjective intensity. In fact, the affectivity of these films calls for the expenditure of a spectator that results in communication/communion: a general economy that is outside of all exchange but is nonetheless imbricated with the ideological value of a restricted economy. In *Dawn of the Dead* the downfall of the political economic exchange system in the world of the film has repercussions that generate affect or intensities because of the necessity to dispose of the 'living dead' in blood-splattering ways. 'Splatter' results in expenditure as 'pure loss' and also communion for the spectator of the film. And yet, these affective moments are still the means of understanding the broader social and economic–political context of these two films.

Shaviro brings these concerns to cinema in his essay 'Film Theory and Visual Fascination' to argue that film is less ideological than affective. He writes:

> Even at its most manipulative, it [cinema] is premised less on the ideological mystification of the spectator than on his or her calculated physiological responses. But beyond and as a result of these very calculations, film also tends towards the blinding ecstasy of Bataillean expenditure. In the cinematic apparatus, vision is uprooted from the idealized paradigms of representation and perspective, and dislodged from interiority. It is grounded instead in the rhythms and delays of an ungraspable temporality, and in the materiality of the agitated flesh.[83]

Beyond ideological cinema, the physiological response is the exchange value with which cinema works. It is what can be exploited and that produces the affective value for cinema. There is expenditure in what Shaviro calls the 'ungraspable temporality' of energies that do not comply with the space and time of a restricted production of representation, as well as in the 'materiality of the agitated flesh'.[84] Such expenditure comprises something more than a physiological response to a film. It is the 'blinding ecstasy' and 'loss' of subjectivity and identity by expenditure.

'Splatter' is a way by which the spectator is exploited and enters exchange: 'splatter' is a type of exploitation cinema. By this we could say that general economy ('loss') is imbricated with restricted economy (exploitation). And yet, we must also refine our definition of exploitation: not exploitation of texts and bodies, but exploitation of energies that, for cinema, is not the exploitation of actual acts but of intensities. As MacCormack writes:

> the affective nature of the images puts end to the stratification and significations of the demand that we "read" images by deferring them to their meanings and possibility of existence in the real world. Horror is all about exploiting—not bodies, but the impossible in the real becoming possible through cinema.[85]

To put it another way, horror exploits, but what it exploits are intensities that are not exploitable; the visceral effects of cinema that have no real presence. This is what the risk of subjectivity amounts to – the risk of intensities 'felt' – and is the 'putting at stake' to cinema.

'Splatter' has the force of affect or *jouissance*. 'Splatter' is also a way by which the spectator is exploited in that 'splatter' produces sensations that are intended to be 'felt' by the spectator of the film. That is, exploitation is not only the exploitation of actors, characters or themes, but is an exploitation of the intensities produced by such films and 'felt' by the spectator. Such an 'opening out' of intensities that 'opens out' the viewer in it, is automutilative and metonymic in ways that characterise the movement and affect of the intensities of the pulse.

How does sovereignty relate to the kind of affective spectatorship seen in horror cinema? What is channelled and exploited by a cinema of the pulse are intensities. The affectivity of such intensities can be described as 'unrepresentable'.[86] In defining affect as Brian Massumi does, the intensities of affect are 'primary, non-conscious, asubjective or presubjective, asignifying, unqualified and intensive'.[87] That is, affects are not conscious qualifications like emotions are, but, as Massumi suggests, are 'unqualified', and significantly, 'asubjective or presubjective', and 'asignifying'. That is, affect gives us something that is always in surplus of what is 'seen' on the screen, and is different to the conscious qualification of emotion. As Shaviro writes: 'Subjects are overwhelmed and traversed by affect, but they *have* or *possess* their own emotions.'[88] For this reason, what we can say of the affect of the pulse is that it shares with general economy the 'pure loss' of subjectivity and also the 'pure loss' of identity, given an intensivity that is communicative in a certain way. Such a 'loss' of subject, however, is also not quite, as Fredric Jameson would have it, a 'disappearance of the individual subject',[89] or rather, it is not a disappearance in the sense that something is absent or lacking, but is better understood, Shaviro writes, as a 'magnification of affect, whose flows swamp us, and continually carry us away from ourselves, beyond ourselves'.[90]

Such affectivity means a 'loss' of mastery given a 'loss' of subjectivity. The pulse by this affectivity cannot be read as having signifying and representational exchange value, just as the film can no longer be read as having signifying and representational exchange value, because there is no longer a subject of mastery to read it. It is Shaviro who provides a way to understand the affective pulse. Affect can be discovered in what Shaviro describes as 'the composition of forces, modulation, and feedback' in cinema (in his analysis, digital works).[91] Similarly, the pulse has the behaviour of forces of intensity that are modulated and fed back through the *dispositif*. The pulse complies with the forces of intensity in the *dispositif* that give us not simply stillness and motion but the micro-movements of an affective spectatorship in which 'immobility' means 'the intensity of extreme *jouissance*'.[92] In my examination of the pulse, this translates to a kind of economy of cinema, but only inasmuch as 'splatter' films can be analysed in a certain affective sense by the 'immobility and excessive movement'[93] of intensities and the exploitation of a certain human 'labour' or response.

Because the affectivity of the pulse does not have signifying or representational exchange value, it is easy to see 'splatter' shots in cinema as a kind of 'rebellion against authority' and thus of order.[94] In fact, what Lyotard says about sovereign films – and he defines neo-realist films as such – is that the 'intense instants, temporal spasms' of such films are 'independent of . . . an authority, indifferent to it'. This is different to classical cinema that is 'servile' in obeying 'the authority of the narrative form'.[95] As such, the 'splatter' of horror cinema is also independent of authority. Lyotard writes:

> Sovereignty is at the antipodes of authority, or rather, it is a stranger to it. It opens up the world, a world neither permitted nor defended, neither good nor bad, neither high nor low, neither black nor white: or rather which is all this, indistinguishably.[96]

In line with what Lyotard describes as the sovereign experience, I argue that 'splatter' shots as the pulsatile 'opening out' to intensities are not a 'rebellion against authority'.[97] We must redefine 'splatter' shots under a general economy; that is, as producing the communication/communion of the sovereign operation that recognises expenditure as 'pure loss'.

Bataille describes particular kinds of bodies or economies of the body that can be used to communicate horror; and for this book, horror cinema. He provides a way by which bodies can be defined in relation to a sacrifice, risking or 'putting at stake'. Such sacrifice, risking, or 'putting at stake' puts bodies in communication/communion that I argue is the mode of sovereign film spectatorship. Of course, the spectator of horror does not really put their life at stake in the way the self-consciousness does in Hegel's account of the master–slave relationship, but they do expose their body to the experience of intensities. The difference is one of preparedness and acceptance; of affective response rather than physical and real sacrifice. As Shaviro writes, cinema is immediate, 'intense', and we 'respond viscerally', but it has no real 'presence'.[98] In other words, there is a *beyond* subjectivity in cinema that is the sacrifice, risking, or 'putting at stake' of sovereignty. In line with the movement of the pulse, the intensities that are 'felt' speed the pulse to erratic movements, risks, or freedoms. For the operation of the *dispositif*, I suggest that the 'putting at stake' to sovereignty means that energy will be expended in the operation of spectatorship and that the spectator will be another sovereign operation in this economy. I conceptualise sovereign experience then, as a 'putting at stake'.

The Pulse as a Sovereign Operation in Horror Cinema

The pulse cannot simply be considered for its physiological response, but for its movement constituted in the pulsing movement of 'blinding ecstasy' and the 'loss' in expenditure.[99] That is, the pulse puts the physiological body in focus, but beyond this 'materiality' is expenditure. An economy of the pulse suggests the flow and flexibility of an affectively 'felt', but unseen, operation; and yet, the pulse also has the force of change. The concept that I refer to as the cinematic pulse is most aptly characterised by an energetic exchange and expenditure between the intensities of the body of the spectator and the force of intensities of the image. The force of energies may be 'felt' in the 'splatter' image in horror by the affective force of blood in such images. In horror cinema, blood acts as the force of affect within a scene. The economy of the pulse then, is momentary (and in cinema, can be likened to the 'pulse' of a 'splatter' shot), but is also the unseen operation.

The intensities of the pulse that are of a general economy resist all concepts by which they might be exchanged and produce meaning. Rather, a general economy describes the expenditure of energies that are of 'pure loss'. Thus, while this chapter undertakes an examination of Bataille's work on economy to identify a general economy and a particular kind of energetic reading that can be identified in the spectatorship of horror, it will suppose a pulse upon this reading only inasmuch as a human 'labour' or response accedes to the 'opening out' of intensities in 'pure loss' where a particular kind of energetic system (*dispositif*), or rather, communication/communion is at play.

Although the quotidian meaning of communication is that of exchange – an exchange of signs, or even, of gifts – what Bataille describes as the sacrifice, risking, or 'putting at stake' of general economy is a different kind of communication: it is the way one enters into communication or communion at the site of un-knowing because it is expenditure without return or reserve of meaning. The 'opening out' of the spectator to intensities is such a 'putting at stake'; that is, a communication/communion of a kind that does not enter exchange but is of 'pure loss'. As Lyotard writes in his essay 'The Idea of a Sovereign Film': 'Sovereignty exchanges nothing', rather it 'give[s] rise to a "communication" (the word is Bataille's), to a communion incomparable to all exchange of signs'.[100] Such communication at the site of 'loss' is seen in horror film as affective expenditure. To be a spectator of the cinematic image is to 'open out' in the affective exchange, by which we might find intimate communication and even communion with others. For Bataille, this 'opening out' to communication and communion with others can be seen before horror and eroticism. Michelson writes: 'For Bataille, indeed, human experience at its fullest – that which he names "communication" or "intimacy" – is sustained by the opening of the self to terror shared.'[101]

In particular kinds of cinema, the communication that takes place between the film and the spectator is found, Lyotard writes, in 'intense instants, temporal spasms'.[102] That is, at the site of sovereignty there is a very different kind of reading, exchange, or communication at play. The 'putting at stake' to the image is an 'at stake' to the 'sensuous immediacy' of the image by which the subject loses herself to expenditure and enters into communication/communion with the image.[103] As MacCormack writes of gore shots in cinema, and which we can assimilate to the kind of communication that Lyotard in a reading of Bataille describes as occurring in the sovereign experience:

> Our brains cannot read these images, and our bodies cannot react to them empathically (we cannot literally empathize with evisceration, like we can in other "body genres" such as coming in porn and crying in melodramas). Our flesh reacts sensorily, reading the images corporeally, while our brains think the inability to think the images sensibly.[104]

Reading and empathy obey the rules of exchange by which the image can be read or responded to in a particular way; that is, they enter the 'interlocutory' or 'socio-economic contractual exchange' of film spectatorship.[105] The sensorial reaction of our flesh and the 'inability to think the images sensibly' can be described as a different kind of communication than that of restricted exchange.[106]

I see this different kind of communication as an outcome of the *dispositif*, which, in Lyotard, channels and exploits intensities. The *dispositif* comprises the investment of components that includes the spectator and forms an assemblage, or what Lyotard also describes in 'The Idea of a Sovereign Film' as a 'constellation'. Lyotard describes this constellation in terms of sovereignty. As Lyotard writes of sovereign film – Lyotard's examples are films such as Michael Snow's *Wavelength*, Andy Warhol's *Sleep* and *Eat*, Hans Richter's *Fuge 20* and *Rhythmus 21*, and also neo-realist films – the camera in cinema does not set out to generate 'narrative sequence', but it is 'as if the sequence-shot suggested a network of associated images, a potential constellation of situations, people, objects'.[107] This *dispositif*, or 'constellation', by its charges and discharges, produces 'arhythmy' – very slow or very fast shots – by which a 'tremendous potential' or *jouissance* may emerge.[108] Lyotard says of such shots, and that we can also say of experimental, B-grade and 'splatter' cinema: 'The intensity of these moments comes from the ambiguity of the realities that they present.'[109] Terrains 'open out' in 'splatter' film in ways that are ambiguous in relation to the real, not just because of the use of special effects, but because there is an impossibility in seeing what is seen. There is a sovereign operation at the core of this impossibility.

'Splatter' films are exemplary of the condition of the affective 'opening out' of intensities by which the spectator is 'opened out'. As MacCormack writes in her essay 'Zombies without Organs: Gender, Flesh, and Fissure' – an essay that has import for redefining a kind of Open as well as redefining the kind of spectatorship that takes place for the zombie film:

> the viewer must form an assemblage with the image so that intensities rather than actual acts are catalysts for refoldings of the flesh and desire. Horror impinges on and creates new thresholds of intensities and undulates as durations and events of corporeal dismantling.[110]

Intensities in alliance with the cinematic assemblage – an assemblage that includes the viewer and the image – act as a *dispositif* for an 'opening out' to communication/communion. Horror films that include the kind of gore shots to which MacCormack refers, produce a heterogeneous assemblage by which components in the *dispositif*, including the spectator, are invested or charged: such shots are only one such *dispositif* that the spectator is heterogeneously 'opened out' in. 'Splatter', by this argument, has the force of *jouissance*. That is, it has the effect of what Ashley Woodward calls the 'sensuous immediacy of the cinematic material' for the spectator in its communication of intensities.[111]

In 'The Idea of a Sovereign Film', Lyotard gives us several ways of understanding the operation of intensities – the 'intense instants, temporal spasms' that make up a kind of communication that is not engaged in exchange[112] – for the sovereign film. The operations of intensities for the sovereign film constitute a 'network of associated images' or a 'constellation',[113] and are the 'antipodes of authority'.[114] These operations can be seen as similar to the energetic cathexis of components in the *dispositif*. The sovereign operation is a heterogeneous 'opening out' of the spectator to intensities that the spectator is already 'opened out' in. We can see such 'opening out' in both examples of the sovereign operation that I have given: automutilation and metonymy.

What then constitutes a sovereign film? If the *dispositif* of cinema generates a 'disintensification' of intensities – the channelling and exploitation of intensities – for cognitive exchange and the interpretation of a film, how can we identify a film that engages in the expenditure of general economy that evokes a sovereign spectator? While we can characterise a general economy as that which is beyond exchange by which there is a sovereign spectator, what we come to is that, as Lyotard writes, no film can be sovereign as such, because in describing a film what one describes is an 'objective totality'.[115] An 'objective totality' – that which is described when one describes a film, including a film's diegesis – is different to the intensities 'felt' by the spectator by which 'I' become engaged in the sovereign operation. To find sovereignty in the image as a particular kind of spectatorial mode – to bring the image into communication/communion, as such – is a different thing altogether to analyse than text or subject; it is to characterise sovereignty as a particular kind of surplus expenditure in which the film spectator is 'at stake'.

According to Lyotard, sovereign film is 'incompatible' with 'objective totality': a textual analysis of a film that is sovereign – a sovereign film – is impossible.[116] If the pulse is a particular kind of spectatorship that is sovereign, this means that the pulse can only be seen as a particular kind of spectatorship that is an 'idea' of spectatorship as sovereign but that is ultimately impossible.[117] While there is evidence of a general economy in Bataille's own writing and in both the films I have analysed, the pulse entails intensities – the force of ecstasy or *jouissance* – that have no productive return or exchange. The pulse has the general economy of surplus or 'loss'. What the pulse gives is a way of thinking about a particular kind of energetic surplus or communication/communion. The pulse is both what defines the coherence of a system as discrete and integrated, and as a return that is not followed through because it is Open. However, in an analysis of Bataille's writings and of film, what occurs is an impossibility to grasp the pulse and situate it in cinema. The pulse gives us a certain way of thinking about an energetic surplus and an experience for a film spectator, but it cannot be limited to a reading of a film's diegesis, composition, or even its shots. In other words, this chapter, as the climax of the book, should have led to a reading of the pulse through sovereign film. What we find instead is a failure at the site of this reading because a general economy of expenditure does not enter into exchange and therefore into meaning. The pulse can be characterised by an energetic surplus that communicates and generates communion for spectators – the pulse is 'felt' and even sometimes it is not – but it cannot necessarily be identified in the textual analysis of a film. The pulse is then a strange theory for cinema, which gives a reading for a 'felt' film spectatorship but is compromised at the site of a textual analysis of the film itself. The pulse is found in the 'felt' intensities it produces, and not necessarily in the reading of the film text per se.

This inability of the pulse to be textually analysed seems counter to the way that scriptwriters, for instance, talk about there being a pulse or iambic metre in successful screenplay dialogue.[118] It also seems counter to the way that scriptwriters indicate a significant emotional turning point in a scene by using the parenthetical 'beat' in a screenplay. Choreographers and editors use movement and rhythm – the latter choosing takes and cuts, and using the rate of cuts – to supply a pulse to film.[119] (It is interesting that, via the choreographer, this third example also enables the gestural body on screen to generate a pulse for cinema.) If the pulse is a sovereign operation, or presupposes the sovereignty of the spectator, the pulse in film is not in the text and cannot be textually analysed, but is in the energetic exchange between the spectator and the image. The pulse is in the *dispositif*.

The films that I have chosen to analyse in this chapter demonstrate the movement and affect of the pulse. For, after all, the 'opening out' to *jouissance* – the ecstasy that opens the body to an outside in automutilation – is just another 'excessive movement' in the midst of 'immobility'. The 'contagion' of metonymy is just another way to characterise the Open of duration; Open because it puts identity 'at stake' to derive the contiguity of 'contagion'. The resistance that the pulse poses to textual analysis is itself also interesting. In light of the pulse, automutilation and metonymy resist being delimited by meaning and interpretative acts. If the pulse is the channelling and exploitation of intensities at the site of the 'opening out' of the libidinal band/skin by the *dispositif*, sovereignty is a resistance to authority; a resistance that is not a 'rebellion' or an 'appeal', but an inadvertent yearning for communication/communion.[120] What these films precipitate then, because intensities are outside of exchange and enter into communication/communion nonetheless, is the operation of a general economy of the pulse.

Notes

1. Lyotard, 'Acinema', pp. 34–5.
2. Lyotard, 'Acinema', p. 39.
3. Derrida, 'From Restricted to General Economy', p. 254.
4. Lyotard, 'Acinema', p. 34.
5. Variations include Germany, where it was released as *Voodoo, Horror Island of Zombies*, and the UK and Australia, where it was released as *Zombie Flesh Eaters*.
6. Arnzen describes Romero's *Night of the Living Dead* (1968) as 'the "primordial" splatter film because it was the first to use gore and graphic violence to reveal "an amoral world where evil cannot be easily contained"' (Arnzen, 'Who's Laughing Now?', p. 177).
7. Derrida, 'From Restricted to General Economy', p. 254.
8. Bataille, *Inner Experience*, p. 191.
9. Bataille describes a 'sustained' continuum in experience when he writes of laughter: 'I do believe in the possibility of beginning with the experience of laughter and not relinquishing it when one passes from this particular experience to its neighbour, the sacred or the poetic' (Bataille, 'Un-knowing', p. 93).
10. Lyotard, 'Acinema', p. 34.
11. Lyotard, 'Acinema', p. 35.
12. Lyotard, 'The Idea of a Sovereign Film', p. 62.
13. Trahair, 'The Comedy of Philosophy', p. 159.
14. Bataille, 'Un-knowing', p. 93.
15. Bataille, *Inner Experience*, p. 16.
16. Derrida, 'From Restricted to General Economy', p. 255.
17. Derrida writes: 'To rush headlong into death pure and simple is thus to risk the absolute loss of meaning, in the extent to which meaning necessarily traverses the truth of the master and of self-consciousness. One risks losing the effect and profit of meaning which were the very *stakes* one hoped *to win*' (Derrida, 'From Restricted to General Economy', p. 255).
18. Bataille, *Inner Experience*, p. 191.
19. Bataille, *Inner Experience*, p. 191.
20. As James Creech writes in a footnote to his essay 'Julia Kristeva's Bataille: Reading as Triumph': 'Inasmuch as it is a meaningful term (which is already the crux of the problem), "sovereignty" is in a diacritical relation to the Hegelian term of "mastery". As such, it seeks but necessarily fails to denote the absolute other, radically outside of the dialectical movement in which

mastery is encompassed. Essentially, mastery seeks by risking itself to recuperate all losses in the end, and thereby sustain itself as mastery. Sovereignty retains nothing, spending or losing everything "sans réserve". It is for this reason that sovereignty is absolutely sovereign, that is, absolutely different from mastery, owing it nothing. The matrices of sovereign sacrifice for Bataille are the erotic, the poetic, the sacred, the comic.

The difficulty which one encounters in trying to speak of the absolutely other without compromising its otherness can not be surmounted by speaking in the Hegelian terms which are themselves dialectical and which therefore appropriate alterity' (Creech, 'Julia Kristeva's Bataille', footnote 3, p. 63).

21. Shaviro, 'Post-Cinematic Affect', p. 5.
22. Massumi, *Parables for the Virtual*, pp. 27, 125.
23. Bataille, 'The Use Value of D. A. F. de Sade', pp. 94–5.
24. Bataille, 'Sacrifice', p. 61.
25. Derrida writes: 'Laughter alone exceeds dialectics and the dialectician: it bursts out only on the basis of an absolute renunciation of meaning, an absolute risking of death, what Hegel calls abstract negativity' (Derrida, 'From Restricted to General Economy', p. 256).
26. Trahair, *The Comedy of Philosophy*, pp. 25–7.
27. Krauss, 'The Im/Pulse to See', p. 51.
28. Krauss, 'Antivision', p. 149.
29. *Oxford English Dictionary Online*. Available at <https://www.oed.com/view/Entry/13367?rskey=wQ1uro&result=9> (last accessed 19 January 2020).
30. Shaviro, 'Contagious Allegories', p. 87.
31. Krauss, 'Antivision', p. 154.
32. Bataille, 'The Economy Equal to the Universe', p. 34.
33. Bataille, 'The Economy Equal to the Universe', pp. 34–5.
34. Bataille, 'Rotten Sun', p. 57.
35. Bataille, 'Rotten Sun', p. 57.
36. Bataille, 'Sacrificial Mutilation', p. 68.
37. See Shaviro, 'Film Theory and Visual Fascination', pp. 52–3; Bordwell, 'Mimetic Theories of Narration', pp. 3–15; Grodal, *Moving Pictures*; Smith, *Engaging Characters*; Rutherford, 'What Makes a Film Tick?'
38. Lyotard, *Libidinal Economy*, p. 17.
39. Waite, *Oxford Dictionary*, p. 398.
40. Carroll, *The Philosophy of Horror*, p. 52.
41. Bataille writes in *Eroticism*: 'We are discontinuous beings, individuals who perish in isolation in the midst of an incomprehensible adventure, but we yearn for our lost continuity' (Bataille, *Eroticism*, p. 15). And continues: 'In essence, the domain of eroticism is the domain of violence, of violation . . . Only violence can bring everything to a state of flux in this way, only violence and the nameless disquiet bound up with it' (Bataille, *Eroticism*, pp. 16–17).
42. Grant, 'Glossary', p. x.

See Roman Jakobson and Morris Halle in their 1956 essay 'Two Aspects of Language and Two Types of Aphasic Disturbances', and also Lacan, for a description of Freudian 'displacement' in terms of metonymy. Lacan uses the association of metaphor with condensation and metonymy with displacement to argue that the unconscious is 'structured like a language' (Jakobson and Halle, 'Two Aspects of Language', p. 81; Lacan, 'The Agency of the Letter', p. 147).

43. de Man, 'The Rhetoric of Temporality', p. 207.
44. Jakobson and Halle, 'Two Aspects of Language', p. 81.
45. Bataille writes: 'There is no longer subject=object, but "gapping [sic] breach" between one and the other and, in the breach, subject and object are dissolved, there is a passage, communication, but not from one to the other: *one* and the *other* have lost their distinct existence' (Bataille, *Inner Experience*, p. 64).
46. Barthes, 'The Metaphor of the Eye', p. 126.
47. Bataille, *Story of the Eye*, pp. 9–67.
48. Barthes, 'The Metaphor of the Eye', p. 119.
49. Barthes, 'The Metaphor of the Eye', p. 122.
50. Bataille, *Story of the Eye*, p. 66.
51. Bataille, *Story of the Eye*, p. 54.
52. Bataille, *Story of the Eye*, p. 54.
53. Barthes, 'The Metaphor of the Eye', p. 124.
54. Bataille, *Story of the Eye*, p. 53.
55. Bataille, *Story of the Eye*, p. 54.
56. Barthes, 'The Metaphor of the Eye', p. 125.
57. Barthes, 'The Metaphor of the Eye', pp. 121, 125.
58. Bataille, 'Un-knowing', p. 93.
59. Barthes, 'The Metaphor of the Eye', p. 126.
60. Barthes, 'The Metaphor of the Eye', p. 126.
61. Barthes writes about this 'violation': 'It makes possible, at the very level of speech, a counter-division of objects, usages, meanings, spaces, and properties that is eroticism itself' (Barthes, 'The Metaphor of the Eye', p. 126).
62. Bataille, *Inner Experience*, p. 64.
63. Lyotard, 'Acinema', p. 35.
64. Lyotard, 'Acinema', p. 35.
65. Available at <http://sensesofcinema.com/2004/perversion/perversion_intro> (last accessed 17 January 2020).
66. Bataille, 'The Use Value of D. A. F. de Sade', pp. 94–5.
67. Lyotard, 'Acinema', p. 35.
68. Bergson, *Matter and Memory*, p. 258.
69. Bataille, *Inner Experience*, p. 97.
70. Barthes writes about Bataille's *Story of the Eye*: 'The Eye's substitutes are *declined* in every sense of the term: recited like flexional forms of the one word; revealed like states of the one identity; offered like propositions none of which can hold more meaning than another; filled out like successive

moments in the one story. On its metaphorical journey the Eye thus both varies and endures; its essential form subsists through the movement of a nomenclature like that of a physical space, because here each inflexion is a new noun, speaking a new usage' (Barthes, 'The Metaphor of the Eye', pp. 120–1).
71. Bataille, 'Sacrificial Mutilation', p. 70.
72. Bataille, *Inner Experience*, p. 125.
73. Shaviro writes in his text *Passion and Excess* on the uncategorisability of the *expérience-limite* (*limit-experience*): 'Thought, at the limit, is uncategorizable, because it is entirely visceral: *literally* spasmodic and excremental' (Shaviro, *Passion and Excess*, pp. 85–6).
74. Bataille, 'The Obelisk', p. 222.
75. Shaviro, *Passion and Excess*, p. 37.
76. Bataille, 'Propositions', p. 200.
77. Bataille, 'Propositions', p. 200.
78. Bataille writes of 'pure loss' in life as the 'limit of growth': 'Life being unable to endlessly invest itself usefully consumes itself in *pure loss*' (Bataille, 'The Economy Equal to the Universe', p. 35).
79. *Dawn of the Dead*'s setting in a shopping mall has seen it regaled as a parody of society's consumerism. The ideological concerns of Fulci's films are based in Catholicism and soul possession, which are not seen in *Dawn of the Dead*'s consumer world despite the catchline and emphatic reflective summation by Peter as he recollects a line his grandfather used to recite as a voodoo priest in Trinidad: 'When there's no more room in hell, the dead will walk the earth.'
80. Shaviro, 'Post-Cinematic Affect', p. 3.
81. Baudry, 'Ideological Effects', pp. 286–98.
82. Woodward, 'A Sacrificial Economy of the Image', p. 143; Lyotard, 'The Idea of a Sovereign Film', p. 62.
83. Shaviro, 'Film Theory and Visual Fascination', p. 45.
84. Shaviro, 'Film Theory and Visual Fascination', p. 45.
85. MacCormack, 'Zombies without Organs', p. 98.
86. Shaviro, 'Post-Cinematic Affect', p. 6; quoting from Jameson, *Postmodernism*, pp. 53–4.
87. Shaviro, 'Post-Cinematic Affect', p. 3.
88. Shaviro, 'Post-Cinematic Affect', p. 3.
89. Shaviro, 'Post-Cinematic Affect', p. 5; quoting from Jameson, *Postmodernism*, p. 16.
90. Shaviro, 'Post-Cinematic Affect', p. 5.
91. Shaviro, 'Post-Cinematic Affect', footnote 14, p. 16.
92. Lyotard, 'Acinema', pp. 35–6.
93. Lyotard, 'Acinema', p. 35.
94. Lyotard, 'The Idea of a Sovereign Film', p. 62.
95. Woodward, 'A Sacrificial Economy of the Image', p. 149.
96. Lyotard, 'The Idea of a Sovereign Film', p. 69.

97. Lyotard, 'The Idea of a Sovereign Film', p. 62.
 98. Shaviro, 'Film Theory and Visual Fascination', p. 26.
 99. Shaviro, 'Film Theory and Visual Fascination', p. 45.
100. Lyotard, 'The Idea of a Sovereign Film', p. 62.
101. Michelson, 'Heterology', p. 112.
102. Lyotard, 'The Idea of a Sovereign Film', p. 62.
103. Woodward, 'A Sacrificial Economy of the Image', p. 143.
104. MacCormack, 'Zombies without Organs', p. 95.
105. Lyotard, 'The Idea of a Sovereign Film', p. 62.
106. MacCormack, 'Zombies without Organs', p. 95.
107. Lyotard, 'The Idea of a Sovereign Film', p. 66.
108. Lyotard, 'The Idea of a Sovereign Film', p. 66; quoting from Bazin, 'André Gide', p. 74.
109. Lyotard, 'The Idea of a Sovereign Film', p. 68.
110. MacCormack, 'Zombies without Organs', p. 96. MacCormack writes about the 'assemblage' in line with Deleuze and Guattari's body without organs. See Deleuze and Guattari, *A Thousand Plateaus*, p. 159.
111. Woodward, 'A Sacrificial Economy of the Image', p. 143.
112. Lyotard, 'The Idea of a Sovereign Film', p. 62.
113. Lyotard, 'The Idea of a Sovereign Film', p. 66.
114. Lyotard, 'The Idea of a Sovereign Film', p. 69.
115. Lyotard, 'The Idea of a Sovereign Film', pp. 69–70.
116. Lyotard, 'The Idea of a Sovereign Film', p. 69.
117. Lyotard, 'The Idea of a Sovereign Film', p. 69.
118. Boyle, 'Visual Mindscape'. Available at <http://www.scriptmag.com/features/visual-mindscape-pulse-screenplay-dialogue> (last accessed 17 January 2020).
119. In *Cutting Rhythms: Shaping the Film Edit*, Karen Pearlman defines the pulse: 'A single pulsation is the extra effort placed on one part of a movement compared to the less intensively energetic other parts of the movement. So, just as in the beating of a heart, there is a continuous on/off of emphasis points, accents on words, gestures, camera moves, colors, or any other pro-filmic event. Actors may develop characters in part by developing a distinguishing pulse; that is, the energy and speed with which they put emphasis on words, gestures, etc. Pulses are shaped by the energy or intention behind movement or speech and make that energy or intention perceptible to the spectator.' And later: 'Pulses in movement are shaped by choreographers and editors into phrases' (Pearlman, *Cutting Rhythms*, pp. 28, 29).
120. Lyotard, 'The Idea of a Sovereign Film', p. 62.

CHAPTER 5

Blood and Convulsive Affect: Vectors of the Pulse as Sovereign Operations

In Stanley Kubrick's *The Shining* (1980), blood represents the horrific past of the isolated snowbound hotel, the Overlook. Brushing his teeth in front of his bathroom mirror, young Danny Torrance (Danny Lloyd) receives a clairvoyant 'shining' from 'Tony', who is a 'little boy that lives in [his] mouth' and who is characterised for Danny in a voice that comes from the back of his throat and the puppet-like movement of his index finger. 'Tony' confirms that Danny's father Jack Torrance (Jack Nicholson) has been offered a job at the Overlook Hotel, and Danny receives a vision of the two large art deco doors of the elevator in the hotel lobby. Blood rushes through the two doors and fills the lobby. The occupants of the hotel, two girls (played by Lisa and Louise Burns), each wearing a blue party dress, hold hands as the blood surges around them. With the girls' backs to the elevator doors, the blood enveloping them, the blood gushes towards Danny in this clairvoyant vision and the spectators of the film. Later Wendy Torrance (Shelley Duvall), Danny's mother, has the same vision as she stumbles through the hotel away from her axe-wielding husband.

The blood in this scene represents the hidden past of the hotel, which was the site of the horrific murder in 1970 (ten years earlier) of the two girls and their mother at the hands of their father Charles Grady, the former winter caretaker of the hotel. After killing them with an axe, he stacked their bodies in a room in the west wing and then committed suicide with a double-barrelled shotgun. Blood also points to the 'loss' of self that is at the core of the film. Jack Torrance is lured into the psychic horror and murderous intentions of the former occupants of the hotel. The engulfing stream of blood signifies the engulfing horrors of the hotel as the Torrance family rapidly find themselves victims of the hotel's murderous past, their own subjectivity occupied by the actions and subjectivities of the hotel's former occupants. Blood, in other words, is the link between the present and the past in this film. In this chapter, I adopt possession, and even dispossession, to consider what we 'possess', or share, in blood, and also the trajectory of the 'loss' of self by expenditure – a dispossession – through affective blood.

In Brian De Palma's *Carrie* (1976), blood remains safe only as long as it is recognised within the strictures of society. Blood disturbs, and is representative of humiliation and loss of control. In the gymnasium shower Carrie (Sissy Spacek) finds herself 'inexplicably' bleeding. At her outburst, the other girls turn on Carrie, pelting her with tampons and chanting 'plug it up'. Chris Hargenson (Nancy Allen), banned from the prom owing to her part in Carrie's humiliation, plots to ruin Carrie's prom experience. Exchanging the prom king and queen ballot, Chris has Carrie delighted to be made prom queen by her fellow class members, only to further humiliate her as a bucket of pig's blood tumbles down from the rafters, covering Carrie's face and dress. While Carrie vents her anger and returns her peer's 'joke' twofold by literally 'bringing the house down' using her telekinetic powers, what is demonstrated by the film is that it is not blood, but the emotions around blood, that are destructive. Blood acts as the vector for the affective release of humiliation and 'loss' of self that occurs in this affective release. That is, the affective intensity of blood gives rise to the magnitude and direction of the 'loss' of self in this humiliation.

In Terry Gilliam and Terry Jones's *Monty Python and the Holy Grail* (1975), there is an excess of blood, which spurts vigorously from severed limbs. Blood instigates a relationship between characters that threatens proximity. In a scene in which King Arthur (Graham Chapman) progressively lops off the limbs of the Black Knight (John Cleese) who guards the pass over the bridge, blood spurts from the Black Knight's 'flesh wounds', bringing into question the conservative decorum of the wounded.[1] Arthur's witty response to the Black Knight's threats, 'What are you going to do, bleed on me?', gestures towards the ineffectual threat of the Black Knight who has lost both his arms and one leg, although the irony lies in the potential threat of blood, which, spurting forth, disrupts the (contained) subjectivity of those bleeding and those potentially bled upon.

Blood is everywhere in cinema. That is, blood is in images, in metaphors, in dialogue, and appears across all genres. Blood is everywhere in cinema in the sense that it is a shared relation with the spectator. This chapter will consider what blood does in cinema in relation to the pulse. In notable 'horror' scenes in Kubrick's *The Shining*, De Palma's *Carrie* and Gilliam and Jones's *Monty Python and the Holy Grail*, it is possible to find a relation to blood that demonstrates both the affective operation of blood and the expenditures of a 'loss' of the unified self. In all three films blood is figured as excess and proximity. Blood signifies a literal 'loss' of the self and a potentially intimate communication between bodies in proximity to or contact with blood. Blood is a real threat to the affective body: of intimacy, of 'loss' of self.

I will show how the pulse, and the 'exposure' of the pulse in the spillage of blood, has a particular kind of movement in film. The contraction and dilation of the heart muscle, and the resulting bursts or shocks of blood as the heart valves open and close, cause the pulsatile wave of distension in the arteries. The movement of the pulse is erratic and jerky, extending to freedoms and contracting in a way that settles into an organic, but convulsive, kind of rhythm. Because the organic pulse is convulsive in its movement at the same time as it is the minimal condition for sensation, it is a 'convulsive affect'. Convulsive affect, by my theorisation, is found in moments of horror and eroticism because they induce the spasms of the affect of terror and ecstasy. Convulsive affect, as the possession of emotions that gives rise to the dispossession of the self, is different from conceptions of affect which understand the spectator as a unified subject. My conception of convulsive affect recognises intensity 'coming into being' for a subjectivity that is breached, 'opened', or expended, giving way to a dispossession of self and 'continuity' with others. As we saw in Chapter 2, the Open relation of spectator and image generates a continuum of communication in the network of relations. I propose here that the convulsively affective nature of the movement of blood allows for an Open relationship for communication between the spectator and the image.

I determine what a spectatorship of convulsive affect and dispossession would be by demonstrating the way Andrzej Żuławski's *Possession* (1981) implicates the spectator in a form of intimate communication by an economy of affect that leads to a dispossession of the self.[2] The film features scenes in which blood flows from bodies. As with so many horror films, spilled blood comprises a kind of ritualistic dispossession of the self. However, I suggest that this is a dispossession of the self that occurs in the experience of eroticism and violence and, in these moments, makes the self 'continuous' with others. The erotic and violent experience is an experience of convulsive affect, 'amorous frenzy', or expenditure.[3] In these experiences, the sacrifice of self or 'putting at stake' has already occurred, or is in a constant state of occurring. As of 'loss', there is no originary or unified subject in Bataille's notion of sovereignty, just an operation. In this sense, there is no unified subjectivity of characters or spectators, simply affective expenditure and a 'yearning' for 'continuity' with others that requires a kind of dispossession of the self for communion to take place.[4]

This chapter develops my characterisation of the pulse by describing the vectors of the pulse that make affect pass from movement to relations:

the vector is the force (magnitude and direction) of transmission (the transport), just as the pulse is the force of transmission (the transport) for blood. The convulsive and affective behaviour of the pulse is constituted of vectors, and sovereignty's 'putting at stake' is the magnitude and direction of these vectors. Insofar as the vector is the means of relating one point to another I find that the excessive movement of blood, and the dispossession of the individual self through blood, creates an intimate communication between characters, film and spectators that brings about the complicity in the affect of horror.

Andrzej Żuławski's *Possession* (1981)

Żuławski's *Possession* is a film about love, or rather, the question of whether it is possible to possess love, and the violence one does to oneself because of love. The scenario details the relationship of a married couple, Mark (Sam Neill) and Anna (Isabelle Adjani). Mark is a secret agent who arrives home after an assignment to a troubled marriage: Anna tells him she wants to leave him. They disagree over the care of their son Bob (Michael Hogben).[5]

The question of what one possesses in love and indeed, whether one can possess the love of the 'other' by a self-generation of it, is raised by the production of two doppelgängers in *Possession*: Mark produces a doppelgänger of Anna in Helen (also played by Isabelle Adjani) and Anna produces a doppelgänger of Mark (also played by Sam Neill). Delivering Bob to school, Mark meets Bob's school teacher, Helen, and mistakes her for Anna. Mark seeks out Heinrich (Heinz Bennent) with whom Anna has been having an affair, though they both soon discover a more shocking union in which Anna is involved. Mark's hired private detective (Carl Duering) is glassed by Anna with a broken wine bottle after he follows her to her new apartment and discovers her secret – an inhuman, half-formed creature in the bathroom. After the disappearance of the private detective, the head of the detective agency and lover of the private detective, Zimmermann (Shaun Lawton), decides to follow one of his leads and is also maliciously murdered by Anna. Given information by Mark, Heinrich follows Anna to her apartment. After finding the apartment, seeing the body parts of the detectives in the refrigerator, and the monster, Heinrich flees. When Heinrich arranges a meeting with Mark in a bar to tell him of what he has seen, Mark knocks him out and drowns him in the bathroom toilet bowl. Mark arrives at Anna's apartment to find her making love to the creature. From her sighs of 'Almost . . . almost . . . almost . . .' and the various stages of development in which the creature has been witnessed, it can be supposed that, fed on meat (the flesh of Anna's victims, as well as meat she minces for this purpose) and with Anna's love, this creature is slowly being brought to realisation.

Possession shows how the production of doppelgängers by Mark and Anna requires the expenditure of energy. In an earlier sequence, Anna tells Mark where she has been. Having left a church, Anna is carrying milk and eggs in a string shopping bag through a subway tunnel. Seized by convulsions that cause her to throw herself and the shopping bag in a vodoun-like trance against the tiled walls of the tunnel, Anna throws herself 'suddenly *outside of*' herself in a literal bloody miscarriage.[6] Anna calls this the miscarriage of 'sister faith' (which she then had to protect in her apartment), leaving her with 'sister chance'. The splatter of the milk and eggs against the tiled walls as Anna convulses pre-empts the milky vomit and blood that splatters onto the tiled floor from Anna's body moments later.

Later, Anna introduces Mark to the 'completed' creation, Mark's doppelgänger. At this moment the police arrive and shoot Mark and Anna. Anna, however, makes the fatal suicidal shot and Mark tumbles from the stairs to die at the bottom of the stairwell. Mark's doppelgänger escapes the scene. Helen (the school teacher), who is looking after Bob, hears a knock on the front door of her apartment. Bob hurries from the room, repeating 'Don't answer it, don't answer it, don't answer it . . . ' Helen goes to answer the door. At this moment Bob throws himself into the bathtub full of water where he floats face down, and a bombing raid begins outside. It is the creation and meeting of this new breed of doppelgänger (of Mark and of Anna) made on, as Anna says, the miscarriage of 'sister faith' and the possibility of 'sister chance', that signifies the apocalyptic at the close of the film.

Possession and Dispossession

The definition of the word 'possession' will inform the analysis I make of Żuławski's film, which further feeds into the kind of cinematic spectator constructed in this book. *Possession* possesses quantities of movement and affect – the film is convulsively affective – even as these aspects dispossess characters and even spectators. 'Possession' is variously defined in the *Oxford Dictionary of English* as:

> 1. *[mass noun]* The state of having, owning, or controlling something.
> 1.1 *Law* Visible power or control over something, as distinct from lawful ownership; holding or occupancy as distinct from ownership.
> 2. (usually **possessions**) Something that is owned or possessed.

2.1 A territory or country controlled or governed by another.
3. *[mass noun]* The state of being controlled by a demon or spirit.
3.1 The state of being completely dominated by an idea or emotion.[7]

The verb 'possess' also gives the literary meaning: '3. *literary* (of a man) have sexual intercourse with'.[8]

While these definitions are largely characterised by mastery and self-possession as they relate to control and ownership, in fact, a preserve of the law, I contend that the ideas or emotions that one is in possession of, or is possessed by, are those which, impossibly excessive, drive one to a state of convulsive affect, and to, in fact, dispossession.

The literary meaning of the verb 'possess', quoted from the *Oxford Dictionary of English* – 'have sexual intercourse with' – also suggests a possible reading of Żuławski's *Possession*. In this film Anna creates a literal doppelgänger of Mark by having sexual intercourse with the embryonic doppelgänger. One could say that Anna possesses herself by putting herself in the 'state of being completely dominated by an idea or emotion'.[9] Anna is possessed of emotions when she has sexual intercourse with the embryonic doppelgänger. This possession is, in fact, a dispossession because she sacrifices herself to an expenditure of these emotions for the creation of the doppelgänger. It is this possession in dispossession that entails the absolute 'other' of mastery and subjectivity. Possession in dispossession is not so much a contradiction as the absolute 'other' of the dialectical movement, which is expenditure and sacrifice. Expenditure, in this case, is Anna's convulsive and affective 'loss' in sexual intercourse by which the dispossession of self also occurs. Another reading can be made in which the film spectator is similarly possessed of emotions and dispossessed by convulsive and affective expenditure in relation to the image.

Dispossession is not simply an opposition to possession. In his essay 'Hegel, Death and Sacrifice', Bataille writes about how possession is associated with the emotions of horror and pleasure released in sacrifice and, for this reason, has more in common with dispossession:

> possession was associated in its time with the image of sacrifice; it was a sacrifice in which woman was the victim ... That association from ancient poetry is very meaningful; it refers back to a precise state of sensibility in which the sacrificial element, the feeling of sacred horror itself, joined, in a weakened state, to a tempered pleasure; in which, too, the taste for sacrifice and the emotion which it released seemed in no way contrary to the ultimate uses of pleasure.[10]

Yet in *Eroticism* he seems to contradict his earlier contention by arguing that the erotic, as a matrix of sovereign sacrifice, is an opening of the self to intimate communication. Dispossession, in this sense, is found in the act of sacrifice at the same time as dispossession enables intimate communication or communion. The erotic is a transition from one state to another – a drive to dissolution of the self and 'continuity' with the 'other'. The opening of the self to intimate communication breaches the discontinuity between self and other. Eroticism is dispossession in the scissiparity that is inherent in cell division in sexual reproduction,[11] as well as the dispossession of self as an emotional state – a 'state of flux'.[12] We can say that there is this operation of dispossession in the creation of the doppelgängers in *Possession*. Anna's creation of the doppelgänger is generated through the 'amorous frenzy' or convulsive affect of the vodoun-like trance and also by the cell division intrinsic to sexual reproduction.[13]

In *Possession*, dispossession is induced by the expenditures operative in movement and affect. These expenditures mean that dispossession is the absolutely 'other' of the dialectic because it retains nothing and expends everything. Characters are in a constant state of movement in *Possession*. There is expenditure in the movement that the characters engage in: it is a kind of excessive movement for its own sake. Mark, in his depressive delirium after Anna leaves him, for example, thrashes back and forth on the bed, and, while waiting for Anna to get home and watching the video made by Heinrich of Anna teaching ballet, violently rocks himself back and forth in a rocking chair. Heinrich, for his part, twists and turns in the stairwell while talking to Mark about Anna's whereabouts. In the detective's office explaining how he wants Anna followed, Mark again swings back and forth in the office chair, while Zimmermann, the head of the detective agency, swings in *his* chair. The rhythm of one chair bounces off the rhythm of the other, as each man demonstrates his level of ease through the speed of the rhythm at which he swings – Mark more vigorously than Zimmermann. While speaking to Heinrich's mother on the telephone – a conversation in which she claims to have found Heinrich's body (but not his soul) – Mark flicks a light switch on and off. In contrast, Anna's convulsive movements culminate in her throwing herself against the walls of the subway in a vodoun-like trance.

There is a dispossession of the self that occurs via the intention to possess the other through the production of doppelgängers. Mark and Anna both miscarry their love for each other by recreating the other outside of themselves as doppelgängers. This generation of doppelgängers is a very literal metaphor for love as dispossession of the self for possession of the 'other'. The self by love or erotic expenditure must be dispossessed to give birth to the 'other', which is more self than 'other'. But love in *Possession* is also a casting out – a dispossession – of the love for the 'other'. This

Figure 5.1 Mark thrashes back and forth on the bed. *Possession* (Andrzej Żuławski, 1981)

Figure 5.2 Anna grinding meat turns the electric knife on her own throat. *Possession* (Andrzej Żuławski, 1981)

love is what Anna calls protecting 'faith', but is also the casting out – the dispossession – that takes time; the self must be actively expended.

Mark walks into Anna's apartment to find her making love to a monster, and as he approaches the bed Anna sighs between each thrust: 'Almost . . .

almost . . . almost . . . ' With each 'almost' the monster is being brought to life through her love – the monster 'almost' complete, the love-making 'almost' at its climax, the goal 'almost' achieved. Although, as in every love-making act, every goal, this 'almost' is never complete but is always 'almost'. For Bataille, eroticism and the ecstasy of the act bring one closer to 'continuity' with others, but continuity always fails. As Bataille writes: 'We are discontinuous beings, individuals who perish in isolation in the midst of an incomprehensible adventure, but we yearn for our lost continuity.'[14] Continuity with the other is impossible, though we 'yearn' for it, and in the 'amorous frenzy' of copulation we 'throw' ourselves '*outside of*' ourselves.[15] To be possessed is to be convulsively affected by the ecstasy of the erotic moment that is dispossessive.

Possession is about a possession that can never take place, even in the creation of something outside of oneself, which Mark and Anna achieve. In 'throwing out' the creation from oneself, one not only throws out the possibility of possessing the creation, but also the possibility of the possession of oneself: one throws out the self as one would throw out the baby with the bath water. Another form of possession entails spiritual or demonic possession – a reading can be made in which Anna's protection in her apartment of the inhuman miscarried 'faith' is what spiritually or demonically 'possesses' the people who lay eyes upon it. There is also the begging of the question 'whatever possessed you?' I argue, however, that in *Possession*'s sense of 'possession' it is not about being

Figure 5.3 Anna throwing herself, milk and eggs, against the walls of the subway tunnel. *Possession* (Andrzej Żuławski, 1981)

Figure 5.4 Anna seized by convulsions. *Possession* (Andrzej Żuławski, 1981)

Figure 5.5 Anna's miscarriage in the subway tunnel. *Possession* (Andrzej Żuławski, 1981)

in possession of 'something' but rather about being possessed by the 'amorous frenzy' itself; convulsively affected. And this is the meaning of Anna's 'Almost . . . almost . . . almost . . . ' in *Possession*. It is the 'almost' expense to the point at which there is nothing left to lose, and by which all is annihilated.

Body Horror and Convulsive Affect

The movement of the pulse is convulsive because it is not regular or rhythmic. The organic quality of the pulse means that its movement is sudden and jerky. In the *Oxford Dictionary* definition, the pulse also denotes 'a throb or thrill of life, emotion'.[16] The pulse has affective or emotional force. I use these aspects of the pulse to express the movement of bodies and blood in *Possession* and their affective force. Convulsive affect characterises the movement and affective nature of the pulse in horror cinema.

I take the idea of convulsive affect from Linda Williams. In her essay 'Film Bodies: Gender, Genre, and Excess', Williams describes pornography, horror and melodrama, and the bodies on the screen in these 'body genres', in terms of excess. In these genres, she writes, bodies are 'beside [them]sel[ves]' in 'uncontrollable convulsion':

> Visually, each of these ecstatic excesses could be said to share a quality of uncontrollable convulsion or spasm—of the body "beside itself" with sexual pleasure, fear and terror, or overpowering sadness. Aurally, excess is marked by recourse not to the coded articulations of language but to inarticulate cries of pleasure in porn, screams of fear in horror, sobs of anguish in melodrama.[17]

It is these kinds of ecstatic bodies 'beside themselves' working through, not 'articulations', but pertinently, 'inarticulations' of sexual pleasure, fear and terror, or sadness, that resemble the excessive bodies of which I wish to speak. Each of the 'body genres' (pornography, horror, melodrama) as Williams describes them, share 'the spectacle of a body caught in the grip of intense sensation or emotion'.[18] Focusing on 'what could probably best be called a form of ecstasy', bodies on screen 'share a quality of uncontrollable convulsion or spasm'.[19]

The spectators of horror cinema are bodies that are 'beside themselves' as they play out the 'actions' of sexual pleasure, fear, and terror, or the sadness of characters on screen. For the bodies of spectators are bound to the operations of 'uncontrollable convulsion' and the inarticulate cries of sexual pleasure, fear, and terror, or sadness as seen in the operation of bodies on screen. Body horror is the 'display of sensations that are on the edge of respectable' and the importance lies in the effect of this 'on the edge of' on the bodies of spectators.[20] This is not to say that the spectator ever simply mimics the bodies on the screen. As Williams notes: 'we may be wrong in our assumption that the bodies of spectators simply reproduce the sensations exhibited by bodies on the screen'.[21] Rather, what we must take into account are the ways in which body genres enact a scene of desire, as opposed to an object of desire. In the relationship between movement and affect, it is precisely the scene of the phantasy and the arrangement of intensities in the *dispositif* that build up or release tension in the body of the spectator.

Where for Williams the 'ecstatic excesses' seen in pornography, horror, and melodrama 'share a quality of uncontrollable convulsion or spasm – of the body "beside itself" with sexual pleasure, fear and terror, or overpowering sadness',[22] in Bataille's work the 'ecstatic excesses' of both eroticism and violence equally have qualities of uncontrollable convulsion and of the 'rapturous escape from the self'.[23] The body 'beside itself' can be defined in two ways: in the colloquial sense of a body in ecstatic convulsion applied when sensations are high, and in the literal sense, of a body that stands apart from itself, which sees itself convulsed in the pleasures, terror, or sadness of, for example a film, but also stands apart from these sensations in analytical attention to the mechanical apparatus of film and its role in producing these sensations (this standing apart from oneself is a strange way of thinking about the doppelgängers in *Possession*).

The body 'beside itself' also appears in Bataille's essay 'Sacrifices' and even more so, in the ninth section of the essay 'The Pineal Eye' titled 'The Sacrifice of a Gibbon', as a self who exists in a moment of dread, who is also aware of the production of that dread. In his essay 'Sacrifices' Bataille writes:

> *Me*, I exist—suspended in a realized void—suspended from my own dread—different from all other being and such that the various events that can reach all other being and not *me* cruelly throw this *me* out of a total existence. But, at the same time, I consider my coming into the world—which depended on the birth and on the conjunction of a given man and woman, then on the moment of their conjunction. There exists, in fact, a unique moment in relation to the possibility of me—and thus the infinite improbability of this coming into the world appears. For if the tiniest difference had occurred in the course of the successive events of which I am the result, in the place of this *me*, integrally avid to be *me*, there would have been "an *other*."[24]

Bataille writes here about the suspension 'from [his] own dread', by which he seems to experience dread as a body 'beside itself', in awareness of the production of that dread. Furthermore, in this moment of dread 'I' become even more fragmented by the realisation that 'my own' existence has depended on the ecstasy of someone else (my parents), who in a past moment, have produced a 'me' that is a unique moment in the production of 'me'.[25] Both the possibility of experiencing an event, and the realisation of my existence that is dependent on others, fragments 'my' very being.

'I' am the 'here' and 'now' but I am also outside of myself, and even outside the production of myself.

Bodies, in *Possession*, literally put themselves 'beside themselves' by generating doppelgängers. In *Possession*, Mark and Anna both exorcise their love for the other in convulsive affect, recreating the other outside of themselves in the image of their love. Feelings exorcised as subjects are recreated as doppelgängers. In both cases it takes energy to work oneself up to the necessary convulsions by which one loses oneself and forces the other, or love for the other, outside of oneself. These doppelgängers are a horrific self-creation of one's own love. The doppelgänger creations are not a production in the true sense of the word, but a production that is more in the realm of convulsive affect, and thus promote a general economy in which the self is consumed by one's own expenditure. That is, the production of doppelgängers is not machinic, but organic and chancy. The doppelgänger is not self/other but a kind of copy – an asexual reproduction – of one's love for the 'other' produced by the convulsions of an excessive expenditure that forces the 'other' outside the self. The doppelgänger exceeds self and is disseminated.

In cinematic terms, it is not just the characters of film who we see transformed by convulsive affect. The spectator, brought into contact with the film, can only but be transformed: the spectator's individual self is 'lost' to the economy of affect that the film perpetuates. Żuławski claims of cinema: 'This is an instrument of mega force; to go into you, to change you, shape you.'[26]

The Copula and the Copulation of Bodies: The Convulsions of Language and Self, Even (Fucking Language)

The action of the grammatical copula, as Bataille writes about it, is like the action of copulation: the subject is changed or transformed in the 'amorous frenzy' between terms.[27] The operation of the copula is an operation that, as 'the vehicle of amorous frenzy', convulsively affects subjects.[28] Like bodies in erotic encounters, the action of the copula makes the subject and the complement continuous in expenditure, and by this action dispossesses the subject. Using the copula, I show how bodies in erotic and violent states move toward expenditure and dispossession.

Bataille develops the notion of the copula first in relation to parody. In 'The Solar Anus', he conceives of the world as 'purely parodic', wherein each thing is but 'the parody of another', 'is the same thing in a deceptive form'.[29] Such 'total identification' of one thing with another, as well as of the subject and the complement in writing, occurs through the copula.

The copula connects the subject to the complement, but the copula is also a verb or an operation, whereby the complement acts on the subject. This operation of the copula is the 'irritation' to identification that Bataille describes. 'Irritation' evokes movement and affect at the site where subject and complement are joined to one another. Bataille writes: 'But the *copula* of terms is no less irritating than the *copulation* of bodies. And when I scream I AM THE SUN an integral erection results, because the verb *to be* is the vehicle of amorous frenzy.'[30] It is this bringing together of subject and complement in the copula and of bodies in copulation that multiplies the 'frenzy' of meanings and bodies. The 'amorous frenzy' designates movement, force, irritation, operation.

In Bataille's statement 'I AM THE SUN', the copula 'AM' assigns something to the 'I', just as copulation is the operation between, or assigns something to, bodies. It is this 'AM' that situates me in relation to the 'SUN'. 'The copula ["AM"] assigns the subject ["I"] either a description or a definition or a location (geographical or existential) or an occupier.'[31] The 'SUN' (the complement) describes, defines, locates, or occupies the subject. The 'SUN' does not exist as an object in itself, but only 'acts on' the subject, and transforms the subject through the copula 'AM'. The copula/copulation then, refers to the action between terms and bodies that irritates at the form of terms and bodies, transforming them in the 'amorous frenzy'. The operation of the 'AM' degrades the subject and complement to material qualities, just as bodies are degraded to material qualities in copulation. In this copula statement, the subjectivity of the 'I' and the 'SUN' are 'put at stake' – are at the edge of their identity. Something happens to both the 'I' and the 'SUN' in the copula of terms. This 'something' is expenditure, but it is an expenditure that is caused by the operation of the copula and the movement of 'amorous frenzy' between subject and complement.

Bataille, who goes against the grain of conventional grammar, suggests that the copula of terms and copulation of bodies enact a flow of qualities or actions that moves between and dispossesses subjects and complements. The limits of the subject and the complement become unstable as they act on each other – they come to exist at the edge of their own identity whereby the copula is capable of assigning or subtracting. The subject and complement move toward 'continuity' with each other in the 'amorous frenzy'.

In the same essay, Bataille describes all things as, or to be, in copulation:

> The two primary motions are rotation and sexual movement, whose combination is expressed by the locomotive's wheels and pistons.
> These two motions are reciprocally transformed, the one into the other.

> Thus one notes that the earth, by turning, makes animals and men have coitus, and (because the result is as much the cause as that which provokes it) that animals and men make the earth turn by having coitus . . .
>
> An abandoned shoe, a rotten tooth, a snub nose, the cook spitting in the soup of his masters are to love what a battle flag is to nationality.
>
> An umbrella, a sexagenarian, a seminarian, the smell of rotten eggs, the hollow eyes of judges are the roots that nourish love.
>
> A dog devouring the stomach of a goose, a drunken vomiting woman, a sobbing accountant, a jar of mustard represent the confusion that serves as the vehicle of love.[32]

Bataille shows how even the most unlikely objects are transformed by their 'mechanical combination' in copulation.[33] To describe all things with the aid of the copula focuses on the subject as it is transformed in relation to the complement. For example, in the above quote, an abandoned shoe, an umbrella, a dog devouring the stomach of a goose, and so on, are transformed by the location, identification and occupation that the complement assigns. Transformation comes about by the copula 'love'. The use of the copula 'love' assimilates the subject to the 'amorous frenzy' of the erotic experience and, in doing so, transforms and, by making continuous, dispossesses the subject. In this sense, Bataille places importance on the action or 'task' of the copula that 'puts at stake', and even dispossesses the subject.

The transformation of the subject occurs through 'amorous frenzy', movement or materialising force, and the copula insists that the subject has no stability of form. Just as the copula transforms the subject, making it only in relation to its complement, the subject or autonomous 'I' is transformed in relation to the complement, bringing it down to 'base materialism' (*bassesse*). In the instant of representation, the 'I' loses mastery in its relation to the construction of meaning: it is 'put at stake'.

The copula is useful for describing what takes place for the subject in the 'amorous frenzy' or by convulsive affect. Bataille's motive is to demonstrate that sovereign expenditure – a 'putting at stake' or dispossession – is dependent upon those things that cause excessive and disruptive affect, and elicit both 'divine ecstasy and its opposite, extreme horror'.[34] When Bataille writes in the essay 'The Solar Anus', 'I am the *Jesuve*, the filthy parody of the torrid and blinding sun',[35] 'I' am at once produced in this ecstatic moment, in the same instant that the copula in this statement pulls 'me' out of the ecstatic moment and dispossesses 'me'. To be the Jesuve in the copula statement, and to have the qualities of the Jesuve, is to be 'beside oneself' – to be caught up in the ecstatic moment, just as the linguistic signification (and impossibility of that signification) dispossesses and throws 'me' out of 'me'. The 'sacrificial spasm' of ecstasy, Nick Land writes, is not one that is directed to an other for the gain of the self, but rather is a movement of everything being brought into expenditure without return or reserve:

> The ultimate intelligible term of the erotic is not that one negates the other in the interests of self-gratification, but rather that one violates a world which obstructs erotic contact, relinquishing all attachments before the predatory *puissance* of the beloved. Erotic love is an unrestrained violence against everything which stands against communion, and thus against everything that stands; a sacrificial spasm that violates God, cosmos, one's fellows and one's self, in a movement of donation without reserve. As Bataille remarks: 'at the summit the unlimited negation of otherness is the negation of self'.[36]

Like erotic love or copulation, the action of the complement on the subject, put in place by the copula, is that of 'amorous frenzy'.[37] It is a sacrifice or dispossession of self that has the magnitude and direction of the 'rapturous escape from the self'.[38] In this chapter, the magnitude and direction of sovereign expenditure is made visible in cinema in the magnitude and direction of the convulsive movement of characters and the affective force of blood. These characteristics of cinema commit spectators to sovereign expenditure.

The Movement-Image and Vectors of Sensation

The vector is a quantity of magnitude and direction, and in this chapter, has wider meaning in terms of the magnitude and direction of movement and affect. The magnitude and direction of convulsive affect are composed of the sensations that the self possesses and the convulsive movements that dispossess the self. My intention is to understand the magnitude and direction of movement and affect that comprise convulsive affect in *Possession* as vectors of the pulse.

In the glossary of *Cinema 1*, Deleuze defines the vector (or what he also calls the '*line of the universe*') as a 'broken line which brings together singular points or remarkable moments at the peak of their intensity'.[39] We can think about the magnitude and direction of the vector that 'bring together' the 'singular' or 'remarkable moments' of the 'splatter' of blood in horror films in this way. In cinema, vectors bridge the gap between images. That is, the vector lies between images, or is the magnitude and direction of the force that traverses images in what Deleuze calls a 'broken line'.[40]

Generally, eye-line vectors in cinema, like those in a dot-to-dot drawing, work with the logic of connecting the totality of points in space – or the eye-lines of subjects between shots. Such eye-line vectors determine the characters' relation to one another. Vectors suggest totalities (unified subjects) in space, or the relation of frames of film to one another. And yet, vectors are vectors of non-causal movement, precisely because we have moved from the causal world of determinate things to the world of qualities and affects. In Deleuzean terms, qualitative movement is the movement-image's Openness to relations. That is, the vector itself is not in an image, but is the magnitude and direction of intensity and affect in and between images and spectators. The movement-image is characterised by heterogeneous movement, and is irreducible to representation, or rather, the homogeneous space that representation fixes in place (subjects and objects in totality). The vector is then also the magnitude and direction of real movement as the Open of the movement-image, and the force of the intensities that are, I contend, convulsively affective.

Possession is different to films that use eye-line vectors because of the circular and frenzied movement of its characters, but also because of the film's use of mirrors. Mirrors, but more importantly the gulf caused by perpendicular reflections, call attention to the mechanism of reflection and the inability to seal the detachment, bridge the chasm, caused by the two reflections: with this distance, intimate communication and communion seems impossible. Żuławski says of cinema: 'cinema is eyes really, image'.[41] He continues: 'I think that the humility of cinema is to show things, and this is, as I repeat, the glory of it, otherwise do something else.'[42] These two premises – to see and to show – seem surprisingly at odds with *Possession* when we consider the scene in which Mark and Anna are seated at a table in Café Einstein at exterior right angles to one another. They are not facing each other, but are facing away from each other, into the café, even as they converse. There are mirrors behind them so that the point of perspective disappears. The vanishing point has literally vanished between the reflective surfaces of the mirrors that reflect perpendicular views of the café and the gulf caused by those views. Or rather, the trick played on the spectator is that the mirrors are a trap set for the reflecting, reproducing or conveying of something else, and the point at which the camera stands is effaced by the angle of the mirrors. Thus, what is engendered is the gulf, a chasm, into which the camera and camera crew, and even the characters, slip. The division between Mark and Anna is also engendered across and between these two reflective surfaces, so that there is little more that each of them can do than to slip into the trap set by the mirrors.

The forces of inversion set by the mirrors produce a point of 'retortion' by which the skin can be said to be turned in on itself as a kind of dispossession at the moment when one 'hope[s] of taking possession of the

Figure 5.6 Mark and Anna in Café Einstein. *Possession* (Andrzej Żuławski, 1981)

flesh'.⁴³ 'Retortion', like non-production or expenditure, is the moment of dispossession of self. In this sense, Mark's observation of Anna's and his own condition is one that inverts the skin of humanity. Mark does not know how right he is when he questions the humanity (humane-ness?) of Anna's acts.

Anna: I think what you want to do to Bob is . . . [slams hands on table]
Mark: Inhuman? So what you're doing must be human?

There is a point at which ethics is exchanged for the literal act of reproduction, by which a certain kind of non-production takes place. This non-production is expenditure by convulsive affect.

In *Cinema 1*, Deleuze also distinguishes between 'vectorial space' and 'encompassing space'.⁴⁴ While 'vectorial space' is concerned with the intersections or 'peaks' of intensities, where vectors are the force (magnitude and direction) and even the transmitters for intensity, the Encompasser has 'power-qualities as actualised in a milieu'.⁴⁵ Deleuze writes: 'The milieu and its forces incurve on themselves, they act on the character, throw him a challenge, and constitute a situation in which he is caught.'⁴⁶ The milieu as a 'particular space–time, the situation as determining and determinate' is different to the space–time of Deleuze's Open that is an opening of the self to the world and a world that envelops the self.⁴⁷ The Open movement of the pulse whereby the image/world envelops the self is not a determinate space. I want to suggest that the pulse is relevant here to the extent that the pulse also has 'singular points or remarkable moments at the peak of their intensity' like 'vectorial space' does, even if these are out of view or simply 'felt'.[48] What vectors and the pulse have in common – what is measured by the vectors of the pulse – is the force that causes change to come about. Where vectors are the quantities of magnitude and direction that determine the force of the pulse, the pulse has the magnitude and direction of the force of convulsive affect.

We have seen how in Deleuze's *Francis Bacon* a diastole–systole rhythm opens the self to sensation. In the same work Deleuze writes about the 'vector of the sensation' as rhythm.[49] In this text, he analyses Bacon's triptychs, writing:

> Paint the sensation, which is essentially rhythm . . . But in the simple sensation, rhythm is still dependent on the Figure; it appears as the *vibration* that flows through the body without organs, it is the vector of the sensation, it is what makes the sensation pass from one level to another.[50]

What Deleuze suggests here is that rhythm has the force of movement or '*vibration*': 'rhythm takes on an extraordinary amplitude in a *forced movement*'.[51] The movement of rhythm is a vector that enables sensation to pass from one level to another, by which he means the way that sensations pass from one sense to another to be unified into a 'multisensible Figure' by the movement of rhythm.[52] Moreover, the vectors of rhythm have the invisible trajectory of sensation or affect. Deleuze writes that: 'it is not movement that explains the levels of sensation, it is the levels of sensation that explain what remains of movement'.[53] Movement is 'in-place' because in Bacon's work movement is restricted to the single frame of the artwork, or to three images in the triptych. Such movement 'in-place' reveals an intense and violent sensation, which Deleuze writes in Bacon's paintings is characterised as, 'a spasm . . . *the action of invisible forces on the body*'.[54] The single frame has movement by the Opening of self and image/world. That is, rhythm is a 'diastole–systole: the world that seizes me by closing in around me, the self that opens to the world and opens the world itself'.[55] In cinema's reliance on the image, the vector can be expressed in the relation between images or by the Opening of the movement-image in relations. And yet, single frames still have the magnitude and direction of '*forced movement*' that is the vector's valency in sensation.[56]

In returning here to my argument on the difference between the pulse and rhythm from Chapter 2, I want to propose that the movement of the pulse, and not simply rhythm, is vectorial. As much as rhythm is the vector of sensation that makes, as Deleuze writes, 'sensation pass from one level to another',[57] the pulse can be expressed as a vector of convulsive affect that makes affect pass from movement to relations. The magnitude and direction of the vector give the pulse force, so that even though the behaviour of the vector can be formulated mathematically, and the formula used to predict the force and velocity of points or images relative to each other, it is still the affective state of an organic force and velocity that must be taken into account, and which is convulsive by nature.

The Machinic and the Non-Machinic

I have said that the behaviour of the vector can be formulated mathematically, and certainly there is a relationship between the formulation of the vector and the ability of computers to map the magnitude and direction of vectors to predict movement. Here I point to the relationship between the force of the vector and its machinic inscription or register. J. G. Ballard makes it clear that the action of machinic inscription is affective.

In his novel *Crash*, Ballard uses the concept of the vector to talk about an emotional state that is contingent upon the speed and direction of the car-crash: 'Within the car-crash death was directed by the vectors of speed, violence and aggression.'[58] These vectors, for Ballard, are imprinted on the material surfaces of the body. The imprint upon the body in bruises, fractures, and scars made by the car crash are an index of the force of the vector:

> Did Catherine respond to the image of these which had been caught, like a photographic plate or the still from a newsreel, in the dark bruises of my body and the physical outline of the steering wheel? In my left knee the scars above my fractured patella exactly replicated the protruding switches of the windshield wipers and parking lights.[59]

For Ballard, the force of the car crash directed by the vectors of speed is as identifiable as violence and aggression, all of which, in the car crash, are imprinted on the body. Speed has vectors of magnitude and direction, just as the emotional states of violence and aggression do. The force of vectors is described in *Crash* in the moment of collision: 'my knees crushed into the instrument panel as my body moved forwards into its own collision with the interior of the car'.[60] The force of vectors is also apparent in the index of the vector as an imprint upon the body:

> His [Helen Remington's husband] hand had struck some rigid object as he was hurled from his seat, and the pattern of a sign formed itself as I sat there, pumped up by his dying circulation into a huge blood-blister – the triton signature of my radiator emblem.[61]

Analogous to the imprint upon a 'photographic plate or the still from a newsreel' as Ballard describes it,[62] it is not simply the vectors of speed, but the affective forces of violence and aggression in *Crash*, which see the relation between the car and the body as they are imprinted. Ballard thus suggests a relation to the machine, and it is an affective one brought about by the force of the vector.

In his book *The Cinema Effect* Sean Cubitt writes that the vector demonstrates a 'new relation with machines'.[63] Finding this relation of vectors with machines in cinema, Cubitt continues that the vector is found in graphical or animation cinema: 'The secret consciousness of the vector is this human-mechanical hybrid.'[64] In cinematic terms Cubitt differentiates the pixel, the cut and the vector to demonstrate the kind of force that the vector entails:

> Where the cut instigates endings, the vector enacts beginnings. It gives the moving image a future, the possibility of becoming otherwise than it is. The pixel grounds us in the film as a present experience, the cut in the pre-existence of the filmstrip to consciousness of it, the vector in the film as the becoming of something as yet unseen. It is the principle of transformation, the quality of changing what we expect from moment to moment.[65]

Vectors, Cubitt writes, 'enact . . . beginnings' for moving images to become otherwise than they are in cinema. Thus, the vector is what Cubitt defines in graphical terms in relation to cinema: 'a line moving through time and space'.[66] However, the vector does something more, according to Cubitt: 'The vector . . . redefines movement as a function of relations and interactions. Reversing the polarity of the cut, the vector temporalizes space.'[67]

While Cubitt understands the vector as qualitatively changing 'what we expect from moment to moment',[68] I want to suggest that this transformation is not simply a material transformation but is more specifically an affective transformation. The vector is the force of the invisible. The vector is what is found in the operation or the transformation of forms in, as Cubitt suggests, 'becoming'. As Cubitt writes:

> In a strict sense, the unities produced by framing, compositing, and editing make the cinema visible, lifting it from the undifferentiated immanence of the nonidentical to the "being" of the object. The vector takes us one step further: from being to becoming, from the inertial division of subject, object, and world to the mobile relationships between them.[69]

Thus Cubitt writes that vectors take us from 'being' to 'becoming' as subjects; object and world are no longer understood in their static and 'inertial division' from each other, but in the 'mobile relationships' between them.[70] Cubitt writes: 'the vector provides the transformative principle in the frame itself, so every moment of every frame is the result of a unique transformation that might have come out differently'.[71] The vector has a trajectory and this trajectory is transformative.

The vector can be used to refer to the invisible trajectory of force or affect. In computer imaging the vector constructs the outline of shapes in graphic representation. The vector is, in this sense, mathematical, and can be described as existing outside of everything, since it has no visible substance. The magnitude and direction of the vector, however, do have force, and thus the vector's invisible trajectory can be tracked mathematically. The graphic representative form of the vector is not the vector itself, but a technological matrix that provides a graphic language for tracing the vector's force and velocity in the construction of the outline of shapes. In much the same way that Marey's graphic inscriptions are a 'direct writing' of the physiologically subtle rhythms of the body that are given line by the body's connection to a graphic language capable of measuring the magnitude and direction of forces and velocities acting in and on the body, the vector is given line in a graphic language.

The vector of the pulse is found in the cardiograph, and it can be said that the cardiograph is, as an index of the pulse, a 'medium of social exchange' inasmuch as it 'communicates' information about the wellbeing of a patient.[72] The vector is a line that vehiculates social meaning: grief, privilege, tragedy, except that the pulse is not the cardiograph. The pulse is not the graphic inscription of its movement. While the cardiograph is the line of transmission – the vector of illness and its impact, what is inscribed by the cardiograph is the affective force of the pulse, which is not reducible to a line. In relation to my discussion of the literal pulse, the cardiograph is the application of an instrument that makes a graphic inscription of the wave of distension that moves blood along the pliable blood vessels. While the vector colludes with the machinic in the cardiograph, the vector itself has the magnitude and direction of a force which itself is decidedly non-machinic.

As an influx that is unseen and excessive, the vectors of which I speak can only be marked as having meaning by their relations in time and space: by their force or velocity of magnitude and direction. The magnitude and direction of the vector is part of the affective precept for socialisation. Cubitt writes:

> The "cinematic," which in this instance equates to the concept of the vector, moves beyond objectification toward a process in which the film is able to take on the task

of signifying. As a material body that signifies, film becomes an other. Only at this moment does the cinematic subject become a self, capable of social relations. This is when the vector socializes film.[73]

The vector has a socialising force. In an analysis of the cut and the vector in cinema Cubitt writes that while the cut is a vehicle for endpoints that enables representation, the vector is a vehicle for beginnings 'moving through time and space' in a manner that enables communication in 'relations'.[74] Just as in Bataille the magnitude and direction of sovereign expenditure in the experience of horror and eroticism puts the self 'at stake' in the same moment that there emerges a continuity, or a communion, between the self and others, in Cubitt, the magnitude and direction of the vector is a 'becoming' that produces 'social relations'.[75] This is useful in that the magnitude and direction of convulsive affect is also the cause of the magnitude and direction of sovereign expenditure, which results in communication and communion.

The Vector and Communication

The vector is a decisive element in the behaviour of the pulse because it is the quantity of the magnitude and direction of points or images, or the state of points or images in relation. Developing the concept of the vector beyond the magnitude and direction of spectatorial convulsive affect and applying it to the undoing of subjectivity, I argue that the magnitude and direction of the vector has the operation of a 'putting at stake' of mastery and subjectivity. This 'putting at stake' is dispossessive. The spectator of the horror film is at once 'possessed' by affect, even as they, at the site of horror, engage in 'loss' as expenditure or the dispossession of self. Even while this possession/dispossession follows the movement of the contraction and dilation of the rhythm of the pulse, an aspect of this affective 'loss' of self is that this dispossession is also a 'yearning' for 'continuity' with others.[76] Thus, dispossession is also communication/communion in cinema. In developing my understanding of the pulse, the concept of the vector allows me to demonstrate how movement is an affectively 'continuous' force that produces relations and the communication/communion of the sovereign experience.

To characterise vectors as communicative forces is to attest to the affect of their magnitude and direction. Marshall McLuhan writes that machines are the vectors along which information travels. In other words, the 'medium' of machines is an extension of ourselves as it is involved in the interface between human and machine, and personal or social consequences.⁷⁷ While this definition involves subjects and objects, what later work on the vector such as Cubitt's reveals is an abandonment of subjectivity in relation to the mechanical apparatus. Cubitt writes:

> The machine is an instrument of humans, and that instrumental relationship defines the user and the used as subject and object. What Cohl's practice reveals is that another relation is possible, one in which the privilege of subjectivity is abandoned in favor of granting an autonomy to the machine equivalent to that assumed by the user. The new relation between human and machine is then no longer instrumental but ethical.⁷⁸

In line with Chapter 2 and my argument on the Open, what can be seen in this 'new relation' between human and machine is the Openness to affect. This is affect as sensorial *aisthesis* – which has not yet entered cognition – and has the operation of the making of relations. As Cubitt writes: 'Causality, logic, law, interpretation, and dialogue belong to this emergence, though they are only historically specific modes of the vector, which is the openness of thinking to the as-yet unthought, the connection as yet unmade.'⁷⁹ The behaviour of the vector is like the openness of the pulse, and indeed, the movement of the pulse has vectors.

Cubitt continues with respect to the vector's characteristic to make connections or relations: 'It is as if the vector's subjectivity is constantly launching itself outward.'⁸⁰ However, not only is the vector 'launching itself outward', it is also the vector's effect on subjectivity that causes a 'launching [of oneself] outward'. The subject, in Bataille's sense, is caught in a sovereign operation of expenditure without reserve and sacrifice without return: this is a 'putting at stake' of the subject that can best be characterised by a 'launching [of oneself] outward'. I propose that the vector is the magnitude and direction of the 'putting at stake' or sacrifice of self in sovereign expenditure.

The vector entails the magnitude and direction of expenditure that cannot be considered to have productive return, even if it does have potential or 'hope'. Cubitt writes about the difference between the cut and the vector: 'The cut is teleological, determined by its ending . . . The vector is eschatological: its future is open, governed only by hope.'⁸¹ The potential or 'hope' of the vector is derived from its action of 'launching itself outward'. Bataille's 'throw[ing] himself suddenly *outside of himself*' which is like a 'launching [of oneself] outward',⁸² is also a 'yearning' for 'continuity' with others. Such 'continuity' with others is the communication that is derived from affective expenditure and the communion derived from the dispossession of self in the experience of horror and eroticism.

The expenditure and sacrifice of self at the site of a 'putting at stake' or 'launching [of oneself] outward', allows for the collective experience of communion.[83] While communion occurs in the experience of horror and eroticism, a part of the sharing of the moment in sacrifice could be said to occur in other settings. Shaviro writes in *Passion and Excess: Blanchot, Bataille, and Literary Theory*:

> The communal feast, like the fascist rally, unites separate individuals into one essence. But sacrifice, or collective vomiting, creates a complicitous communal relation in which the integrity of separate individuals is lost, and yet the difference as such is maintained. Community does not abolish, but is affirmed on the basis of—and in the midst of—distance and separation.[84]

Equally cinema could be said to be a space for community or even communion. The affective experience suggests a complicity – a communion or sharing of the event – even while the heterogeneity of spectators and sensations, and the difference of response is maintained. It is the 'sacrifice' of self that enables this communion.

In Bataille's work, the excesses and contestations of 'sacrifice', 'collective vomiting' or 'excretion' exist both within and between the heterogeneities of the body and of society – an excess and contestation of affects, the body, and social institutions – that are capable of taking us to the limits of ourselves as individuals and as community. This is what James Creech describes as the 'los[ing] more than is *given* to be lost' of sovereign expenditure.[85] What is 'lost' is the self and in the sacrificial moment, just as in the act of ecstatic copulation, the self is dispossessed and brought into continuity and even communion with others.

Communion sustains the heterogeneity of spectators in a material sense. For Cubitt, the dimension of the vector as signifier is the material of signification: 'The vector is the dimension of the signifier . . . The signifier is the material of signification, and its task is not to represent but to be exchanged.'[86] Thus, we can also say that the 'task' of the material, blood, in cinema, is not to 'represent', but to cause an affective and communicative exchange. And yet, the magnitude and direction of blood is not simply toward affective and communicative exchange, since the self is also engaged in sovereign expenditure. Just as Cubitt's vector is caught up in the 'production of meaning' as a signifying moment in communication, the moment of signification is also an impossible destination. As Cubitt writes, vectors are 'uncapturable transformations'.[87]

The Magnitude and Direction of Vectors that Result in Possession and Dispossession

This chapter uses the vector to refer to the relation between the self and others through affective blood; the vector is the magnitude and direction of the 'loss' of self because of excessive expenditure, but also the 'continuity' with others inspired by affective relation. Vectors are the quantity of magnitude and direction, and in this chapter, are the magnitude and direction of the convulsive movement of affect. Convulsive affect has vectors or quantities of magnitude and direction, however, in convulsive affect we see how magnitude builds up and direction becomes frenzied. While such movement demonstrates the movement of two points relative to each other, the vector 'possesses' its own force and velocity, and yet, is found to act out the convulsive affect of dispossession. It is the relationship between the kinds of movement of bodies employed and the spilling of blood that makes *Possession* convulsively affective, giving rise to possession/dispossession.

Through the magnitude and direction of blood, the vector is an affective and communicative force. The expenditure of affective sacrifice gives rise to communication and communion. Vectors also have a communicative function via machines. As we saw in Chapter 3, blood takes on a different meaning when an apparatus or machine enacts the spillage of blood.

In *Possession*, in a scene in which Anna is preparing mince in the kitchen with an electric meat mincer and Mark questions her about her lover and the kind of relationship she wants to have with Mark and their son Bob, the relationship between the agitating movement of the meat mincer and the electric knife, the agitated movement of characters, and the magnitude and direction of the blood spilled, has the effect of a 'frenzy' at the same time as, by affect, it has the effect of intimate communication.

Mark: It's disgusting.
Anna: Yes.
Mark: Look what we've become.
Anna: Yes.
Mark: Talk to me. I don't want you to be like this. You know, when I'm away from you I think of you as an animal or a woman possessed and then I see you again and all this disappears. You must try and help me. Tell me. Make me want to help. Are you happy? [Anna nods]. Do you love him? [Anna nods]. Does he love you? Do you want to live together and have a family, and am I in your way and Bob too? [Anna shakes her head].

Then there's something else you must tell me. Why are you afraid to tell me? Are you afraid of me? [Anna shakes her head]. Are you afraid I'll get

mad again and beat you? [Anna shakes her head]. Are you afraid I won't like you?
Anna: Yes.
Mark: Anna help me, help me.
[Anna raises the electric knife to her throat and turns it on, cutting herself].
Mark: Anna, Bob, Bob remember. Christ, remember.
[In the bathroom Mark bandages Anna's neck].
Mark: It'll be the way you want it. It'll be the way you want it. You're my whole family.
[In the kitchen, Mark is sitting alone. He picks up the electric knife and calmly slices his arm three times. Anna appears in the doorway].
Anna: I have to go now.
Mark: Will you wait for Bob?
Anna: I can't now.
Mark: Maybe we can both go and pick him up at school?
Anna: I can't. It doesn't hurt.
Mark: No.

In this scene the mechanical agitation of the meat mincer and the electric knife releases a tension that pulverises the self as the meat is pulverised. The violence is done to the self in a returning turn to the body. That the purpose of the pulverised meat is to feed Anna's doppelgänger of Mark demonstrates another violence done to the self in reification of an 'other'. The act of turning the knife on oneself – exemplified when Anna turns the electric knife on her own throat, and later, when Mark turns the knife on his own arm – is precursory to the dispossessing release of sacrificial 'acephalic' decapitation. Batailile writes that: 'Only violence can bring everything to a state of flux in this way, only violence and the nameless disquiet bound up with it.'[88] And it is in this 'state of flux', Bataille also writes, that we are closer to being in 'continuity' with others – in intimate communication. Thus, in turning the knife upon themselves Anna and Mark not only return the hurt upon their own bodies, but Anna and Mark are also brought into a 'state of flux' by which communication at the most intimate level is made possible. That is, Anna demonstrates her innermost pain to Mark in a sacrifice of the self and reason, just as Mark demonstrates his pain to Anna in a sacrifice of the self and reason.

There is, however, contrast between the vehicle of affect in this scene and the material vector of blood. The dialogue – 'It'll be the way you want it' – is undercut by the reconstitution of pulverised flesh in the form of the doppelgänger. Anna minces meat in a whirring mincer as Mark pleads with her. With Mark in mid-sentence, Anna draws the electric knife she has used to dice the meat across her throat, ending the conversation with a gush of blood. Mark's response is an inversion of affect.

After bandaging Anna's wound, he too cuts himself, drawing three bright red lines across his arm. This seemingly unmotivated act is a form of transfer set against the affective exchange of the dialogue. One could say that a vector has moved between Mark and Anna, resulting in the repetition of this self-mutilation – one which sets the material vector of blood against the affect. Like the act of mincing, this conveyed act reconstitutes flesh: beyond describable feeling – beyond feeling at all. Mark draws the oscillating blade across his arm and in response to Anna's statement 'It doesn't hurt', responds 'No'.

It is notable that in this sequence neither Mark nor Anna make eye contact with each other. Both Mark and Anna move around the kitchen, their bodies in a state of convulsive affect in relation to each other, and in relation to the mechanical rhythm and agitation of the meat mincer and the electric knife. Although vectors are quantities that have magnitude and direction, in *Possession* vectors are not those generally made by film in which the magnitude and direction of the eye-line demonstrate the line of communication between characters. The vectors that move the self to intimate communication in *Possession* do not take place at the level of character-to-character eye contact. Rather, vectors in *Possession* turn around on themselves and become clouds of 'circular agitation'. Bataille writes about the erotic moment in this way:

> Existence, in the end, discovers the blind spot of understanding and right away absorbs it completely. It could go otherwise only if the possibility of rest offered itself at some point. But nothing like that happens: what alone remains is the circular agitation—which does not exhaust itself in ecstasy and begins again from it.[89]

It is not that these 'circular agitations' do not have force. It is just that these agitations have a way of turning around on themselves, so that the force of the vectors becomes a necessity to sacrifice the self for intimate communication to take place. In other words, the magnitude and direction of vectors, driven by agitation, is dispossessive by the action of convulsive affect.

Material Vectors and their (Non)sense

In the movement of bodies and the affective spilling of blood a contradiction arises between the magnitude and direction of the vectors of the pulse that are unseen and the vectors of magnitude and direction that are seen in blood. Inasmuch as the pulse can be aligned with the affective force of blood spilled in cinema, this is only as far as the spilling of blood 'exposes' the pulse and the blood that circulates unseen in the body. In cinema, the magnitude and direction of the vectors of the pulse are 'exposed' in the spilling of blood.

Not simply a materiality, or rather, a materiality only as it relates to a change of state, material vectors are, in a way, a (non)sense. Cubitt comes to much the same conclusion when he writes about the action of the vector in Émile Cohl's film *Fantasmagorie* (1908): 'Flowers become bottles become a cannon; an elephant becomes a house; Pierrot becomes a bubble, a hat, a valise.'[90] Cubitt calls this the 'transformative principle' of the vector.[91] Because of this 'transformative principle', material vectors are parodies or violations of functionality: they are nonsense.

Blood only means something when, and as, it invokes affect, where affect is defined as that which acts on or has an effect on somebody or something. Blood has affective force and in this way produces sensorial relations: this is the 'sense' of (non)sense. In cinema, blood spilled is an aesthetic and pictorial representation, and 'exposes' *aisthetic* sensations. By 'exposing' *aisthetic* sensations, blood also 'exposes' the complicity of the self in the experience of horror. That is, blood 'exposes' the communicative and transformative principle of the vector via the affects or sensations that it elicits.

In Chapter 4, I suggested that the scene in Fulci's *L'aldilà* in which a beaker of acid pours onto Mary-Ann's face causing her to disintegrate into a frothing pool of blood, brings about the 'loss' of Jill. The line of contact with the blood flow is a changing coastline. As Land writes: 'Bodies are not volumes but coastlines; irresolvable but undelimitable penetrabilities, opportunities for the real decomposition of space.'[92] In *L'aldilà*, the ever-expanding pool of blood that Mary-Ann represents for her daughter, Jill, is a coastline.

While the material of blood has a coastline, the vector is not a volume or even a coastline. The vector is the magnitude and direction of, in my example, blood flow, which produces the ever-expanding coastline but is not itself that coastline. The vector is the force *unseen* – the magnitude and direction of the blood flow. By its magnitude and direction, the vector is also an affective operation of the subject's undoing in terror. The affective force of blood does not come from the terror that along the coastline are possible points at which the subject might make contact with the material of blood; rather, the affective force of blood is a subject looking into the dizzying void of that tide of blood. That is, blood produces the affectivity of a sovereign operation of self that is a 'putting at stake' to the constitutively 'other'.

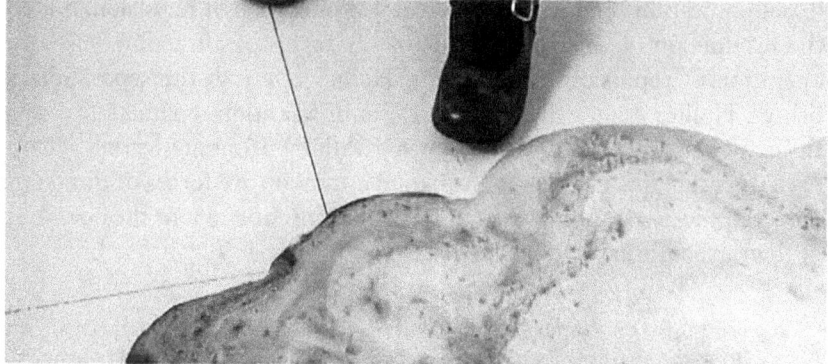

Figure 5.7 The tide of blood approaches Jill's feet. *L'aldilà / The Beyond* (Lucio Fulci, 1981)

The force of the vector is the terror of the vertiginous 'fall' to something other than the self: to a transition in state in which the self sacrifices. By giving the 'projection' of blood the affect of the ecstatic moment, Bataille ties life and death together in moments of eroticism in which the self sacrifices. On the 'horror of blood', Bataille, in the essay 'Sacrifices', writes:

> In the fact that life and death are passionately devoted to the subsidence of the void, the slave's subordinate relation to the master is no longer revealed, but life and void are confused and mingled like lovers, in the convulsive movements of the end. Burning passion is no longer acceptance and realization of nothingness: nothingness is still a cadaver; brilliance is the blood that flows and coagulates.
>
> And just as the freed obscene nature of their organs more passionately connects embracing lovers, so too the nearby horror of the cadaver and the present horror of blood tie the *me* that dies more obscurely to an empty infinity—and this empty infinity is itself projected as cadaver and as blood.[93]

In this sense, blood is not simply material – 'the freed obscene nature of ... organs' – but is the 'projection' of the 'empty infinity' of the void.[94] Bataille argues that what is revealed in these 'convulsive movements' is the 'loss' to sovereign expenditure.[95] The economy of affect is indicative of a dispossession of self, such that, as we saw in Chapter 4, Jill's standing at the edge of the pool of blood is the 'loss' of self to sovereign expenditure.

Blood is a pictorial representation of the sacrifice or dispossession of self, at the same time as the affective force of blood enacts complicity or affective communication and communion. Denis Hollier writes about communication in *Against Architecture: The Writings of Georges Bataille*:

'Communication is nothing other than this operation of repulsion, merely the production of repulsion as one of the terms of attraction.'[96] By the operation of repulsion as attraction, Hollier refers to the separation of beings. Hollier argues that Bataille's 'communication' operates less by a fusion of beings than it does by their separation.[97] Communicating vectors have direction in so far as repulsion and attraction are forces of direction; however, these vectors are consumed by their production, or the operation of their expenditure. Hollier writes:

> If a being exists only through communication, then communication itself is nothing if not the sacrifice of a being: "I propose to acknowledge as law that human beings are never united with each other except through tears or wounds, an idea that has a certain logical force in its favor."[98]

This point by Hollier suggests how communication is bound up not simply in the magnitude and direction of repulsion and attraction, and the dispossession of self via sacrifice and expenditure, but is bound up in material vectors such as tears and wounds. Tears and wounds – and for this chapter, blood – are communicating, because affective, forces.

In *Possession*, the sacrifice of self that takes place for intimate communication to come about makes itself visible in the release of substance: in spilled and affective blood. However, this intimate communication also occurs via the 'amorous frenzy' of the copula – the frenzied 'loss' of self that is 'felt' when the self is brought in relation to the substance blood – and is what marks the operation of this sacrifice. This is why the production of the doppelgängers by Mark and Anna – and specifically the doppelgänger created by Anna, since it is constructed not simply through copulation but also with the meat she feeds it – brings about an intimate communication in which Anna 'loses' herself. The production of the doppelgänger is more lost than the convulsive affect – the 'amorous frenzy' – that was used to generate it. Thus Anna loses herself in the 'amorous frenzy' in the production of the doppelgänger, and when she presents the doppelgänger to Mark, Mark loses himself in the 'amorous frenzy' of actions that will end in death.

In Żuławski's film, the materiality or substance of blood is tied to expenditure in movement and affect. In Anna's apartment, after Heinrich sees the body parts in the refrigerator and the creature Anna is generating, Anna says to Heinrich as she flicks his shirt and chest with the point of a knife: 'You are not different from anyone else. We are all the same, but in different words, different bodies, different versions. Like insects. MEAT.' At this moment, Anna stabs Heinrich in the chest, and the blood from the wound stains his shirt. Blood both rises to the occasion (the wounds caused by the knife and the pouring blood demonstrate this meat), and is lost in this communication (the force of this communication is felt in the 'loss' of self to pain). The doppelgänger Anna creates is just a different version of Mark – a different body to be named in different words. The substantial point is that this different version of Mark is created by Anna's 'amorous frenzy', which is really not a difference at all when we consider what is created by love. The copula of love and the copulation of bodies bring the 'other' in relation to the self. The self 'projects' an image of the 'other' by the self's love for the 'other'. Whether the substance of Mark is an 'other' or, as in Anna's doppelgänger creation, is the substance that results from her own 'projection' of Mark, is unimportant in comparison to the expenditure of that production.

The relationship between substance and copula is further demonstrated in the 'miscarriage' scene. This miscarriage is as much a miscarriage of the self – a dispossession of the self – as it is a state of bodily crisis. That is, in the miscarriage we see again the debate between substance and copula. While the substance of blood finds a simpler path to explaining the magnitude, direction, force, trajectory and duration of the vector in visible effect, in the end it is the copula – the 'amorous frenzy' that arises in Anna to produce an 'other' in relation to self – that demonstrates the magnitude, direction, force, trajectory and duration of the vector. The condition of being possessed of affect or sensation is the sacrifice or dispossession of self because of this possession. And yet, in cinema, the material blood is a pictorial representation of the sacrifice or dispossession of self. The sacrifice or dispossession of self finds its relevance in the tide of blood that flows from Mary-Ann in *L'aldilà* and from Anna in *Possession*.

The vectors of the pulse dispossess in the sense of a dispossession of the unified self that is the operation of sovereignty by which 'I' am 'put at stake'. Affect, and specifically, the aberrant movements of convulsive affect that extend to new freedoms and contract again, are the movements of a sovereign self that sacrifices itself to the freedoms of the 'new', to the feelings found in cinema. However, the dispossession of the 'putting at stake' is also, by erotic and violent sacrifice, a dispossession of self toward continuity with the other, that is, a dispossession that breaches the discontinuity between self and other, and 'yearns' for communication and communion.

The theory of spectatorship I have gleaned from Bataille's work, particularly the spectatorship of the ritual sacrifice, is aesthetically strong but ethically weak. In making the spectator complicit with the event, Bataille separates spectators from the ethical implications of the eroticism and violence of which he speaks, precisely because the spectator is theorised as holding a particular place in operation. Spectators are engaged in, and transformed by, sovereign operations of expenditure.

In terms of blood, the relationship between aesthetics and ethics returns us to Chapter 3, wherein the aesthetics of spilled blood in the 'theater of cruelty' is the result of the 'ethical law'.[99] The effect of the law is found in the aesthetics of spilled blood because this is what the body will sensibly understand. Ethics is secondary to the initial prescription of that which was 'before' in *sanguis* or the blood that circulates. For Żuławski's *Possession*, this means that the violence perpetrated upon characters and of which characters would be ethically culpable, or the pain found in the victim, is not negotiated but instead made the sum of the sensorial and *aisthetic* affect of the sovereign operation. Both Mark and Anna in *Possession* are ethically culpable and are both victims of the violence of the other; but they are also victims to the violence of themselves. It is necessary to acknowledge the ways in which the pain of others and of ourselves takes place alongside what is the absolute 'other' of sovereignty. That is, the dialectics of the 'ethical law' for which we are all subjectivities is not erased or displaced by sovereign operations but stands alongside them. As Lyotard writes in his essay 'Prescription': 'There is no court that can take up the conflict between the aesthetic and the ethical and decide the matter.'[100] And later: 'Only the sacrifice of the body maintains the sanctity of the law.'[101] In Bataillean terms, this would mean that the sacrifice that takes place through the sovereign expenditure of self – the 'putting at stake' – is in fact what also maintains the subjectivity of the ethical self. If rhythm, as I have argued, enacts a restricted economy of the return of meaning and subjectivity, and the pulse a general economy of sacrifice and sovereign expenditure, the two cannot exist in isolation. A restricted economy will always reside beside – or be imbricated with – a general economy. There will always be the rhythm of the pulse.

Notes

1. In true *Monty Python* style, this sequence is a parody of Robert Bresson's *Lancelot du Lac/Lancelot of the Lake* (1974), which also depicts blood spurting from the severed limbs of slain knights.
2. Żuławski's *Possession* was reissued in the US under the title *The Night the Screaming Stops*.
3. Bataille, 'The Solar Anus', p. 5.
4. Bataille, *Eroticism*, p. 15.

5. Interviews with Żuławski confirm that the film was intended to capture something of his own experience of marriage and divorce, even to the extent of including dialogue he had had with his then wife, which he remembered and transcribed (Thrower and Bird, 'Cinema Superactivity', pp. 70–1).
6. Bataille, 'Sacrificial Mutilation', p. 70.
7. Available at <https://en.oxforddictionaries.com/definition/possession> (last accessed 17 January 2020).
8. Available at <https://en.oxforddictionaries.com/definition/possess> (last accessed 17 January 2020).
9. Available at <https://en.oxforddictionaries.com/definition/possession> (last accessed 17 January 2020).
10. Bataille, 'Hegel, Death and Sacrifice', p. 23.
11. Bataille, *Eroticism*, p. 95.
12. Bataille, *Eroticism*, p. 17.
13. Bataille, 'The Solar Anus', p. 5.
14. Bataille, *Eroticism*, p. 15.
15. Bataille, 'Sacrificial Mutilation', p. 70.
16. Waite, *Oxford Dictionary*, p. 1586.
17. Williams, 'Film Bodies', p. 4.
18. Williams, 'Film Bodies', p. 4.
19. Williams, 'Film Bodies', p. 4.
20. Williams, 'Film Bodies', p. 2.
21. Williams, 'Film Bodies', p. 12.
22. Williams, 'Film Bodies', p. 4.
23. Bataille, 'The Sacred Conspiracy', p. 181.
24. Bataille, 'Sacrifices', p. 130.
25. Bataille, 'Sacrifices', p. 130.
26. Thrower and Bird, 'Cinema Superactivity', p. 65.
27. Bataille, 'The Solar Anus', p. 5.
28. Bataille, 'The Solar Anus', p. 5.
29. Bataille, 'The Solar Anus', p. 5.
30. Bataille, 'The Solar Anus', p. 5.
31. Johnson, 'What is a Sentence?' Available at <https://www.englishgrammartutor.com/grammar%20book.htm> (last accessed 17 January 2020).
32. Bataille, 'The Solar Anus', p. 6.
33. Bataille, 'The Solar Anus', p. 6.
34. Bataille, *The Tears of Eros*, p. 207.
35. Bataille, 'The Solar Anus', p. 9.
36. Land, *The Thirst for Annihilation*, p. 193.
37. Bataille, 'The Solar Anus', p. 5.
38. Bataille, 'The Sacred Conspiracy', p. 181.
39. Deleuze, *Cinema 1*, p. 218.
40. Deleuze, *Cinema 1*, p. 218.
41. Thrower and Bird, 'Cinema Superactivity', p. 68.

42. Thrower and Bird, 'Cinema Superactivity', p. 70.
43. Lyotard writes in *Duchamp's TRANS/formers* about the point of tension, or the *limes* of retortion in movement, as the point at which 'appearance' metamorphoses. To elaborate, Lyotard describes the 'body of the trap' that contains the '*limes*' as such:

> It has the power to turn itself inside out, inverting its exterior and its interior. In the Hellenic tradition the fox turns his body inside out when the eagle dives on him; or the octopus, 'which unfurls its internal organs, turning them outwards, stripping off its body like a shirt'; or Hermes who, having stolen the cows of his brother Apollo, confuses the tracks by making the herd walk backwards.
>
> Today the category of these non-reliable bodies, capable of such twists and turns, includes the gloved hand of Roberte as sketched by the 'semiotics' of Pierre Klossowski: For it's just when the aspirant, using his strength, ungloves this hand in the hope of taking possession of the flesh itself that the latter escapes, because the appearance of the epidermis metamorphoses him, the predator, into a prey. Likewise, Ovid's Diana, pursued by Actaeon while she is bathing naked, changes him into a stag and has him hunted down by her hounds.

Retortion, then, is the 'foil' to the 'aim of coupling' because it turns the self inside out (Lyotard, *Duchamp's TRANS/formers*, pp. 44–5).
44. Deleuze, *Cinema 1*, p. 218.
45. Deleuze, *Cinema 1*, p. 142.
46. Deleuze, *Cinema 1*, p. 141.
47. Deleuze, *Cinema 1*, p. 142.
48. Deleuze, *Cinema 1*, p. 218.
49. Deleuze, *Francis Bacon*, p. 72.
50. Deleuze, *Francis Bacon*, p. 72.
51. Deleuze, *Francis Bacon*, pp. 72–3.
52. Deleuze, *Francis Bacon*, p. 42.
53. Deleuze, *Francis Bacon*, p. 41.
54. Deleuze, *Francis Bacon*, p. 41.
55. Deleuze, *Francis Bacon*, pp. 42–3.
56. Deleuze, *Francis Bacon*, p. 73.
57. Deleuze, *Francis Bacon*, p. 72.
58. Ballard, *Crash*, p. 45.
59. Ballard, *Crash*, p. 45.
60. Ballard, *Crash*, p. 20.
61. Ballard, *Crash*, p. 20.
62. Ballard, *Crash*, p. 45.
63. Cubitt, *The Cinema Effect*, p. 82.
64. Cubitt, *The Cinema Effect*, p. 83.
65. Cubitt, *The Cinema Effect*, pp. 71–2.
66. Cubitt, *The Cinema Effect*, p. 71.

67. Cubitt, *The Cinema Effect*, p. 72.
68. Cubitt, *The Cinema Effect*, p. 72.
69. Cubitt, *The Cinema Effect*, p. 71.
70. Cubitt, *The Cinema Effect*, p. 71.
71. Cubitt, *The Cinema Effect*, p. 76.
72. Cubitt, *The Cinema Effect*, p. 80.
73. Cubitt, *The Cinema Effect*, p. 90.
74. Cubitt, *The Cinema Effect*, pp. 71–2.
75. Cubitt, *The Cinema Effect*, p. 90.
76. Bataille, *Eroticism*, p. 15.
77. McLuhan, 'The Medium is the Message', p. 9.
78. Cubitt, *The Cinema Effect*, p. 88.
79. Cubitt, *The Cinema Effect*, p. 72.
80. Cubitt, *The Cinema Effect*, p. 80.
81. Cubitt, *The Cinema Effect*, p. 80.
82. Bataille, 'Sacrificial Mutilation', p. 70.
83. Bataille, 'Sacrificial Mutilation', p. 70.
84. Shaviro, *Passion and Excess*, p. 100.
85. Creech, 'Julia Kristeva's Bataille', p. 63.
86. Cubitt, *The Cinema Effect*, p. 80.
87. Cubitt, *The Cinema Effect*, p. 97.
88. Bataille, *Eroticism*, p. 17.
89. Bataille, *Inner Experience*, p. 112.
90. Cubitt, *The Cinema Effect*, p. 76.
91. Cubitt, *The Cinema Effect*, p. 76.
92. Land, *The Thirst for Annihilation*, p. 161.
93. Bataille, 'Sacrifices', p. 133.
94. Bataille, 'Sacrifices', p. 133.
95. Bataille, 'Sacrifices', p. 133.
96. Hollier, *Against Architecture*, p. 67.
97. Hollier, *Against Architecture*, p. 67.
98. Hollier, *Against Architecture*, pp. 67–8; quoting from Bataille, 'The College of Sociology', p. 370.
99. Lyotard, 'Prescription', p. 180.
100. Lyotard, 'Prescription', p. 181.
101. Lyotard, 'Prescription', p. 181.

Bibliography

Arnzen, Michael A., 'Who's Laughing Now? The Postmodern Splatter Film', *Journal of Popular Film and Television* 21, no. 4, 1994, pp. 176–85.
'auto-, comb. form1', *Oxford English Dictionary Online*, December 2019, Oxford University Press. <https://www.oed.com/view/Entry/13367?rskey=wQ1uro&result=9> (last accessed 19 January 2020).
Ballard, J. G., *Crash* (New York: Picador/Farrar, Straus, and Giroux, 1973).
Barthes, Roland, 'The Metaphor of the Eye', in *Story of the Eye* (London and New York: Penguin Books, 1982), pp. 119–27; Eng. trans. by Joachim Neugroschal from the French 'Le Métaphore de l'œil', *Critique* 195–6, 1963, pp. 770–7.
Bataille, Georges, 'The College of Sociology', in Allan Stoekl (ed.), *Visions of Excess, Selected Writings 1927–1939* (Minneapolis: University of Minnesota Press, 1985), pp. 246–53; Eng. trans. by Allan Stoekl et al. from the French 'Le Collège de Sociologie', in *Œuvres complètes* II (Paris: Gallimard, 1970), pp. 364–74.
Bataille, Georges, 'The Economy Equal to the Universe: Brief Notes Preliminary to the Preparation of an Essay on "General Economy" Forthcoming under the Title *The Accursed Share*', *Scapegoat* 5, Summer/Autumn, 2013, pp. 34–7; Eng. trans. by Stuart Kendall from the French 'L'économie à la mesure de l'univers (1946)', in *Œuvres complètes* VII (Paris: Gallimard, 1976), pp. 7–16.
Bataille, Georges, *Eroticism* (London and New York: Penguin, 2001); Eng. trans. by Mary Dalwood from the French *L'Érotisme* (Paris: Les Éditions de Minuit, 1957).
Bataille, Georges, 'Eye', in Allan Stoekl (ed.), *Visions of Excess, Selected Writings 1927–1939* (Minneapolis: University of Minnesota Press, 1985), pp. 17–19; Eng. trans. by Allan Stoekl et al. from the French 'Œil', *Documents* 4, September 1929, p. 216.
Bataille, Georges, 'Formless', in Allan Stoekl (ed.), *Visions of Excess, Selected Writings 1927–1939* (Minneapolis: University of Minnesota Press, 1985), p. 31; Eng. trans. by Allan Stoekl et al. from the French 'Informe', *Documents* 7, December 1929, p. 382.
Bataille, Georges, 'Hegel, Death and Sacrifice', in *Yale French Studies* 78, 1990, pp. 9–28; Eng. trans. by Jonathan Strauss from the French 'Hegel, la mort et le sacrifice', in *Deucalion* 5, 1955, pp. 21–43.

Bataille, Georges, *Inner Experience* (Albany, NY: State University of New York Press, 2014); Eng. trans. by Stuart Kendall from the French *L'Expérience intérieure* (Paris: Gallimard, 1943).

Bataille, Georges, 'The Obelisk', in Allan Stoekl (ed.), *Visions of Excess, Selected Writings 1927–1939* (Minneapolis: University of Minnesota Press, 1985), pp. 213–22; Eng. trans. by Allan Stoekl et al. from the French 'L'obélisque', *Mesures* 2, 15 April 1938, pp. 35–50.

Bataille, Georges, 'The Pineal Eye', in Allan Stoekl (ed.), *Visions of Excess, Selected Writings 1927–1939* (Minneapolis: University of Minnesota Press, 1985), pp. 79–90; Eng. trans. by Allan Stoekl et al. from the French 'L'œil pinéal', *L'Éphémère* 3, 1967.

Bataille, Georges, 'Propositions', in Allan Stoekl (ed.), *Visions of Excess, Selected Writings 1927–1939* (Minneapolis: University of Minnesota Press, 1985), pp. 197–201; Eng. trans. by Allan Stoekl et al. from the French 'Propositions', *Acéphale* 2, January 1937, pp. 17–21.

Bataille, Georges, 'Rotten Sun', in Allan Stoekl (ed.), *Visions of Excess, Selected Writings 1927–1939* (Minneapolis: University of Minnesota Press, 1985), pp. 57–8; Eng. trans. by Allan Stoekl et al. from the French 'Soleil pourri', *Documents* 3, 1930, pp. 173–4.

Bataille, Georges, 'The Sacred Conspiracy', in Allan Stoekl (ed.), *Visions of Excess, Selected Writings 1927–1939* (Minneapolis: University of Minnesota Press, 1985), pp. 178–81; Eng. trans. by Allan Stoekl et al. from the French 'La conjuration sacrée', *Acéphale* 1, June 1936, pp. 2–4.

Bataille, Georges, 'Sacrifice' (1939–1940), *October* 36, Spring 1986, pp. 61–74; Eng. trans. by Annette Michelson from the French 'Le sacrifice', in *Œuvres complètes* II (Paris: Gallimard, 1970), pp. 238–43.

Bataille, Georges, 'Sacrifices', in Allan Stoekl (ed.), *Visions of Excess, Selected Writings 1927–1939* (Minneapolis: University of Minnesota Press, 1985), pp. 130–6; Eng. trans. by Allan Stoekl et al. from the French *Sacrifices* (Editions G. L. M., 1936).

Bataille, Georges, 'Sacrificial Mutilation and the Severed Ear of Vincent Van Gogh', in Allan Stoekl (ed.), *Visions of Excess, Selected Writings 1927–1939* (Minneapolis: University of Minnesota Press, 1985), pp. 61–72; Eng. trans. by Allan Stoekl et al. from the French 'La mutilation sacrificielle et l'oreille coupée de Vincent Van Gogh', *Documents* 8, 1930, pp. 10–20.

Bataille, Georges, 'The Solar Anus', in Allan Stoekl (ed.), *Visions of Excess, Selected Writings 1927–1939* (Minneapolis: University of Minnesota Press, 1985), pp. 5–9; Eng. trans. by Allan Stoekl et al. from the French *L'Anus solaire* (Paris: Éditions de la Galérie Simon, 1931).

Bataille, Georges, *Story of the Eye* (London and New York: Penguin Books, 1982); Eng. trans. by Joachim Neugroschal from the French Lord Auch, *Histoire de l'œil* (Paris: René Bonnel, 1928).

Bataille, Georges, *The Tears of Eros* (San Francisco: City Lights Books, 1989); Eng. trans. by Peter Connor from the French *Les Larmes d'Éros* (Paris: Jean-Jacques Pauvert, 1961).

Bataille, Georges, 'Un-knowing: Laughter and Tears' (1953), *October* 36, Spring 1986, pp. 89–102; Eng. trans. by Annette Michelson from the French 'Non-savoir, rire et larmes (9 février 1953)', in *Œuvres complètes* VIII (Paris: Gallimard, 1976), pp. 214–33.

Bataille, Georges, 'The Use Value of D. A. F. de Sade (An Open Letter to My Current Comrades)', in Allan Stoekl (ed.), *Visions of Excess, Selected Writings 1927–1939* (Minneapolis: University of Minnesota Press, 1985), pp. 91–102; Eng. trans. by Allan Stoekl et al. from the French 'La valeur d'usage de D. A. F. de Sade', in *Œuvres complètes* II (Paris: Gallimard, 1970), pp. 54–69.

Bataille, Georges, 'Van Gogh as Prometheus', *October* 36, Spring 1986, pp. 58–60; Eng. trans. by Annette Michelson from the French 'Van Gogh Prométhée', in *Œuvres complètes* I (Paris: Gallimard, 1970), pp. 497–500.

Baudry, Jean-Louis, 'Ideological Effects of the Basic Cinematographic Apparatus', in Philip Rosen (ed.), *Narrative, Apparatus, Ideology* (New York: Columbia University Press, 1986), pp. 286–98; Eng. trans. by Alan Williams from the French 'Effets idéologiques de l'apparcil cinématographique de base', *Cinéthique* 7–8, 1970, pp. 1–8.

Bazin, André, 'André Gide', *France-observateur* 96 (13 March 1952), in *Qu'est-ce que le cinéma? I. Ontologie et langage* (Paris: Éditions du Cerf, 1958), pp. 71–4.

Benjamin, Walter, 'The Work of Art in the Age of Mechanical Reproduction', in Hannah Arendt (ed.), *Illuminations* (New York: Schocken, 1969), pp. 217–51; Eng. trans. by Harry Zohn from the German *Illuminationen* (Frankfurt am Main: Suhrkamp Verlag, 1955).

Bennington, Geoffrey, *Lyotard: Writing the Event* (New York: Columbia University Press, 1988).

Bergson, Henri, *Matter and Memory* (London: George Allen & Unwin; New York: Macmillan, 1911); Eng. trans. by Nancy Margaret Paul and W. Scott Palmer from the French *Matière et mémoire* (Paris: F. Alcan, 1896).

Bergson, Henri, *Creative Evolution* (Mineola, New York: Dover Publications, 1911); Eng. trans. by Arthur Mitchell from the French *L'Évolution créatrice* (Paris: F. Alcan, 1907).

Bois, Yve-Alain, and Rosalind E. Krauss, *Formless: A User's Guide* (New York: Zone Books, 1997).

Bordwell, David, 'Mimetic Theories of Narration', in *Narration in the Fiction Film* (London: Routledge, 1986), pp. 3–15.

Boyle, Bill, 'Visual Mindscape: The Pulse of Screenplay Dialogue', *Script* Magazine, 2 December 2013, <http://www.scriptmag.com/features/visual-mindscape-pulse-screenplay-dialogue> (last accessed 17 January 2020).

Braun, Marta, *Picturing Time: The Work of Étienne-Jules Marey (1830–1904)* (Chicago: University of Chicago Press, 1992)

Briggs, John, and F. David Peat, *Seven Life Lessons of Chaos: Timeless Wisdom from the Science of Change* (New York: HarperCollins, 1999).

Cabanne, Pierre, *Dialogues with Marcel Duchamp* (London: Thames and Hudson, 1971).

Carroll, Noël, *The Philosophy of Horror: Or, Paradoxes of the Heart* (New York and London: Routledge, 1990).

Castle, William, *Step Right Up! I'm Gonna Scare the Pants Off America* (New York: G. P. Putnam's Sons, 1976).

Chappell, Sophie Grace, 'Plato on Knowledge in the *Theaetetus*', in Edward N. Zalta (ed.), *The Stanford Encyclopedia of Philosophy*, Winter 2013 edn, <https://plato.stanford.edu/archives/win2013/entries/plato-theaetetus> (last accessed 17 January 2020).

Clover, Carol J., 'Her Body, Himself: Gender in the Slasher Film', *Representations* 20, Fall 1987, pp. 187–228.

Clover, Carol J., *Men, Women and Chain Saws: Gender in the Modern Horror Film* (Princeton, NJ: Princeton University Press, 1992).

Conley, Tom, 'Movement-Image', in Adrian Parr (ed.), *The Deleuze Dictionary* (Edinburgh: Edinburgh University Press, 2013), pp. 179–80.

Crary, Jonathan, 'Modernizing Vision', in Hal Foster (ed.), *Vision and Visuality* (Seattle, WA: Bay Press, 1988), pp. 29–49.

Creech, James, 'Julia Kristeva's Bataille: Reading as Triumph', *Diacritics* 5, no. 1, Spring 1975, pp. 62–8.

Cubitt, Sean, *The Cinema Effect* (Cambridge, MA and London: The MIT Press, 2004).

Curtis, Neal, 'The Body as Outlaw: Lyotard, Kafka and the Visible Human Project', *Body & Society* 5, 1999, pp. 249–66.

Dagognet, François, *Étienne-Jules Marey: A Passion for the Trace* (New York: Zone Books, 1992); Eng. trans. by Robert Galeta with Jeanine Herman from the French *Étienne-Jules Marey: La Passion de la trace* (Paris: Editions Hazan, 1987).

Deleuze, Gilles, *Cinema 1: The Movement-Image* (Minneapolis: University of Minnesota Press, 1986); Eng. trans. by Hugh Tomlinson and Barbara Habberjam from the French *Cinéma I. L'Image-mouvement* (Paris: Les Éditions de Minuit, 1983).

Deleuze, Gilles, *Empiricism and Subjectivity: An Essay on Hume's Theory of Human Nature* (New York and West Sussex: Columbia University Press, 1991); Eng. trans. by Constantin V. Boundas from the French *Empirisme et subjectivité. Essai sur la nature humaine selon Hume* (Paris: Presses Universitaires de France, 1953).

Deleuze, Gilles, *Francis Bacon: The Logic of Sensation* (London and New York: Continuum, 2003); Eng. trans. by Daniel W. Smith from the French *Francis Bacon: Logique de la sensation* (Paris: Éditions de la Différence, 1981).

Deleuze, Gilles, 'What is a *Dispositif?*', in Timothy J. Armstrong (ed.), *Michel Foucault Philosopher* (New York and London: Harvester Wheatsheaf, 1992), pp. 159–68; Eng. trans. by Timothy J. Armstrong from the French 'Qu'est-ce qu'un dispositif?' *Michel Foucault philosophe*, Rencontre internationale, Paris, 9–11 janvier 1988 (Paris: Éditions du Seuil, 1989), pp. 185–95.

Deleuze, Gilles, and Félix Guattari, 'The Body without Organs', in *Anti-Oedipus: Capitalism and Schizophrenia* (Minneapolis: University of Minnesota Press,

1983), pp. 9–16; Eng. trans. by Robert Hurley, Mark Seem and Helen R. Lane from the French *L'Anti-Œdipe* (Paris: Les Éditions de Minuit, 1972).

Deleuze, Gilles, and Félix Guattari, 'Oedipus at Last', in *Anti-Oedipus: Capitalism and Schizophrenia* (Minneapolis: University of Minnesota Press, 1983), pp. 262–71; Eng. trans. by Robert Hurley, Mark Seem and Helen R. Lane from the French *L'Anti-Œdipe* (Paris: Les Éditions de Minuit, 1972).

Deleuze, Gilles, and Félix Guattari, *A Thousand Plateaus: Capitalism and Schizophrenia* (Minneapolis and London: University of Minnesota Press, 1987); Eng. trans. by Brian Massumi from the French *Mille plateaux* (Paris: Les Éditions de Minuit, 1980).

Deleuze, Gilles, and Claire Parnet, *Dialogues* (London: The Athlone Press, 1987); Eng. trans. by Hugh Tomlinson and Barbara Habberjam from the French *Dialogues* (Paris: Flammarion, 1977).

de Man, Paul, 'The Rhetoric of Temporality', in *Blindness and Insight: Essays in the Rhetoric of Contemporary Criticism* (Minneapolis: University of Minnesota Press, 1983), pp. 187–228.

Derrida, Jacques, 'From Restricted to General Economy: A Hegelianism without Reserve', in *Writing and Difference* (Chicago: University of Chicago Press, 1978), pp. 251–77; Eng. trans. by Alan Bass from the French 'De l'économie restreinte à l'économie générale: Un hégélianisme sans réserve', *L'arc: Georges Bataille* 32, May 1967, pp. 24–44.

Dulac, Germaine, 'From "Visual and Anti-Visual Films"', in P. Adams Sitney (ed.), *The Avant-Garde Film: A Reader of Theory and Criticism* (New York: Anthology Film Archives, 1987), pp. 31–5.

Epstein, Jean, 'For a New Avant-Garde', in P. Adams Sitney (ed.), *The Avant-Garde Film: A Reader of Theory and Criticism* (New York: Anthology Film Archives, 1987), pp. 26–30.

Epstein, Jean, '*Bonjour cinéma* and Other Writings', *Afterimage* 10, 1981, pp. 8–39; Eng. trans. by Tom Milne from the French *Écrits sur le cinéma 1–2* (Paris: Éditions Seghers, 1974–5).

Fechner, G. T., *Einige Ideen zur Schöpfungs- und Entwicklungsgeschichte der Organismen* (Leipzig: Breitkopf & Härtel, 1873).

Fletcher, John, and Martin Stanton (eds), *Jean Laplanche: Seduction, Translation, and the Drives* (London: Psychoanalytic Forum: Institute of Contemporary Arts, 1992).

Foucault, Michel, 'The Confession of the Flesh', in Colin Gordon (ed.), *Power/Knowledge: Selected Interviews and Other Writings, 1972–1977* (New York: Pantheon Books, 1980), pp. 194–228.

Freud, Sigmund, *Beyond the Pleasure Principle* (New York and London: W. W. Norton & Company, 1961); Eng. trans. by James Strachey from the German *Jenseits des Lustprinzips* (Leipzig, Vienna and Zürich: Internationaler Psychoanalytischer Verlag, 1920).

Freud, Sigmund, 'A Child is Being Beaten: A Contribution to the Study of the Origin of Sexual Perversion (1919)', in James Strachey (ed.), *The Standard*

Edition of the Complete Psychological Works of Sigmund Freud, Vol. XVII (London: The Hogarth Press, 1961), pp. 175–205; Eng. trans. by James Strachey from the German 'Ein Kind wird geschlagen, Beitrag zur Kenntnis der Entstehung sexueller Perversionen', *Internationale Zeitschrift für ärtzlische Psychoanalyse* 5, no. 3, 1919, pp. 151–72.

Freud, Sigmund, 'The Ego and the Id (1923)', in James Strachey (ed.), *The Standard Edition of the Complete Psychological Works of Sigmund Freud*, Vol. XIX (London: The Hogarth Press, 1961), pp. 12–66; Eng. trans. by James Strachey from the German *Das Ich und das Es* (Leipzig, Vienna and Zurich: Internationaler Psychoanalytischer Verlag, 1923).

Freud, Sigmund, 'A Note upon the "Mystic Writing-Pad" (1925 [1924])', in James Strachey (ed.), *The Standard Edition of the Complete Psychological Works of Sigmund Freud*, Vol. XIX (London: The Hogarth Press, 1961), pp. 226–32; Eng. trans. by James Strachey from the German 'Notiz über den "Wunderblock"', *Internationale Zeitschrift für ärtzlische Psychoanalyse* 11, no. 1, 1925, pp. 1–5.

Freud, Sigmund, 'The Unconscious (1915)', in James Strachey (ed.), *The Standard Edition of the Complete Psychological Works of Sigmund Freud*, Vol. XIV (London: The Hogarth Press, 1957), pp. 159–215; Eng. trans. by James Strachey from the German 'Das Unbewußte', *Internationale Zeitschrift für ärtzlische Psychoanalyse* 3, no. 4, 1915, pp. 189–203.

Ganguly, Suranjan, 'All that is Light: Brakhage at 60', *Sight and Sound* 3, no. 10, October 1993, pp. 20–3.

Grant, Iain Hamilton, 'Glossary', in Jean-François Lyotard, *Libidinal Economy* (Bloomington and Indianapolis: Indiana University Press, 1993), pp. x–xvi.

Gray, Henry, *Anatomy: Descriptive and Surgical*, 9th edn (London: Longmans, Green and Co., 1880)

Grodal, Torben, *Moving Pictures: A New Theory of Film Genres, Feelings, and Cognitions* (Oxford: Clarendon Press; New York: Oxford University Press, 1997).

Hawkins, Joan, *Cutting Edge: Art-Horror and the Horrific Avant-garde* (Minneapolis: University of Minnesota Press, 2000).

Heidegger, Martin, 'Phenomenological Interpretations in Connection with Aristotle', in *Supplements: From the Earliest Essays to* Being and Time *and Beyond* (Albany, NY: State University of New York Press, 2002), pp. 111–46; Eng. trans. by John van Buren from the German 'Phänomenologische Interpretationen zu Aristoteles' (1922), in *Dilthey-Jahrbuch* 6, 1989, pp. 236–74.

Hollier, Denis, *Against Architecture: The Writings of Georges Bataille* (Cambridge, MA and London: The MIT Press, 1989); Eng. trans. by Betsy Wing from the French *La Prise de la Concorde* (Paris: Éditions Gallimard, 1974).

Jakobson, Roman, and Morris Halle, 'Two Aspects of Language and Two Types of Aphasic Disturbances', in *Fundamentals of Language* (The Hague: Mouton & Co., 1956), pp. 55–82.

Jameson, Fredric, *Postmodernism, Or, The Cultural Logic of Late Capitalism* (Durham, NC: Duke University Press, 1991).

Johnson, Sophie, 'What is a Sentence?', *Grammar Book: The Well Bred Sentence*, 2001, <https://www.englishgrammartutor.com/grammar%20book.htm> (last accessed 17 January 2020).

Kafka, Franz, 'In the Penal Colony', in *The Penal Colony: Stories and Short Pieces* (New York: Schocken Books, 1948), pp. 191–227; Eng. trans. by Willa Muir and Edwin Muir from the German *In der Strafkolonie* (Leipzig: Kurt Wolff, 1919).

Kant, Immanuel, 'Analytic of the Beautiful', in *Critique of Judgement* (Indianapolis: Hackett, 1987), pp. 43–95; Eng. trans. by Werner S. Pluhar from the German *Kritik der Urteilskraft* (Berlin and Libau: Lagarde und Friedrich, 1790).

Kendall, Stuart, 'Editor's Introduction: Unlimited Assemblage', in Georges Bataille, *The Unfinished System of Nonknowledge* (Minneapolis and London: University of Minnesota Press, 2001), pp. xi–xliv.

Krauss, Rosalind, 'Antivision', *October* 36, Spring 1986, pp. 147–54.

Krauss, Rosalind, 'The Im/Pulse to See', in Hal Foster (ed.), *Vision and Visuality* (Seattle, WA: Bay Press, 1988), pp. 50–78.

Krauss, Rosalind E., *The Optical Unconscious* (Cambridge, MA and London: The MIT Press, 1993).

Kubelka, Peter, 'The Theory of Metrical Film', in P. Adams Sitney (ed.), *The Avant-Garde Film: A Reader of Theory and Criticism* (New York: Anthology Film Archives, 1987), pp. 139–59.

Lacan, Jacques, 'The Agency of the Letter in the Unconscious, or Reason Since Freud', in *Écrits: A Selection* (New York: W. W. Norton & Company, 1977), pp. 146–78; Eng. trans. by Alan Sheridan from the French *Écrits* (Paris: Éditions du Seuil, 1966).

Lacan, Jacques, *The Four Fundamental Concepts of Psycho-Analysis* (New York and London: W. W. Norton & Company, 1981); Eng. trans. by Alan Sheridan from the French *Le Séminaire de Jacques Lacan, Livre XI. Les Quatre concepts fondamentaux de la psychanalyse* (Paris: Éditions du Seuil, 1973).

Land, Nick, *The Thirst for Annihilation: Georges Bataille and Virulent Nihilism (An Essay in Atheistic Religion)* (London and New York: Routledge, 1992).

Laplanche, Jean, 'Economic Paradox of the Death Drive (1970)', in Sigmund Freud, *Beyond the Pleasure Principle* (Ontario: Broadview Editions, 2011), pp. 260–4.

Leclaire, Serge, *Psychanalyser: Essai sur l'ordre de l'inconscient et la pratique de la lettre* (Paris: Seuil, 1968).

Lloyd, Norman, *The Golden Encyclopedia of Music* (London and Sydney: Paul Hamlyn, 1968).

Lyotard, Jean-François, 'Acinema', in Graham Jones and Ashley Woodward (eds), *Acinemas: Lyotard's Philosophy of Film* (Edinburgh: Edinburgh University Press, 2017), pp. 33–42; Eng. trans. by Paisley N. Livingston from the French 'L'Acinéma', *Revue d'esthétique* 26, nos. 2–4, 1973, pp. 357–69.

Lyotard, Jean-François, 'Anamnesis of the Visible, or Candour', in Andrew Benjamin (ed.), *The Lyotard Reader* (Oxford and Cambridge, MA: Blackwell, 1989), pp. 220–39; Eng. trans. by David Macey from the French Catalogue ADAMI (Paris: Éditions du Centre Georges Pompidou, December 1985).

Lyotard, Jean-François, 'The Connivances of Desire with the Figural', in Roger McKeon (ed.) *Driftworks* (New York: Semiotext(e), 1984), pp. 57–68; Eng. trans. by Anne Knab from the French 'Connivences du désir avec le figural', in *Discours, figure* (Paris: Klincksieck, 1971), pp. 271–80.

Lyotard, Jean-François, *Des dispositifs pulsionnels* (Paris: Union générale d'éditions, 1973).

Lyotard, Jean-François, *Duchamp's TRANS/formers* (Venice: The Lapis Press, 1990); Eng. trans. by Ian McLeod from the French *Les Transformateurs Duchamp* (Paris: Éditions Galilée, 1977).

Lyotard, Jean-François, 'Fiscourse Digure: The Utopia behind the Scenes of the Phantasy', in *Discourse, Figure* (Minneapolis and London: University of Minnesota Press, 2011), pp. 327–55; Eng. trans. by Mary Lydon from the French 'Fiscours, digure, l'utopie du fantasme', in *Discours, figure* (Paris: Klincksieck, 1971), pp. 327–54.

Lyotard, Jean-François, 'The Idea of a Sovereign Film', in Graham Jones and Ashley Woodward (eds), *Acinemas: Lyotard's Philosophy of Film* (Edinburgh: Edinburgh University Press, 2017), pp. 62–70; Eng. trans. by Peter W. Milne and Ashley Woodward from the French 'Idée d'un film souverain', in *Misère de la philosophie* (Paris: Galilée, 2000), pp. 209–21.

Lyotard, Jean-François, *Libidinal Economy* (Bloomington and Indianapolis: Indiana University Press, 1993); Eng. trans. by Iain Hamilton Grant from the French *Économie libidinale* (Paris: Les Éditions de Minuit, 1974).

Lyotard, Jean-François, 'Prescription', in Robert Harvey and Mark S. Roberts (eds), *Toward the Postmodern* (New York: Humanity Books, 1999), pp. 176–91.

Lyotard, Jean-François, 'Several Silences', in Roger McKeon (ed.) *Driftworks* (New York: Semiotext(e), 1984), pp. 91–110; Eng. trans. by Joseph Maier from the French 'Plusieurs silences', *Musique en jeu* 9, November 1972, pp. 64–76.

MacCormack, Patricia, 'Perversion – An Introduction', *Senses of Cinema* 30, February 2004, <http://sensesofcinema.com/2004/perversion/perversion_intro> (last accessed 17 January 2020).

MacCormack, Patricia, 'Zombies without Organs: Gender, Flesh, and Fissure', in Shawn McIntosh and Marc Leverette (eds), *Zombie Culture: Autopsies of the Living Dead* (Lanham, MD, Toronto and Plymouth, UK: The Scarecrow Press, 2008), pp. 87–102.

Macpherson, Gordon (ed.), *Black's Medical Dictionary*, 40th edn (London: A. & C. Black, 2002).

Marcus, Steven, *The Other Victorians: A Study of Sexuality and Pornography in Mid-Nineteenth-Century England* (New York: Basic Books, 1964).

Marey, Étienne-Jules, *Animal Mechanism: A Treatise on Terrestrial and Aerial Locomotion* (New York: D. Appleton and Co., 1874); Eng. trans. from the

French *La Machine animale: locomotion terrestre et aérienne* (Paris: Germer Baillière, 1873).

Marey, Étienne-Jules, *La Méthode Graphique dans les Sciences Expérimentales et Principalement en Physiologie et en Médecine* (Paris: G. Masson, 1878).

Marey, Étienne-Jules, *Movement* (New York: D. Appleton and Co., 1895); Eng. trans. by Eric Pritchard from the French *Le Mouvement* (Paris: G. Masson, 1894).

Marks, Laura U., *Touch: Sensuous Theory and Multisensory Media* (Minneapolis and London: University of Minnesota Press, 2002).

Massumi, Brian, *Parables for the Virtual: Movement, Affect, Sensation* (Durham, NC and London: Duke University Press, 2002).

McGee, Mark Thomas, 'King of the Gimmicks', *Fangoria* 12, April 1981, pp. 34–7.

McLuhan, Marshall, 'The Medium is the Message', in *Understanding Media: The Extensions of Man* (Cambridge, MA and London: The MIT Press, 1994), pp. 7–21.

Merleau-Ponty, Maurice, *Phenomenology of Perception* (London: Routledge and Kegan Paul, 1962); Eng. trans. by Colin Smith from the French *Phénoménologie de la perception* (Paris: Éditions Gallimard, 1945).

Michelson, Annette, 'Heterology and the Critique of Instrumental Reason', *October* 36, Spring 1986, pp. 111–27.

Michelson, Annette, 'Paul Sharits and the Critique of Illusionism: An Introduction', in *Projected Images* (Minneapolis: Walker Art Centre, 1974), pp. 20–5.

Mitry, Jean, *The Aesthetics and Psychology of the Cinema* (Bloomington and Indianapolis: Indiana University Press, 1997); Eng. trans. by Christopher King from the French *Esthétique et psychologie du cinéma* (Paris: Groupe Mame, 1963).

Pearlman, Karen, *Cutting Rhythms: Shaping the Film Edit* (Amsterdam and Boston, MA: Focal Press/Elsevier, 2009).

Rabinbach, Anson, 'Time and Motion: Étienne-Jules Marey and the Mechanics of the Body', in *The Human Motor: Energy, Fatigue and the Origins of Modernity* (Berkeley and Los Angeles: University of California Press, 1992), pp. 84–119.

Richter, Gregory C., 'Translator's Note', in Sigmund Freud, *Beyond the Pleasure Principle* (Ontario: Broadview Editions, 2011), pp. 37–48.

Richter, Hans, 'The Badly Trained Sensibility', in P. Adams Sitney (ed.), *The Avant-Garde Film: A Reader of Theory and Criticism* (New York: Anthology Film Archives, 1987), pp. 22–3.

Rutherford, Anne, '"What Makes a Film Tick?": Cinematic Affect, Materiality and Mimetic Innervation', PhD, University of Western Sydney, 2006.

Sanouillet, Michel, and Elmer Peterson (eds), *The Writings of Marcel Duchamp* (New York: Da Capo Press, 1989).

Scarry, Elaine, *The Body in Pain: The Making and Unmaking of the World* (New York and Oxford: Oxford University Press, 1985).

Shaviro, Steven, 'Contagious Allegories: George Romero', in *The Cinematic Body: Theory Out of Bounds* 2 (Minneapolis and London: University of Minnesota Press, 1993), pp. 83–105.

Shaviro, Steven, 'Film Theory and Visual Fascination', in *The Cinematic Body: Theory Out of Bounds* 2 (Minneapolis and London: University of Minnesota Press, 1993), pp. 1–81.

Shaviro, Steven, *Passion and Excess: Blanchot, Bataille, and Literary Theory* (Tallahassee: The Florida State University Press, 1990).

Shaviro, Steven, 'Post-Cinematic Affect: On Grace Jones, *Boarding Gate* and *Southland Tales*', *Film-Philosophy* 14, no. 1, 2010, pp. 1–102.

Sitney, P. Adams, 'Introduction', in P. Adams Sitney (ed.), *The Avant-Garde Film: A Reader of Theory and Criticism* (New York: Anthology Film Archives, 1987), pp. vii–xlv.

Skal, David J., *The Monster Show: A Cultural History of Horror* (New York and London: W. W. Norton & Company, 1993).

Smith, Murray, *Engaging Characters: Fiction, Emotion, and the Cinema* (Oxford: Clarendon Press; New York: Oxford University Press, 1995).

Sobchack, Vivian, *The Address of the Eye: A Phenomenology of Film Experience* (Princeton, NJ: Princeton University Press, 1992).

Stevenson, Angus (ed.), 'possession, noun', *Oxford Dictionary of English*, 3rd edn (Oxford: Oxford University Press, 2010) <https://en.oxforddictionaries.com/definition/possession> (last accessed 17 January 2020).

Stevenson, Angus (ed.), 'possess, verb', *Oxford Dictionary of English*, 3rd edn (Oxford: Oxford University Press, 2010) <https://en.oxforddictionaries.com/definition/possess> (last accessed 17 January 2020).

Thrower, Stephen, and Daniel Bird, 'Cinema Superactivity: Andrzej Żuławski interviewed by Stephen Thrower and Daniel Bird', in Stephen Thrower (ed.), *Eyeball Compendium: Writings on Sex and Horror in the Cinema from the Pages of* Eyeball Magazine, *1989–2003* (Godalming, UK: FAB Press, 2003).

Trahair, Lisa, 'The Comedy of Philosophy: Bataille, Hegel and Derrida', *Angelaki: Journal of the Theoretical Humanities* 6, no. 3, December 2001, pp. 155–69.

Trahair, Lisa, *The Comedy of Philosophy: Sense and Nonsense in Early Cinematic Slapstick* (Albany, NY: State University of New York Press, 2007).

Trahair, Lisa, 'Jean-François Lyotard', in Felicity Colman (ed.), *Film, Theory and Philosophy: The Key Thinkers* (Montreal and Kingston: McGill-Queen's University Press, 2009), pp. 222–32.

Waite, Maurice (ed.), *Oxford Dictionary and Thesaurus*, 2nd edn (Oxford and New York: Oxford University Press, 2007).

Waters, John, 'Whatever Happened to Showmanship?', *American Film: A Journal of the Film and Television Arts* 9, no. 3, December 1983, pp. 55–8.

Weiss, Allen S., 'Impossible Sovereignty: Between "The Will to Power" and "The Will to Chance"', *October* 36, Spring 1986, pp. 128–46.

Williams, James, *Lyotard: Towards a Postmodern Philosophy* (Cambridge, UK: Polity Press, 1998).
Williams, Linda, 'Film Bodies: Gender, Genre, and Excess', *Film Quarterly* 44, no. 4, Summer 1991, pp. 2–13.
Williams, Linda, 'Learning to Scream', *Sight and Sound* 4, no. 12, December 1994, pp. 14–17.
Woodward, Ashley, 'A Sacrificial Economy of the Image: Lyotard on Cinema', *Angelaki: Journal of the Theoretical Humanities* 19, no. 4, 2014, pp. 141–54.

Filmography

The Act of Seeing with One's Own Eyes, directed by Stan Brakhage. USA, 1971.
L'aldilà/The Beyond, directed by Lucio Fulci. Italy, 1981.
Anémic Cinéma, directed by Marcel Duchamp. France, 1926.
Arnulf Rainer, directed by Peter Kubelka. Austria, 1960.
Ballet mécanique, directed by Fernand Léger. France, 1924.
Carrie, directed by Brian De Palma. USA, 1976.
La Chute de la maison Usher/The Fall of the House of Usher, directed by Jean Epstein. France, 1928.
Cinéma de notre temps: Franju le visionnaire, television series, directed by André S. Labarthe. France, original airdate 1 January 1997.
Cœur fidèle/The Faithful Heart, directed by Jean Epstein. France, 1923.
Dawn of the Dead, directed by George A. Romero. USA, 1978.
Day of the Dead, directed by George A. Romero. USA, 1985.
Diary of the Dead, directed by George A. Romero. USA, 2007.
Dog Star Man, directed by Stan Brakhage. USA, 1961–1964.
Eat, directed by Andy Warhol. USA, 1963.
Fuge 20/Fugue 20, directed by Hans Richter. Germany 1920.
House on Haunted Hill, directed by William Castle. USA, 1959.
I Walked with a Zombie, directed by Jacques Tourneur. USA, 1943.
Lancelot du Lac/Lancelot of the Lake, directed by Robert Bresson. France, 1974.
Land of the Dead, directed by George A. Romero. USA, 2005.
The Last Man on Earth, directed by Ubaldo Ragona. USA, 1964.
Macabre, directed by William Castle. USA, 1958.
Monty Python and the Holy Grail, directed by Terry Gilliam and Terry Jones. UK, 1975.
Night of the Living Dead, directed by George A. Romero. USA, 1968.
Paura nella città dei morti viventi/City of the Living Dead, directed by Lucio Fulci. Italy, 1980.
The Plague of the Zombies, directed by John Gilling. UK, 1966.
Polyester, directed by John Waters. USA, 1981.
Possession, directed by Andrzej Żuławski. France/West Germany, 1981.
Psycho, directed by Alfred Hitchcock. USA, 1960.

Quella villa accanto al cimitero/The House by the Cemetery, directed by Lucio Fulci. Italy, 1981.
Rhythmus 21/Rhythm 21, directed by Hans Richter. Germany, 1921.
Le Sang des bêtes/Blood of the Beasts, directed by Georges Franju. France, 1949.
The Shining, directed by Stanley Kubrick. USA, 1980.
Sleep, directed by Andy Warhol. USA, 1963.
Survival of the Dead, directed by George A. Romero. USA, 2009.
The Tingler, directed by William Castle. USA, 1959.
Tol'able David, directed by Henry King. USA, 1921.
The Undead, directed by Roger Corman. USA, 1957.
Vancouver Island Films, directed by Stan Brakhage. USA, 1991–2000.
The War Game, directed by Peter Watkins. UK, 1965.
Wavelength, directed by Michael Snow. USA/Canada, 1967.
White Zombie, directed by Victor Halperin. USA, 1932.
Window Water Baby Moving, directed by Stan Brakhage. USA, 1959.
Les Yeux sans visage/Eyes without a Face, directed by Georges Franju. France/Italy, 1959.
Zombie Flesh Eaters, directed by Lucio Fulci. Italy, 1979.
Zorns Lemma, directed by Hollis Frampton. USA, 1970.

Index

absence, 69, 71–3, 85, 88, 90; *see also* presence
abstraction, 31, 36–8, 67
acephalia, acephalic, acephalus, 70, 71, 72, 192
acinema, 130, 132–3, 143–4
The Act of Seeing with One's Own Eyes, 13
aesthetics, 9–12, 17, 19, 39, 81, 82–4, 86–7, 98–9, 103–11, 114, 119, 125, 138, 198
affect, 9, 12, 124–6, 134–5, 152–6, 168–9, 179, 182, 184–5, 187, 188–9, 191–8
 convulsive, 16, 18, 20, 168, 171, 172, 176, 178, 180, 181, 183–5, 188, 191, 193, 196–7
affection, 1–2, 6, 29
A-grade film, 124
aisthesis, 9–12, 15, 17, 19, 98, 103–4, 106–11, 112, 114, 117, 119–20, 122–6, 189
L'aldilà/ The Beyond, 12, 17, 19–20, 130–1, 147–52, 194–5, 197
American avant-garde, 12, 18, 25, 30–3, 39
amorous frenzy, 168, 172–5, 178–81, 196–7
analogue, 49, 50, 52, 73, 119, 121
 figural, 121–5
anamnesis, 90–2

Anémic Cinéma, 13, 37–40
apparatus,
 cinematic, 4, 7, 13, 68, 100, 110, 111–12, 114, 124–6
 execution, 100–1, 104–6, 112, 124
 mechanical, 7, 35, 36, 46, 48–9, 71, 114, 118, 177, 189
 psychical, 49, 52–3, 57, 66–7, 68
appropriation, 114
arhythmy, 158
Arnulf Rainer, 32
assemblage, 34–5, 86–7, 158–9
attraction, 196
authority, 106, 114, 155, 159, 160–1
automatic writing, 46–7
automutilation, 17, 20, 131–2, 135–9, 140, 142, 143–6, 152, 159, 160

Bacon, F., 79, 80
Ballard, J. G., 185–6
Ballet mécanique, 37, 38–9
Barthes, R., 140, 141–2
base materialism, 138, 180
Bataille, G.,
 on eroticism, 20, 139, 140–2, 157, 171–4, 177, 178–81, 188, 189–90, 195, 197
 on general economy, 20, 134–8, 157, 159
 on loss, 10–11, 23n, 134–5, 137–8, 143, 164n, 195

Bataille (*Cont.*)
  on putting at stake, 10–11, 20, 23n, 130, 134–5, 142, 155, 157, 180, 189–90
  on restricted economy, 137, 143
  on sacrifice, 155, 157, 171–2, 177, 189–90
  on the sovereign operation, 10–11, 133–5, 152, 155, 189
  on surplus, 134, 136, 141
Baudry, J.-L., 7, 153
Bazin, A., 83
Bazin, J., 83
beat, 3, 4, 22n, 28, 29, 32, 42, 55, 73, 82, 85, 91, 121, 135, 147, 160
becoming, 7, 77, 81, 116–17, 133, 186–7, 188
before, 9–10, 90, 103–4, 107–9, 111, 120, 198
Beier, S., 28
Benjamin, W., 4
Bennington, G., 87, 88, 91
Bergson, H., 42, 75–7, 81, 151
B-grade film, 15, 124, 158
block, blocking, 3, 8, 21n, 23n,
blood, 9, 10–11, 12, 16, 17–18, 19, 20, 27–8, 31, 63, 65, 67, 78, 84, 92–3n, 99, 101–3, 104–11, 114, 120, 123, 125, 135, 143, 145, 147–52, 153, 156, 166–9, 170, 176, 181, 187, 190–8
  circulating (*sanguis*), 106, 109, 114, 125, 198
  spilled (*cruor*), 106, 109, 114, 125
body genres, 13, 15, 157, 176
body horror, 12, 14–15, 17, 176
boredom, 143
Brakhage, S., 13, 18, 31
Briggs, J., 28, 29, 81

candour, 90–1, 111
capture, 66, 92; *see also* escape
cardiograph, 5, 45, 47, 66, 69, 78, 187
carnal, 2–3

Carrie, 167–8
Carroll, N., 139
Castle, W., 12, 17, 19, 97–100, 107, 111, 119, 121, 124–5, 126n
cathexis, 7, 9, 39, 49, 54, 56–7, 87–8, 112, 118–19, 125, 159; *see also* charge and investment
Cézanne, P., 79
charge, 5, 7–9, 21n, 22n, 49, 52–4, 56, 71; *see also* discharge
chiasmus, 91
chronophotography, 12, 40–4, 47–8
La Chute de la maison Usher/ The Fall of the House of Usher, 13
Cinéma de notre temps: Franju le visionnaire, 83–4
circular agitation, 193
close-up, 13, 34–5, 37, 151
Clover, C. J., 14–15
Cœur fidèle/ The Faithful Heart, 13
cognition, 5, 133, 146, 189
comedy, 123–5, 135
communication, 5, 9, 15, 16, 20, 23n, 39, 81–2, 91, 130–1, 132–5, 139–40, 142–4, 147, 151, 153, 155, 156–9, 161, 168–9, 172, 182, 188–93, 195–7
communion, 5, 15, 20, 130–1, 132, 134–5, 139–40, 142–4, 146–7, 151, 153, 155, 156–61, 168, 172, 181–2, 188–91, 195, 197
condensation, 143, 163n
Conley, T., 33
constellation, 158–9
contagion, 17, 21, 132, 138–44, 147, 149, 151, 160
contiguity, 121, 139–42, 149, 160
continuity, 20, 31, 33, 41–2, 44, 50–1, 131, 139–40, 142, 162n, 168, 172, 174, 179, 188–92, 197; *see also* discontinuity

copula, 178–81, 196–7
corporeal, corporealised,
    corporealisation, 1, 2, 4, 100,
    108–9, 119, 123, 135, 158
Crary, J., 3
cruelty, 10, 12, 88, 104, 106–14,
    119–20, 123–5, 128n, 198
Cubitt, S., 186–90, 194
Curtis, N., 111, 120

Dadaist cinema, 12, 18, 25, 30, 36–40
Dagognet, F., 45–6
Dawn of the Dead, 12, 17, 19, 130–1,
    143–6, 152–3
Day of the Dead, 131
declined, 151
de/formation, 73, 87, 120
Deleuze, G.,
    on affection, 1
    on the body without organs, 65,
        165n, 184
    on diastole–systole, 79–82
    on lines of subjectification, 116
    on the movement-image, 64–5,
        74–8, 182
    on the Open, 64–5, 75, 77, 183
de Man, P., 140
Derrida, J., 11, 130
desire, 3–5, 7, 9, 13, 15, 21n, 25, 30,
    38–9, 48–9, 53–5, 57, 66–8, 88,
    90–2, 108, 123–4, 126, 135, 146,
    151, 158, 177
détour, 55
Diary of the Dead, 131
diastole–systole, 2, 18–19, 78–82, 184
difference, 8, 21n, 22n, 72, 74, 87
différend, 111–12
direction, 3, 18, 20–1, 91, 115–16,
    167, 169, 181–5, 187–91, 193–7
discharge, 5, 8–9, 21n, 22n, 49, 53–4,
    56, 71; *see also* charge
discipline, 100, 107, 112, 114, 127n
discontinuity, 33, 42, 51, 55, 172, 197;
    see also continuity

discursive, 72–3, 115, 117, 120;
    see also non-discursive
disjunction, 117
displacement, 17, 20–1, 51, 63, 83–4,
    132, 140, 142–3, 163n
dispositif, 4, 5–9, 12, 13, 17, 18, 20–1,
    49, 54, 57, 63–6, 68, 72–3, 78,
    82, 88–9, 91–2, 111–20, 124, 133,
    138, 140, 152, 155–6, 158–60,
    177; *see also positif*
disposition, 7–9, 112, 118, 123–5
dispossess, dispossession, 18, 20,
    166–9, 170–3, 178, 180–1, 182–3,
    188–9, 191, 195–7; *see also*
    possess
disruption, 87, 119
disseizure, 114; *see also* seizure
divisible, 56, 60n, 74–5
Dog Star Man, 31
doppelgänger, 169–70, 171–2, 177–8,
    192, 196–7
drive, 23n, 28, 53, 55–6, 138, 172;
    see also instinct, pulsion, *Trieb*
Duchamp, M., 3, 18, 36–40
Dulac, G., 18, 35
duration, 5, 41, 44–8, 74–80, 82, 160,
    197

Eat, 158
ecstasy, 8, 133, 135, 142, 146, 151–2,
    153, 156, 159, 160, 168, 174,
    176–7, 180–1, 193
élan vital, 55
embodiment, 7
ephemeral, 6–7, 65–8, 70, 86–8, 91,
    138
episteme, 115
Epstein, J., 13, 18, 33–5
erotic, eroticism, 9, 10, 14, 20, 88,
    134, 139, 140–2, 157, 168, 171–4,
    177, 178–81, 188, 189–90, 193,
    195, 197
escape, 12, 92, 116–17, 126, 177, 181;
    see also capture

ethics, ethical, 83, 105, 108, 119, 183, 197–8
event, 18, 68, 70, 107, 119, 120, 177, 190, 197
excess, 2, 15–16, 116–17, 119, 120–1, 135, 138, 152, 167, 176, 190
excessive movement, 16, 133, 143, 149, 155, 160, 169, 172; *see also* immobility
exclusion, 73, 117
excretion, 138, 190
expenditure, 7, 10–11, 14, 16, 17, 19–20, 48, 81, 114, 130, 132, 134–8, 142, 144, 147, 151–3, 155, 156–7, 159–60, 167, 168, 170, 171–2, 178–81, 183, 188–91, 195–8
experimental cinema, 12–13, 25, 30–1, 158
exploitation, 12, 17, 92, 123–4, 131, 133, 152, 154–5, 159, 160
exploitation cinema, 12, 15, 124, 131, 153
exposed, exposure, 5, 6, 9–12, 15, 17, 19, 85, 98, 100, 103–4, 107–8, 110–11, 112, 114, 119, 124–6, 168, 194
exterior, 5, 41, 73, 122, 200n; *see also* interior

failure, 120, 123–5
fall, 151–2, 195
Fechner, G. T., 53
feedback, 31, 155
Figure, 79, 81–2, 184
Figure with Meat, 80
film spectatorship, 1–2, 7, 12, 14, 63–4, 67, 79, 89, 92, 111, 124, 136, 138, 155, 157, 160
filmstrip, 5, 7, 13, 26, 30–3, 35, 36, 67, 70–3, 86, 92, 186
flow, 3, 5–8, 19, 20, 28–9, 39, 54, 65, 67–8, 75, 84, 90, 142, 156, 179

formation, 66, 67, 73, 115, 117–18; *see also* de/formation
Foucault, M., 114–15, 117
Franju, G., 83–4
freedom, 10–12, 28, 81, 108–9, 111, 114, 134, 141
French Impressionist cinema, 12–13, 25, 30, 33–5
Freud, S.,
  on the death drive (*Thanatos*), 49, 55–7
  on the life drive (*Eros*), 49, 55–7
  on perception-consciousness (*Pcpt.-Cs.*), 50–2, 91
  on the pleasure principle, 3, 6, 53–7
  on the unconscious, 18, 50–7, 65, 91
Fuge 20/ Fugue 20, 158
Fulci, L., 131

Ganguly, S., 31
general economy, 4, 5, 20, 130, 134–8, 140, 143, 146, 147, 152, 153–7, 159–61, 178, 198
geometrical chronophotography, 40–4, 47
Gidal, P., 31
Grant, I. H., 72–3, 87, 118
graphic inscription, 40–2, 45–8, 52, 187
Gray, H., 29
great ephemeral skin, 86–7

heart, 1, 9, 27–8, 34, 41, 44–5, 47–8, 78, 81, 89, 98, 119, 121–5, 165n, 168
heartbeat, 1, 27, 36, 103, 112, 121–2
Heidegger, M., 9
heterogeneous, heterogeneity, 7, 9, 23n, 47, 60n, 67–8, 70, 74–5, 79, 86, 87, 91, 114–15, 118, 120, 136, 138, 151, 158, 159, 182, 190; *see also* homogeneous
Hollier, D., 195–6
homeostasis, 6, 54
homogeneous, homogeneity, 26, 60n, 74, 76, 116, 138, 182

horror cinema, 10, 12, 14–15, 110, 114, 132, 133–4, 136, 139, 154–8, 168, 176, 181, 188
House on Haunted Hill, 98, 99

identification, 14–15, 25, 99, 140, 178–80
identity, 10–11, 17, 19, 130, 131–4, 138–43, 147, 149, 153–4, 160, 179
ideology, ideological, 7, 86–7, 153
imbricate, imbrication, 5, 18–19, 56, 69, 73, 85, 87, 92, 133, 143, 153, 198
immobility, 133, 143, 149, 155, 160; *see also* excessive movement
imperceptions, imperceptible, 22n, 25, 34, 35, 107
index, 1, 32, 47, 185, 187
inertia, 6, 55
infancy, 103–4, 107, 120
informe, 4
inscription,
  surfaces of, 18, 65–71, 73, 88–9, 92
instinct, 49, 54–7, 118, 132; *see also* drive
intensity,
  force of, 4, 8, 81, 82, 111
  passages of, 9, 18–19, 63–70, 73, 85–6, 89, 118
interior, 12–13, 34, 40–1, 46–8, 98, 122, 200n; *see also* exterior
intractable, 107
investment, 3, 6, 7–8, 13, 17, 18, 20–1, 48, 49, 53–4, 63, 65, 68, 69, 71, 84, 85–6, 88–9, 92, 114, 117–21, 131, 132–3, 136, 140, 142–3, 152, 158; *see also* cathexis
I Walked with a Zombie, 131

Jakobson, R., 140,
Jameson, F., 154
jouissance, 8, 130, 135, 143–4, 146, 154, 155, 158, 159, 160

Kafka, F., 10, 19, 100, 104–5, 107–8, 120–1, 125
Kant, I., 90, 103,
knowledge, 3, 110, 115–16, 133, 146
Krauss, R. E., 2–4, 135–6
Kubelka, P., 18, 32–3

Labarthe, A. S., 83
Lacan, J., 6, 163n
lack, lacking, 88, 119, 154
Lancelot du Lac/Lancelot of the Lake, 198n
Land, N., 181, 194
Land of the Dead, 131
language, 10, 11–12, 46–7, 70, 72, 104, 105, 107, 108, 114, 116, 120, 140–2, 176, 178, 187
Laplanche, J., 53
The Last Man on Earth, 131
law, 10–12, 69, 100, 104–10, 112, 119–20, 124, 125, 171, 189, 196, 198
LeGrice, M., 31
libidinal band/skin, 6–7, 20, 63, 65–74, 85–9, 117, 119–20, 123–6, 138, 160
libidinal economy, 8, 18, 66, 70–3, 88–90, 92, 114, 118–19
loss, 10–11, 17, 19–20, 23n, 132, 134–5, 137–8, 142–3, 147, 151–7, 159, 161n, 164n, 166–8, 171, 188, 191, 194–7
Lyotard, J.-F.,
  on *aisthesis*, 9–12, 103–4, 106–10, 119
  on the *dispositif*, 7–8, 63–5, 66, 68, 72–3, 88–90, 91–2, 117–19, 124, 138, 158–9
  on the libidinal band/skin, 6–7, 20, 63, 65–74, 85–89, 117–19, 138
  on passages of intensity, 18–19, 63–70, 73, 85–6, 89, 118
  on prescription, 9–10, 103–10, 198

Lyotard (*Cont.*)
  on surfaces of inscription, 18, 65–71, 73, 88–9
  on the turning of the bar, 74, 117
  on uncompensated loss, 130, 132–3, 135
  on the zero, 71, 73, 88

Macabre, 99
MacCormack, P., 146, 154, 157–8
machine, 31, 47, 50, 71–2, 100, 106, 108, 110, 111–14, 125, 147–8, 186, 188–9, 191
McLuhan, M., 188
magnitude, 3, 18, 20–1, 167, 169, 181–5, 187–91, 193–7
Marey, É.-J., 12, 18, 40–9, 52, 92n, 187
Marks, L. U., 126n
masochism, 8, 16
Massumi, B., 154
master–slave dialectic, 133, 156
mastery, 10, 19, 130, 133–5, 155, 161–2n, 171, 180, 188
materiality, 31, 153, 156, 194, 196
matrix, 21n, 22n, 171, 187
mediate, mediation, 4–5, 11, 13–14, 29
Mekas, J., 30, 32
memory, 11, 18, 27, 31, 34, 36–9, 69–73, 86, 90, 119
Merleau-Ponty, M., 81, 91
Metaphor, metaphoric, 123, 140–2, 163n
metonymy, metonymic, 17, 20–1, 121–3, 131–2, 138–43, 147, 149, 151, 152, 154, 159, 160, 163n
metre, 26, 32
  iambic, 160
metric, metrical, 6, 25, 32–3
Michelson, A., 31, 157
mimesis, 136, 138
Mitry, J., 26–7, 30, 32–3
Moebius strip/band, 87, 89, 117
Monty Python and the Holy Grail, 167

music, 2, 27, 30, 32–3, 45, 47, 79, 81, 82
Muybridge, E., 42
Mystic Writing-Pad, 49, 50–3, 57, 70, 87

negation, 22n, 72–3, 181
Night of the Living Dead, 130–1, 144
non-discursive, 115, 117, 120; *see also* discursive
non-realized, 88
(non)sense, 193–4

Open, 1–2, 4–6, 7, 9, 12, 13–14, 15, 17, 18–19, 57, 64–5, 75, 77–82, 85, 90–2, 98, 111, 118, 132, 133, 158, 160, 168, 182–3, 189
operation, 4, 7, 8, 10–11, 12, 16, 17, 19, 20, 48, 49, 51, 54, 57, 98, 100, 118, 130, 132, 134, 136, 139–43, 147–51, 152, 156, 159, 167, 168, 172, 176, 178–9, 186, 188–9, 194, 196–8
organic, 1, 5, 27, 28, 29, 36, 47, 55, 65, 68, 90, 110, 136, 168, 176, 178, 185

Paura nella città dei morti viventi/ City of the Living Dead, 131
Pearlman, K., 165n
pellicule, 63, 85–7, 92
perception, perceptible, 5, 9, 27, 33, 35, 37, 42, 49–53, 75; *see also* imperception
periodicity, 26, 32–3, 52, 57
persistence of vision, 26–7
phantasy, 3, 8, 177
photogénie, 34
physiological response, 1, 15, 133, 153, 156
The Plague of the Zombies, 131
Plato, 9
pleasure principle, 3, 6, 53–7
Polyester, 99

positif, 9
possess, possession, 149, 154, 166–7, 168, 169, 170–5, 182, 188, 191, 197; *see also* dispossess
Possession, 12, 17–18, 20, 168, 169–70, 171–8, 181, 182–3, 191–3, 196–8
potential, potentiality, 7, 11–12, 70, 74, 112, 117, 120, 124, 158, 189
pouvoir, 119
prescribe, prescription, 9–10, 12, 17, 97–8, 100, 103–6, 107–9, 111–12, 114–18, 119–20, 122–5, 198
presence, 14, 21n, 69, 71–3, 85, 90, 154, 156; *see also* absence
preserve, preservation, 66, 69–70, 73, 77
proportion, 26, 30, 33
proximity, 98, 140, 142, 149, 153, 167–8
Psycho, 99–100
puissance, 119, 181
pulse,
 corporeality, 2, 135–6
 film viewer, 121–2
 force, 10, 14, 53, 57, 67, 88, 184, 187
 intensity, 39
 unseen, 1, 14, 19, 48, 57, 156
pulsion, pulsional, 118, 132; *see also* drive

Quella villa accanto al cimitero/ The House by the Cemetery, 131

Rabinbach, A., 42, 46, 47
Real, 87
recurrence, 86, 87
relations, 28, 34–5, 37, 65, 75, 77–82, 87, 91, 114–16, 120, 140, 168, 182, 184–5, 186–9, 194
repulsion, 196
restricted economy, 5, 137, 143, 146, 153, 198
retortion, 182–3, 200n

rhythm
 consciousness, 26–7, 39, 50–2
 film viewer, 91
 inscription, 50–3, 65–6
 perception, 5, 26–7, 49–53, 67, 68, 93n
 visuality, 2, 3, 30–1, 81–2
 see also arhythmy
Rhythmus 21/ Rhythm 21, 36–7, 158
Richter, H., 18, 36–7
Romero, G. A., 12, 17, 19, 130–1, 143, 147

sacrifice, 20, 132, 134–5, 155–6, 157, 168, 171–2, 177, 181, 189–90, 191–3, 195–8
sadism, 8, 16
sadomasochism, 16
Le Sang des bêtes/ Blood of the Beasts, 12–13, 19, 63–4, 65, 82–4, 85–6
savage, savagery, 11, 109, 112, 114, 115, 124
Scarry, E., 108, 120
scream, 80, 97, 98, 99–100, 101–3, 111–12, 115, 117, 120–6, 149, 151, 179
seizure, 114; *see also* disseizure
sensation, 1–2, 5, 6, 9–12, 14, 17, 19, 29, 39, 65, 78–82, 83–4, 97–8, 99, 104, 107, 111, 117, 119, 122, 124, 125, 132, 139, 141, 142, 143, 168, 176, 184–5, 197
sequence, sequential, 6, 25, 26, 28, 30, 33, 36, 51, 56, 57, 86, 110, 158
Shaviro, S., 13–14, 136, 138, 151, 152–6, 190
The Shining, 166–8,
signification, 6, 11, 53, 71, 87, 123, 133, 140, 141, 143, 180, 190
Sitney, P. A., 32, 37
Skal, D. J., 99
Sleep, 158
Smith, H., 30
Sobchack, V., 12

INDEX

sovereign operation, 10–12, 17–18, 19, 130, 131–5, 136, 151, 152, 155–60, 171, 180–1, 188–90, 194–5, 197–8
The Sower, 137
space–time, 34, 37, 103, 183
spasm, spasmodic, 15, 16, 79, 82, 133, 151, 155, 157, 159, 168, 176–7, 181, 184
sphygmograph, 44–5, 46
splatter, 15, 17, 19, 130, 131, 135, 143–4, 152–6, 158, 170, 181
Structuralist/Materialist cinema, 12, 13, 18, 25, 30–3
Survival of the Dead, 131

tableau, tableaux, 82–4, 85
tensor, 116
theatre, theater, 35, 71, 72, 104, 106–11, 114, 116, 117, 119–21, 123–5, 198
threshold, 116, 151, 152, 158
time, 6, 12–13, 18, 22n, 25, 26–8, 30, 32–4, 37, 40–2, 44, 46–7, 49, 51, 54, 56, 67, 71–2, 74, 75–7, 86–7, 105, 110, 151–2, 153, 173, 186–8; *see also* timeless
timeless, 56–7
The Tingler, 12, 17, 19, 97–103, 110, 111–15, 117, 120, 121–6
Tol'able David, 103, 112, 121–2
touch, 5, 10, 41, 81, 101, 104, 107–10, 119–20, 141
transgression, transgressive, 4, 88
Trieb, 118, 132; *see also* drive

unconscious, 18, 21n, 22n, 25, 30, 37–9, 46–7, 49, 50–7, 65, 67–8, 70, 71–2, 91–2, 104

The Undead, 131
un-known, un-knowing, 133–4, 157

value, 9, 19, 35, 53, 69, 116–17, 123, 130, 133, 135, 152–3, 155
Vancouver Island Films, 31
van Gogh, V., 136–7
vector, 17, 18, 20, 21, 116, 167, 168–9, 181–97
velocity, 41, 44, 185, 187, 191
video nasty, 131
virtual, virtuality, 14, 28, 86, 90
vital, vitality, 2, 6, 22n, 47, 57, 79, 81
volume, 72–3, 88, 194

The War Game, 13
Waters, J., 98–9, 124
Wavelength, 158
Weiss, A. S., 11
White Zombie, 131
whole, 26, 27, 41, 47, 75, 77–9, 119, 121, 140, 151
Williams, J., 66, 70, 72, 73, 74, 88, 123, 124–6
Williams, L., 15–16, 99–100, 120, 176–7
Window Water Baby Moving, 31
Woodward, A., 158–9

zombie, 130–2, 136, 144, 147, 149, 158
Zombie Flesh Eaters, 131
Zorns Lemma, 32
Żuławski, A., 12, 17, 20, 168, 169, 170–1, 178, 182, 196, 198

EU representative:
Easy Access System Europe
Mustamäe tee 50, 10621 Tallinn, Estonia
Gpsr.requests@easproject.com